Praise for *Raising Wild*

"This book is not exactly about wild landscapes but the life of a house-holding family placed out there with two verge-of-puberty daughters. It is about our daily reality, not our fantasy possibilities, and who knows today what these girls will have to say later? So it is remarkably interesting, lively, non-theoretical, and hopeful. The wild might be wildfire or bushy-tailed woodrats under the floor—not just to live with but to know them. Michael Branch's book points forward, not back."

—GARY SNYDER

"I have long considered Michael Branch one of the true visionaries of western American literature—and here is further proof. This beautiful, often raucous account of fatherhood and (wild) faith takes us even deeper into his remarkable kinship with northwestern Nevada. A place where, through the 'daily practices of love, humility, and humor,' we can all learn to be at home in this world."

—JOHN T. PRICE, author of
  Daddy Long Legs: The Natural Education of a Father

"Reading Michael Branch's prose is like attending a great and raucous party. A party held around a campfire in a secret corner of the wilderness full of intense talk, laughs, liquor, and deep insights. That the kids are invited this time makes it even better. A profound and moving book that just might change some lives."

—DAVID GESSNER, author of *All the Wild That Remains*

"At last! A home for Michael Branch's joyous dispatches from the high desert, which I have long followed with delight. If you're unfamiliar with Branch, prepare for your first encounter with a singular sensibility, bracing yet affable. In part a memoir of building a unique home in an extraordinary place, in part a treatise on cultivating, protecting, and loving the wild, and each other therein, *Raising Wild* is a wholly defiant, tender book bristling with spirit, intelligence, and mountains of laughs."

—CLAIRE VAYE WATKINS, author of
Battleborn and *Gold Fame Citrus*

"Michael Branch has been an essential figure in western letters for years. Now, in his marvelous *Raising Wild*, he brings us an intimate look at one remarkable family's lucky life situated more deeply into their place than most will ever know. Hugely loving but ardently unsentimental, open and curious yet skeptical as desert dust, Mike's dispatches shimmer. They mean so much, I could enjoy reading them even upside down, or back to front."

—ROBERT MICHAEL PYLE, author of
Sky Time in Gray's River: Living for Keeps in a Forgotten Place

"Not since Rachel Carson's *Sense of Wonder* has there been such a lively and evocative account of intergenerational experiences in nature. Michael Branch's *Raising Wild* offers breathtaking lyricism, sage wisdom, and big belly laughs in equal measure. Most importantly, this collection is a testament to the value of marrying memory and place— especially while in the company of those we love."

—KATHRYN MILES, author of *Adventures with Ari,*
All Standing, and *Superstorm: Nine Days Inside Hurricane Sandy*

Raising
Wild

Raising Wild

DISPATCHES FROM A HOME
IN THE WILDERNESS

Michael P. Branch

ROOST BOOKS

BOULDER

2017

Roost Books

An imprint of Shambhala Publications, Inc.

2129 13th Street

Boulder, Colorado 80302

roostbooks.com

9 8 7 6 5 4 3 2

Printed in the United States of America

♾ This edition is printed on acid-free paper that meets the American National Standards
Institute Z39.48 Standard.

♲ Shambhala Publications makes every effort to print on recycled paper.
For more information please visit www.shambhala.com.

Roost Books is distributed worldwide by Penguin Random House, Inc.,
and its subsidiaries.

Designed by Jess Morphew

THE LIBRARY OF CONGRESS CATALOGUES THE HARDCOVER EDITION OF THIS
BOOK AS FOLLOWS:

Names: Branch, Michael P.
Title: Raising wild: dispatches from a home in the wilderness / Michael P. Branch.
Description: First edition. | Boulder: Roost Books, 2016.
Identifiers: LCCN 2016000871 | ISBN 9781611803457 (hardcover: acid-free paper)
ISBN 9781611804591 (paperback)
Subjects: LCSH: Branch, Michael P. | Branch, Michael P.—Homes and haunts—Great
Basin. | Wilderness areas—Great Basin. | Branch, Michael P.—Family. | Parenting—
Great Basin. | Sustainability—Great Basin. | Great Basin—Biography. | Great Basin—
Description and travel. | Great Basin—Environmental conditions. | BISAC: NATURE
/ Essays. | BIOGRAPHY & AUTOBIOGRAPHY / Personal Memoirs. | FAMILY &
RELATIONSHIPS / Parenting / Fatherhood.

For Hannah Virginia and Caroline Emerson

contents

Learning to Walk

"Off the trail" is another name for the Way, and sauntering off the trail is the practice of the wild. That is also where— paradoxically—we do our best work.

—GARY SNYDER, *The Practice of the Wild*

I earned my whiskers as a desert rat out in the remote, hilly, high-elevation western Great Basin Desert, scurrying across the land, scrabbling up every dome, running each ridge, scouring all the canyon draws, poking my snout into any rocky crevice I could find. My life's ambition had been to inhabit a place so remote as to provide immediate access to solitude and big wilderness. After many years of making incremental decisions that inched me closer to this dream, at last I took the leap. I put my life savings down on a parcel of raw land in the hinterlands of northwestern Nevada. My new property was not only suitably isolated and rendered nearly inaccessible by mud, snow, and unmaintained access roads, it was also at 6,000 feet in elevation and adjacent to public lands stretching west all the way to the foot of the Sierra Nevada mountains in neighboring California. Never mind walking the dog—I'd be able to launch solo backpacking trips from my own front door. Of course I had no front door and no house to hang it on—just an exposed, windy patch of sand and sagebrush out on the threshold of a vast, beautiful high desert wilderness.

My first hike from the secluded hilltop where I would eventually build a passive solar home began at sunrise. I set off alone, tromping west up a nearby hill that I would later name Moonrise. From the crest of Moonrise I looked out across a sage-filled draw that swept gracefully up to the rocky cliffs ornamenting a higher summit ridge I would later call Palisades. Another hour of stepping out brought me to the top of Palisades, from which an even higher ridge came into view. Harder scrambling brought me to the boulder-strewn crest of that third ridge, which I would name Prospect. From Prospect I gazed west over my dream landscape. Below me steep slopes of sage and scree, dotted yellow-green with mounds of ephedra, fell away to a deep, broad, sweeping valley. Several miles away, on the far side of that wild valley, rose my home mountain, an impressive, 8,000-foot-tall, fifteen-mile-long sleeping giant whose rocky north-facing flanks held streaks of late-season snow. From Prospect Ridge I enjoyed an expansive view of a high desert montane landscape on the monumental, inhuman scale that is its signature. A small cluster of pronghorn antelope could be seen gliding across the bitterbrush-stippled flank of the distant mountain. Two glossy black ravens wheeled silently beneath me. I felt the exhilaration of solitude.

Descending the ridge in a long, semicontrolled slide down the scree slope, I soon reached the broad canyon and made my way across its sunny, sage-strewn expanse to the foot of the big mountain. From the wildfire-scorched bitterbrush flats at the mountain's base I began an 1,800-foot ascent into the cloudless azure sky. Halfway up the mountain I discovered a small seep, where I paused to refill my water bottles. Looking back from there across the Great Basin I saw broken hills and alkali-white playas separated by juniper-dotted ridges rolling east to the horizon. Above me to the west twisted a faint game trail, rising through copses of bitter cherry and coyote willow and dodging between granite cliffs tattooed with chartreuse lichen.

Finally cresting the mountain's 8,000-foot ridge, I found myself in a sweeping summit meadow that reclined between a brace of rocky peaks and was graced with groves of gnarled aspens and the occasional green dome of a snowberry bush. Spreading out before me in all directions was an undulating yellow blanket of flowering tower butterweed. As I stood in the swell and ripple of that wild meadow, I gazed even farther west, first to the valley 3,000 feet below and then out over green California, its thick conifer forests and towering granite turrets and gables ignited by shafts of high-elevation sunlight. I was a man alone in the wilderness, and in that moment of summit bliss I imagined there was nothing that I could not see. Only later would I discover that, even from that high peak, what mattered most remained invisible to me.

Ever since they were toddlers, our daughters, Hannah and Caroline, have had as their life's ambition to achieve the summit of Moonrise, to finally stand with their fists in the air on the crest of what is in fact a modest bump in this immense landscape. An officially nameless little knoll of the sort that are numberless here in the Great Basin, Moonrise is less than a mile from our front door and perhaps only four or five hundred feet above us. It is the kind of "summit" a desert rat scurries over on his way to bigger, wilder quarry. But to a kid Moonrise looks imposing, and the idea of gaining a ridge carved so high into the sapphire desert sky has proven irresistible to the girls. The first ridge westward from our house, Moonrise is in sight on every walk we take together. It is what you notice when you walk Beauregard the dog, what you look up at when Dad pulls you over-land in the sky-blue toboggan. The girls see it clearly from their play structure and from their tree house, too. If the window shades are up,

Hannah and Caroline can see the etched crest of the ridge as they lie reading stories with my wife, Eryn, in their bunk beds. To a little kid, Moonrise fills the western sky.

On her fourth birthday, Hannah blew out the candles on her birthday cake and then turned immediately to me.

"Dad, am I old enough to climb Moonrise now?" she asked, as if the process of extinguishing the candles had suddenly brought her to a new level of readiness for outdoor adventure.

"Not yet, Bug. How about if we go up on your seventh birthday?" I replied.

"How about birthday six instead?" she persisted. The look on her face was both plaintive and determined.

"OK, kid, six it is. Two years from today. Put it on your calendar."

"Can CC come?" Hannah asked, looking down at her six-month-old sister, Caroline, who was at that moment pulling herself upright by grasping the seat of the kitchen stool upon which Hannah sat. "It wouldn't be fair not to take her with us for something this important."

"Good point," Eryn replied. "Sure, you guys can take CC. It will be the first ascent of Moonrise for both Branch girls!"

During the two intervening years, Moonrise was never out of sight, either literally or figuratively. For Hannah it was as if the days were being counted down, the anticipation rising as her sixth birthday approached. She often told Caroline stories about the upcoming "Moonrise Expedition," as she called it, an expedition that also appeared in Hannah's writings and drawings and even in her dreams.

In an attempt to document insights gleaned from one dream of the great expedition, Hannah drew a detailed map, which she reasoned we could use to navigate safely to summit and thus avoid the explorer's fate of becoming forever lost in this vast desert wilderness. I explained that because our house would never be out of sight during the hike, we'd probably be fine, but I thanked her for the map just the same, and we agreed that it would be a good idea for her to add it to the day pack whose contents she had begun assembling more than a month before the epic climb was to take place.

When the day of her sixth birthday arrived, Hannah shouldered her little red day pack, and Eryn lifted Caroline into the baby backpack I had buckled around my waist and chest. After we made sure we had everything needed for the Moonrise Expedition, Eryn took pictures of the momentous occasion, and I set off with the girls toward the western horizon.

By the time we finished bushwhacking up the brushy draw behind the house, Hannah was tired and thirsty, and she had been caught a few times on the sharp thorns of the desert peach bushes that choked the ravine. But she was tough, continuing to slog uphill, her sinewy little legs driving downward as she leaned into the grade, pumping her elbows side to side like an old Scotsman striding into the wind. Hannah kept this up for two more hours, when at last she plopped down on the steep southern exposure of Moonrise. At this elevation the brushy canyon slopes had given way to open, sandy desert dotted with wild rye and ephedra. Patches of snow hid in the shade of a few boulders across the canyon, while the delicate yellow flowers of sagebrush buttercup were visible here and there in damp spots in the granitic sand.

On this steep desert slope we all drank water, ate snacks from Hannah's pack, and marveled at how tiny our house appeared, so far below us down in the sage. "You've come a long way today, Bug," I affirmed, looking homeward. "This is your biggest hike ever. How do you feel?"

"I'm pretty pooped, Dad. Do you think I can make it?" She looked tired, flushed, and also a little worried about the fate of the expedition.

"I do. It is so steep from here to summit that you'll have to use your hands, though, and scramble up like a desert monkey. We can go home anytime you want. Moonrise will always be here for you. But if you want to go all the way up, I think you can make it." She sat quietly, gazing out over the Great Basin. I couldn't tell what she was thinking or if she even knew. There were countless occasions on which I had taken the long view across our home desert with that same exhausted, exhilarated, open-hearted gaze.

"What do you think we'll find at the top?" she asked, as if weighing the prize of the summit against the cost of her fatigue.

"The thing about climbing a mountain is you never know what you'll find at the top. You'll just have to go up and see. But you don't have to do it today, honey."

Hannah paused for a moment and then stood up, though I still wasn't sure what decision she had made. "Let's go see what's at the top of Moonrise," she said resolutely, as she began to clamber up the final pitch with renewed energy. I trudged along behind, using my hands now and then for balance, watching Hannah rising into the sky above me as Caroline bounced in her pack on my shoulders.

Thirty minutes later our expedition's leader shouted back, "Dad, I think I'm almost there!"

"Just a little farther, Bug," I replied. "You go ahead and be the first up there, and we'll be along soon."

Five minutes later, panting with the weight of Caroline on my back, I crested the ridge and lifted my head. There, on the rocky summit of Moonrise, stood my six-year-old daughter, wearing the widest grin her little face could contain and holding up an immense, gracefully curved, many-fingered, bone-white mule deer antler—the largest and most perfect imaginable.

"Look what was on top of Moonrise!" Hannah exclaimed in delight. "Did you know this was up here?"

I stood in silence, genuinely astonished at the remarkable antler. "No, honey, I didn't," I finally managed to reply, breaking into a wide smile to match hers. "I think your expedition was a success. Happy birthday, Bug."

I looked down at our little home, a small island in a vast sagebrush ocean, a sanctuary huddled among the scattered green dots of wild juniper trees below. It was a more meaningful view than I'd ever achieved from a higher ridge or even from the summit of my majestic home mountain. In that moment it occurred to me that maybe Moonrise actually *was* my home mountain. Our home mountain.

For more than a decade now we have lived together—my wife, Eryn, and our two girls, Hannah and Caroline—in these high, dry wilds, on this windy knoll, amid the remote ridges and canyons of the western Great Basin. A vast 200,000-square-mile expanse of sagebrush steppe high desert, the Great Basin extends from the Columbia Plateau up north to the Mojave and Sonoran Deserts down south, from the Rocky Mountains all the way out here to northwestern Nevada, where we live among the arid hills that ripple out beneath the rain shadow of the towering granitic escarpment of the Sierra Nevada.

The Great Basin is the largest and least familiar of American deserts, and it is among the most extreme landscapes in North America. To call conditions here "extreme" hardly does justice to the apocalyptic nature of life in this isolated high desert place. Since making our home here we've seen temperatures close to 110 degrees on the top end and 20 below at the bottom, while day-night swings of 40 degrees occur often. We've had high winds whip up into impenetrable sandstorms of swirling alkali dust, while other periods have been so breathless and stultifying that it seemed the earth had ceased to turn on its axis. Some spells have been so dry that we went six months without feeling a drop of rain, while other years have brought thunderstorms so intense as to trigger flash floods, which blasted through this open desert in broad sheets led by roiling, muddy, foot-tall snouts, sweeping our road away and leaving us stranded. Because we're in one of the most active seismic zones in the country, earthquakes have on occasion rattled books off our shelves, and smaller tremors are common. And, of course, this is fire country. There have been wildfires on the nearby public lands almost every summer or fall, and we have twice been subject to emergency evacuation as a curtain of wind-driven flames raced toward us across the desert plains beneath billowing black clouds of acrid smoke. Although we've occasionally been forced out by fire, we've more often been snowbound on our isolated hill, sometimes for days and often without electricity, huddled by the wood stove, gazing out at the beauty of snow that has sometimes been wind driven into drifts five feet deep.

The critters here are as wild as the weather. Mountain lions hunt our high valley each winter, and on several occasions a bobcat has tried to make a meal of the few laying hens we keep. This is winter range for mule deer, which join us in autumn to avoid becoming the snowbound prey of lions up in the Sierra, and it is also the year-round home of pronghorn antelope, which we see gliding effortlessly through the open desert at speeds of up to sixty miles per hour. Coyotes are everywhere in this landscape, loping through the sage and bitterbrush by day and yipping by night in bands whose shrill chorus is carried downcanyon on moonlit wind. Desert cottontails are dwarfed by seven-pound black-tailed jackrabbits, which are struck from above and eviscerated by big redtails and by the fierce, silent great horned owls that have repurposed our home's peaked roof as a hunting perch. The golden eagles are much larger—so immense that they prey successfully on pronghorn fawns—while the white pelicans that glide high above us in splintered Vs on their way from one remote desert lake to another are larger still, each one a cross of alabaster drifting through the azure sky on a ten-foot wingspan that is second in length only to that of the California condor.

There are plenty of smaller brute neighbors, too. Our home ground is also residence to California and antelope ground squirrels, kangaroo rats, pocket gophers, broad-footed moles, grasshopper mice, and that most amazing of desert rodents, the bushy-tailed pack rat. Snakes are common, and while most are Great Basin gopher snakes, I once discovered an eleven-button rattler shading himself in our garage. It seems that a scorpion hides beneath every rock, with plenty left over to inhabit the ductwork of our house. One year hordes of shield-backed katydids (a large sagebrush-country insect often called a "Mormon cricket") invaded, blanketing these hills so thickly that their mushed guts rendered the paved roads slick as ice, even prompting the closure of a major highway. Whenever we get a big rain after an especially hot summer day, the western harvester ants whose colonies dot this desert sprout wings and rendezvous to mate at the highest point in the local landscape, which is the top of our chimney, on top of our house, on top of our home hill. From there they descend the chimney in untold thousands and writhe in a foot-deep mass behind the glass doors of the wood stove's firebox. Our shared life on this isolated patch of high desert has provided an unbroken string of such challenges.

If this place doesn't sound like paradise, then perhaps I've taken the wrong tack in describing it. Maybe I should say that this is an open, wild country of extreme beauty, that its undulating, muscular hills hide life-giving springs and seeps, that these canyons and arroyos wind sinuously between knobs crowned with palisades of granite slung gracefully between ridges of sand and sage. Perhaps I should mention that the western horizon is etched by the serrated ridgeline of our spectacular 8,000-foot home mountain, which conceals a soaring split summit brimming with tangled stands of mountain mahogany and rolling meadows flowing in lavender waves of wild iris. Maybe I should explain that the elevation and aridity here create a sky bluer than any imagining of it could ever be. This landscape has a clarity and presence unmatched by any other I've experienced, a quality of light that keeps the hard splendor of the world before us in high relief. This is the place where the moon draws your long shadow across snow and granite, the place where the forking path of the Milky Way seems always within reach.

I could offer a great deal more in this lyrical vein, but I don't want to do that. I'd prefer to return to a celebration of our home landscape as vast, alien, and fierce. This place is not remarkable in spite of its blizzards and droughts, its fires and floods, its rattlers and scorpions. It is astonishing because of them. This is a landscape so full of energy, surprise, and struggle that it constantly challenges our ideas about nature and about ourselves. To dwell in this vast desert requires that we relinquish any pretense of control over the circumstances of our wild existence. Living here offers the salutary reminder that control is nothing more than a human idea, an abstract concept that this marvelous landscape is under no obligation to recognize. It is the fantasy of control that is itself most vulnerable, because in this land a humbling corrective is only one fire, blizzard, or rattler strike away.

The passionate desire to inhabit this extreme landscape is not easily explained, even by those few of us who have been so rash as to act upon it. Yet harder to explain is why anybody would choose to raise their children out in this open wilderness. This is a question I am still trying to answer, one that I find intriguing and useful even after a decade of meditating on it. I could, of course, point to the exquisite beauty of the high desert landscape, to the way a single glint of alpenglow on a distant snowcapped desert peak sweeps away all doubt. Or I might claim that there is a certain resourcefulness or strength of character that develops in those who struggle to make a life in this unforgiving place. I could say that our geographical isolation has strengthened us as a family, providing opportunities to bond deeply through shared experiences that other modes of living do not provide. I could suggest that for kids, outdoor adventure and play are essential forms of engaging with the world, and I might offer a corollary lament that for many of us grown-ups the thrill of adventure and the joy of free play have by now receded into the ghostly world of memory. Speaking as a man who is still learning to be a father, I could share my deep belief that this wild desert is teaching my daughters things that I cannot.

These sorts of claims point to a deeper issue concerning the relationship between domesticity and wildness. Wilderness, and the wildness it both embodies and expresses, has received eloquent praise within American literary culture. In many ways the flight to nature in order to transcend the perceived limitations of the domestic world describes the arc of the quintessential American journey. Consider Lewis and Clark hunting their way across the broad continent; Herman Melville's Ishmael bolting to a life on the high seas; Henry Thoreau retreating to his writer's shack at Walden Pond; John Wesley Powell shooting the rapids of the uncharted Colorado; John Muir riding out a windstorm in the tossing crown of a towering Doug fir up in the nearby Sierra; Mark Twain's Huck Finn rolling on the big river and then "lighting out for the territory"; the heroes of Jack London's tales answering the call of the wild western wilderness; my fellow desert rat "Cactus Ed" Abbey soloing across the glowing red-rock mesas of the Colorado Plateau. Even those who never returned tell a similar story: Everett Ruess vanishing into a labyrinth of canyons in southern Utah's Escalante or Chris McCandless perishing in the sublimity of the Alaskan wilderness.

While plenty of counterexamples might be cited, the dominant narrative of engagement with wildness in American culture has been one that features men, often operating in solitude, removing themselves from the sphere of home and children in order to enter a distant green world where opportunities for heroism and adventure abound. To judge from the mainstream of American environmental literature, a reader might be forgiven for assuming that the concepts of family and wildness are in fact mutually exclusive. But when we assume that the wild does not exist within the family—or that the family cannot exist within the wild—we radically limit our conception of what wildness means and so also limit what it can teach us.

In perpetuating an understanding of wildness that depends upon the far-flung exploits of men heroically working alone (or with other men), we overlook the wildness that is inherent both to parenting and to children. The wildness of conception and birth only initiate young lives in which a spontaneous wildness is strikingly apparent. I am keen to avoid romanticizing the relationship of children to nature, because to do so often leads to a self-indulgent, Wordsworthian sentimentality that is rife with problems. That said, anybody who has attended carefully to how a young kid's universe operates can't help but notice the many ways in which children appear to be more like wild animals than human beings. Watch a kid climb a tree, build a shelter, dig a tunnel, imagine and then inhabit a magical forest or underwater hideout or secret desert cave, and you'll witness a visceral form of animal engagement. Children's stories are so often framed as animal parables, not only because we grown-ups aim to use all those rabbits and coyotes to impart moral lessons but also because children are already in such close communication with the animal world. Of course we grown-ups are animals too, but we've had the time and training necessary to forget that, while our children have not. In this sense our kids are the keepers of a wild flame that may be nearly extinguished in ourselves; they are emissaries between the adult world and the wild world from which we emerged and upon which we have so often turned our backs.

This book's title, *Raising Wild*, is intended to suggest a very different approach to how we conceive the relationship between wildness and domesticity. We tend to think that something that is "raised" cannot also be "wild" and that something that is "wild" must not have been "raised." (Think salmon here.) But rather than figure the wild as other than and apart from the family, this book explores the ways in which living as a family in a wild landscape reveals the wildness at the heart of both childhood and parenthood. Raising daughters in this amazing place has tested many of my own assumptions, leading me to question our culture's association of wildness with adulthood, masculinity, and solitude. Some of what I've gleaned from my experience appears in the following dispatches from our remote home in this high desert wilderness.

The complete text of W. S. Merwin's elegant little poem "Witness" reads as follows:

> *I want to tell what the forests*
> *were like*
>
> *I will have to speak*
> *in a forgotten language*

I am moved by Merwin's suggestion that the language we use to express our understanding of nature is itself the fruit of nature—and also by his warning that an ancient connection between words and world is weakened when the world upon which language depends is imperiled.

Among the innumerable joys and challenges of parenthood is the recognition that kids often speak in this forgotten language. We see in them some glimmer of how the natural world once appeared to us: immediate, new, strange, funny, waiting to be touched and played with. While it is we who teach our children the names of things, it is they who engage the things themselves, often spontaneously employing modes of perception, imagination, and intimacy that are no longer immediately available to us. If it is a truism that children can teach as well as be taught, it is equally certain that in order to fully communicate with our kids we'll need to remember some of what we've forgotten about how we once saw this world. While some might argue that a language, once forgotten, is destined for extinction, my experience suggests that substantial relearning is not only possible but necessary to parenting, especially in this wild place.

I do not subscribe to the notion that wildness is reserved for adult male adventurers who are defined by their escape from the constraints of home and family. Instead, I have come to view childhood as a valuable repository of wildness from which we grown-ups might derive insight and draw inspiration. As the father of daughters, I am also convinced that our association of wilderness and wildness with masculinity is not only archaic but profoundly misinformed from the start. And I am troubled that the so-called retreat narrative—a stylized way of telling the wild that valorizes solitude as the correct mode of encounter with the natural world—authorizes a view of wildness that necessarily excludes children. It is certainly not that I fail to appreciate the value of solitary wilderness experiences. Since the day of that first epic hike over Moonrise, Palisades, and Prospect—those three ridges still unnamed on every map—and up to the forked summit of our high home mountain, I have walked more than 13,000 solitary miles in the desert hereabouts (during which I encountered a grand total of two recreational hikers). Having logged so many miles in all seasons and all weathers, I've witnessed miracles and wonders too numerous to tell. Nevertheless, I have found the experiences I share in nature with my daughters to be instructive and liberating in ways that my solo hikes are not.

I too have retreated to the wild, but I have retreated *with* my family, rather than *from* them. In so doing I have discovered wildness in my children and in myself, as well as in the remote hills and canyons of the high desert. This experience has been more fascinating and valuable than any heroic male wilderness adventure could possibly be. Here, in the wildness of home, Moonrise is our Everest and our Denali.

One of the most surprising and useful things I've learned is that inhabiting the desert and raising children have many things in common. Both enterprises begin with genuine passion, but it is a passion born of an uninformed idealism that blinds us to the challenges and blessings of the actual condition we're about to enter. I look back on my pilgrimage to this desert place in much the same way I view the fact that I once read how-to books to prepare myself for fatherhood.

Even as a confirmed bibliophile, I now freely acknowledge as laughable the idea that anyone could become prepared for fatherhood by any means other than being a father. So too with this hard, bright landscape: language can only obliquely approximate the experience of it. One must be immersed in desertness to have an inkling of what ennobling challenges full engagement with it might offer.

Eking out a living in this unforgiving landscape requires a high tolerance for frustration and failure, for this is a place that, if it is not exactly hostile, is impressively indifferent to human ambition. Parenting can be similarly exasperating, because, like the desert, it constantly forces upon us an awareness of our limitations. In this sense, both raising children and dwelling in arid lands help us to acquire a necessary humility, an acknowledgment of our weaknesses, without which either enterprise would be perilous. Both experiences strip us of superfluity, deprive us of naive assumptions about ourselves and the world, render absurd any coveted delusion that we are superior to our kids or to the nonhuman natural world. Self-congratulation is an affectation that neither parents nor desert dwellers can long sustain.

Making a home in the high desert and making a home for children also have in common that they entail a constant process of self-examination and growth—one facilitated by the enforced humility I've described. *Raising Wild* shares the story of how my girls' intuitive understanding of self and nature has provided a profound challenge to my own. In their disarmingly honest approach to me and to their home landscape, Hannah and Caroline have innocently exposed many of my unquestioned assumptions about myself as a man, a father, an environmentalist, and a lover of wild places. My shared experiences with the girls have often forced me to admit the absurdity or hypocrisy of my own values or actions, ultimately helping me to revisit core questions about why we engage both children and nature as we do. Even my most cherished self-image—that of an independent man whose journey to this remote place was motivated by a passion for galvanic, unmediated contact with wildness—has been sorely tested, as I have confronted both the daunting realities of desert living and also my own weaknesses as a man who is still learning how to be a good father.

"As soon as you have made a thought, laugh at it." So proclaimed Lao-tzu, who understood that humor is an inevitable and redeeming by-product of humility. Laughter is the sound we make in the moment we acknowledge, perhaps even begin to accept, our own mistakes or inadequacies. A laugh is a marker of recognition, a sign that we have momentarily seen ourselves in some new light. As humor theorist Gina Barreca puts it, "Humor, like shame or wisdom, is a product of understanding." My efforts to make a home in the high desert and to become a good dad have been so riddled with missteps, absurd inconsistencies, and failed grand plans that I couldn't survive a day without humor. For this reason, *Raising Wild* often approaches the braided challenge of parenting and environmental engagement in comical ways that differ considerably from the solemn attitude often adopted by environmental writers. Unfortunately, a great deal of writing about nature (and, for that matter, about children) is humorless and predictable, relying on threadbare tropes that give readers the false impression that the writer's relationship to nature is a fait accompli—a static achievement that can be used to manufacture calculated epiphanies celebrating the sacredness of nature. But those of us who care deeply about the natural world have good reasons to laugh, because our relationship to nature is often inherently comical, and also because humor provides a sustainable form of resilience that we desperately need in this trying time of environmental crisis. James Thurber was right in identifying humor as "one of our greatest earliest natural resources, which must be preserved at all cost." Humor is also an essential element of parenting, because laughter generates the flexibility and acceptance that are necessary for one to develop patience and express love. I have found that, even in its most earnest moments, parenting is very much a laughing matter.

Much like living in the desert, becoming a mindful father requires an ongoing and often chastening process of attempt, failure, insight, and growth—and then, ever and always, *attempt*. Practice does not make perfect but rather makes more practice, and it is this practice of reflective parenting and attentive dwelling in place that has led me to discover enriching forms of intimacy within my family and within the wild landscape we inhabit. There is no place I love more than this high desert, no people I love more than my daughters. And yet there is a wonderful sense in which I do not know them yet. Even in the open desert much remains hidden. Hannah and Caroline too are deserts—each an exquisite mystery I have not yet solved. I need one more day, or year, or another decade; just one more walk, another mile, then 13,000 more. I am still learning to pay attention.

Parenting, like walking in the desert, is a meandering art of improvisation. The adventure never turns out quite as we planned it, the inner and outer weather remain unpredictable. We are in sympathy but never in control. We take conditions as we find them, putting one foot in front of the other as we navigate a topography of uncertainty, trying to make the most of each day's pilgrimage back to the heart and to the land. We carry water toward our lovely garden, but end up using it to put out a fire. We set out for the spring but follow pronghorn tracks instead, intend to witness the rise of the crescent moon but are drawn to the huddled glow of the Pleiades. We search for ways to reshape our experiences into narrative, to transform a shared life into a story that can be given to our children, mapped onto the high, dry landscape of their only home.

In this wide open desert there are no trails, which is to say that any route you choose becomes a trail only as it is walked, becomes a story only as it is told. Before our children can fully engage the world they must first learn to walk. As a father I am still exploring the hard beauty of this wild landscape, learning slowly, with the help of my family, how to walk with and within it.

PART ONE

Birthing

To know the spirit of a place is to realize that you are a part of a part and that the whole is made of parts, each of which is whole. You start with the part you are whole in.

—GARY SNYDER, *The Practice of the Wild*

Chapter 1

Endlessly
Rocking

It's true that on the day Eryn and I decided to have a kid we had been drinking quite a lot of gin. Gin, the product of fermented juniper berries; juniper, the wild trees that surround our home in the high-elevation, western Great Basin Desert—*Juniperus osteosperma,* the seminal one. It is best to achieve a state of extreme lucidity before making a sober determination about something as weighty as the eternal fate of one's sperm or eggs.

After many years of wandering in the glaring sun and desiccating wind of the Great Basin, I had come, as we all eventually must, back to the sea, to the cradle Walt Whitman rightly described as "endlessly rocking." The sea here was the late-winter Pacific, gray-green and breaking gently along the rocky shores of Monterey Bay, on California's central coast. In addition to the harbor seals, sea otters, and sea lions that hang around the wharves and rocky islands, you see here a variety of shorebirds and occasionally notice the rolling of dolphins or the spouting of whales—mostly gray whales this time of year, though the big humpbacks and hundred-foot-long blues will return come summer. What remains invisible is even more remarkable, for not far offshore is a submarine canyon of incredible proportions. The top of the walls of Monterey Canyon are a mile beneath the ocean's surface, and from there the canyon descends another mile—the approximate depth of the Grand Canyon—to the frigid darkness of the seafloor far below. This remarkable canyon was cut by a giant river, and though the river hasn't run for eight million years, its massive canyon remains, a precipitous chasm snaking from the bay out to the broad Pacific beyond. What swims in the nearly 12,000-foot-deep ocean in and above this grand submarine canyon? Better to ask what doesn't swim there, so wild and vast is that invisible labyrinthine world beneath the waves.

My main objective in leaving my home desert to visit this place was to sit on the chilly beach and stare at the horizon. Maybe study the tip of a surf rod stuck in a sand spike by the cooler. Maybe unwrap a C harp from a green bandana and bend a few blues lines around the booming G-ish bass of surf on sand. Maybe decide, once and for all, who would take the National League pennant in the upcoming season. Maybe resolve to have a child. It was a modest agenda, but I have always believed that with enough gin and time all problems are solvable. Or at least soluble: capable of being diluted with equal parts distilled juniper berries and seawater.

Hiking on an exposed expanse of bare beach in February, squinting into the wind, pelted by flying sand, buried beneath the sound of roaring waves—these things are surprisingly comforting to a desert dweller. If you can excuse there being water present, the rest is keenly familiar: leaning into the gust-driven gyre that lifts surging blasts of sand, you tilt toward a deep gray horizon of dusty green swells that rise like shiny billows of mountain mahogany and creosote bush and bitterbrush—breakers undulating like shimmering waves of *Artemisia tridentata*, big sage, each desiccated three-lobed leaf reminiscent of Neptune's trident. Even the distant battleship clouds rise in broken, serrated ridgelines like desert mountains, low ranges lipping an overflowing world-round cup that contains both gray whales and pronghorn antelope.

It is best to visit visited places when they are unvisited, both to avoid the throng of folks who shatter the solitude necessary for problem solving—and questions of pennant races and procreation promise to be close calls this year—and also because we sometimes enjoy people's presence most when we register their absence. The best kind of solitude is created when people not only aren't around but *might* have been around and aren't. Even in praising the beauty of a "deserted" beach we reveal the awareness that it was once inhabited—betray the recognition that its charm is created not by its beauty alone but also by the people who once were there but have now moved on, blown away, *deserted*.

Melville observed that all paths lead to water—that an irresistible force constantly and silently pulls us benighted terrestrials back to our watery home. Even in the desert it is true that all paths terminate at either a glistening spring or a pile of powdered bones. Like everything else in life, it's simply a matter of choosing the correct fork in the canyon's sandy wash-bottom game trail. But there is something compelling about this limitless mass of life-filled water, roiling around the globe, pulled by moon and pushed by wind. It is a truism that we carry the ocean in our veins and tears, but that seems a thinly clinical way to measure the affiliation. My body is a gin-powered carbon-based flesh satchel that is essentially saltwater—so far so good. But think of the wildness of the sea, with its innumerable underwater canyons and mountain peaks, its turreted and gabled reefs, its fissures and crypts, vents and vaults. Think of a myriad of minute life-forms spiraling around towering spires of swaying kelp, of the high-pressure, frigid, eternal darkness above which bright, fish-filled rivers of animated current run. Think of the battle between whale and giant squid that is raging in the depths at this moment somewhere, the giant cephalopod frenetically twining its eighty-foot tentacles around the snapping jaws of a hundred-foot cetacean that is glaring, coldly, out of its tiny eye.

But think, too, of ourselves. Of how we crawled, frame by time-lapse frame, out of the pond, rose to our feet, grabbed an ash or maple stick just as our flippers became hands with digits, and smacked a soaring dinger into the left-field bleachers—or invented the quadrant, or wrote *Hamlet*, or created the smartphone, or whatever you think of as the pinnacle of hominid evolution. And just when a giant squid seems the ultimate nasty neighbor, try living on land for a while, always worried about finding shade and fresh water and paying rent and taxes, flinching constantly at all the looming things that can spear you through the back of the neck while you're only trying to grub a few roots. Maybe the whale and its air-breathing marine cousins got it right when they crawled back into the drink: any sensible terrestrial mammal will tell you that leaving the pond wasn't exactly a cakewalk.

I slice another lime with my bait knife, thinking to myself that what would be wildest—and what would connect us with the wildness of our watery home even more powerfully than knowing that we cry salt tears—would be to crawl back in. Not in an underwater robot, like Jacques Cousteau, or with an oxygen tank on our back, like Sean Connery's Bond, James Bond (impossibly cool even in those British secret agent diaper-white swim trunks), but silently and unassisted, simply breathing water as we once did, returning quietly to the calm of our coral caves, leaving the windy beach without regret. *Deserting*.

Since this doesn't seem possible—although the seals and dolphins have managed it rather gracefully—I've been contemplating the terrestrial mammal's best alternative: my wife's suggestion that perhaps we should give birth to a tiny human. This proposition seems at once perfectly natural and extremely reckless. For us nonmarine mammals, being a fluid-breathing fetus floating in the amniotic ocean of our mother's uterus is as close as we'll ever get to turning our backs on this troubled land and sliding back into the silent sea. Still, I can't help but think of the more mundane implications: How long does it take before a thing like that can run a Weedwacker, cut stove wood, or slice limes, even? My father always said that the perfect age for a kid is when they're old enough to run the lawn mower but not old enough to drive the car. Fair enough, but think of the magnitude of the investment, given the extremely narrow preautomotive mowing phase of child development. And these infants—what, exactly, do they do all day? And doesn't much of what they do smell? I've heard poet Galway Kinnell's scatophilic assertion that those who don't poop don't live, while those who do do doo doo do. But still.

As I look out over Uncle Walt's endlessly rocking cradle and consider this question further, I no longer picture the epic battle of cetacean and cephalopod or the spiraling, undulating towers of kelp, but instead imagine a pudgy little human baby, rosy cheeked, bulging eyed, wide smiled, wearing bunchy diapers attached with those big pins (for some reason) and doing the breaststroke underwater as a curtain of bubbles periodically covers its fat face like a belch. An amphibious cherub, more monstrous than cute and not at all as advertised. As the thing swims slowly toward me with its sweet, trusting grin, I think how unlikely it is to survive very long down there, with all the hungry fish folk, so red in tooth and fin—and it so corpulent and awkward and slow-moving, and probably not too chewy. Do I really want to take responsibility for this defenseless monster, neither fish nor ape, that can't hide in a coral nook, or outswim a shark, or even cut a lime? I'll mow my own damned lawn.

As the tiny beast paddles yet closer, a huge mushroom cloud of brown bubbles suddenly bursts from beneath its diaper, blowing the cloth to shreds in underwater slo-mo. I suspect that sharks can smell this. I wince in disgust. Lifting the fruit jar from the sand, I take a healthy belt of sandy gin and tonic, then slowly raise my eyes and look out across the sea again. Somewhere beneath its rocking green cradle is a hypothetical baby—an amphibious infant that, like me, has saltwater in its veins and tears. I look beneath the surf again: against a trailing curtain of brown butt chum the child is still swimming at me placidly, still approaching land, ready to crawl out and stand up and swing a bat. And it is still smiling.

The woman who calls me her husband is from California. But Eryn isn't blond, and she doesn't surf. (As it turns out, California is loaded with brunettes, several of whom don't even know how to surf. Who knew?) She's one of the Crackers of the West, that sturdy Okie stock whose kin came across the Great Basin and Sierra like Ma and Pa Joad, piloting a ramshackle jalopy and looking for the endless orchards of what everybody from Moses to Chuck Berry called the Promised Land. Eryn is the kind of woman who makes you want to do a rash thing like get married, even if you've had a good, long run of knowing better than to enter what I once disparagingly referred to as "the condition."

Make no mistake, marriage is one of the few institutions I respect. Ralph Waldo Emerson was right that most institutions are dead forms: ossified, impersonal, ineffective, inertial, disingenuous, self-promoting, tautological, hermetic, superficial, and fucked up (Emerson didn't actually say "fucked up," but that's what he was thinking). In front of a bus stop at a remote rural crossroads in central Nevada I once saw an old drunk preaching, most righteously, into the vastness of the glaring desert: "Beware the *institution,* for there's two things, *two things* that it never can do, *never can do,* and that is anything, *anything,* for the first or the last time . . . *first or last,* brother, first or last, *beware!*" There are prophets everywhere. But I don't think the crazy wise man intended his divinely inspired admonition to apply to the institution of marriage, which is, as none less than lascivious old Ben Franklin recognized, a fine condition into which even freedom-loving men should rightly enter. But it somehow never seemed a good idea for *me* to enter it. Marriage wasn't like baseball—a game meant to be both played and watched—but rather like horse racing, something you watched, wagered on, and drank at, but didn't actually participate in.

Even with the weight of the evidence regarding "the condition" on the other side of the question, I married Eryn—or, more accurately, she was generous enough to marry me. Eryn is smart, patient, and generous. She's also witty, stubborn, and optimistic. And though she is Californian, her peach-picking lineage in the Central Valley is substantially redeeming. She's a good friend, and she's resourceful and interesting, which is saying something. It would have been good if I had thought of some of this stuff to put in my crappy, bootlegged, eleventh-hour wedding vows—if you're hung over and you end-run the Bible you're left with crap for vows, as it turns out. I love being married to Eryn.

But just as I'm feeling at peace with my new and improved life, the specter of the swimming diaper-blasting insanely grinning non-lime-slicing not-yet-lawn-mowing amphibious proto-dinger-smacking belching cherub has come upon me from right field—a place things should go to rather than come from. Somehow this strikes me as unfair. I've just taken a deep breath and said, yes, I'm quite pleased with this whole marriage condition, when this fat-faced hypothetical baby comes along, with all its expulsing bodily fluids, to sour my gin and trouble the wide oceans and attract poop-sniffing sharks. It's like sliding safely across home plate and then being tagged out—and by the umpire. But safety, so hard to come by in this world, is especially elusive when freakish babies are paddling around the juniper juice in your noggin.

It happened this way. Eryn and I had just come back from a nearly ideal lovers' evening walk along the chilly, deserted strand of beach with my dog, a thick-headed mystery mutt Eryn generously characterized as "good-natured." I should explain that I had vexed my family by foolishly naming the dog Cat, which I thought sounded cool (as in "cool cat") but which I bestowed primarily, and smugly, to illustrate the power of behavior modification and operant conditioning. "This dog doesn't think about the fact that it's a dog," I philosophized over an IPA one summer afternoon after returning from the SPCA with the new addition to the family. "I could call him Cat, and he'd still come when I called him, so long as he was trained, like Pavlov's dog, through use of a clearly structured series of rewards and punishments." By the time the words tumbled out of my mouth I was already in trouble. First of all, it should have occurred to me that this sort of conditioning had failed when my parents tried it on me. In characteristic form, that morning at the campsite Cat had licked the coagulated bacon grease out of the bottom of the frying pan while I was peeing on the other side of the dune, and when we later walked him down to the ocean he immediately rushed into the surf and attacked the first wave he could reach as it broke on shore, shotgunning a bucketful of ocean as a chaser for his slimy breakfast, after which he dragged along all morning, hacking up sand and saltwater as he went.

So we had just come back from a wonderful evening walk along the beach, and we were sitting comfortably in the tent as a light sea breeze rippled the sloping nylon walls and the glow of the rising moon poured through the mesh windows. We were half-tucked into our sleeping bags when evening damp began to fall, and we were on the sandy shoulder of the infinite sea, and we were laughing, and we were simultaneously playing and drinking gin. Cat, who was curled up in the corner of the tent, snoring happily and occasionally farting, had even stopped yacking. I was fully inhabiting the role of the proverbial happily married man. The situation was as close to ideal as it is likely to get on this side of the vale of tears.

"Do you ever think about having a baby?" Eryn asked, absolutely unprovoked. I could hear her voice winging in from right field as I stood, incredulous, once again tagged out after safely crossing the plate. At that exact moment I was slicing a lime, and I damn near cut my finger off, though it did flash through my mind that if nine and a half fingers was good enough for the Grateful Dead guitarist Jerry Garcia, it ought to be good enough for me.

"Huh?" I replied. Before she could rephrase the question I rebounded, wittily: "I'd like to, but I don't think it's anatomically possible. Perhaps you've mistaken me for a sea horse?"

"Michael, be serious," she said. My long first name plus a command, encapsulated incisively in a three-word sentence. This was clearly inauspicious. Happily married man meets buzz-crushing topic of adult conversation.

"Hey, feel free to call me Mike. Besides, what do you want with one of those?" I asked, desperately invoking levity where it had so little chance of success. "I hear they're expensive and noisy and they smell bad. Really, things are so perfect right now."

"But maybe they would be *more* perfect if we were a real family," Eryn said with disturbing sincerity.

I objected, grasping at semantic straws. "You can't have '*more* perfect'—'perfect' is as good as it gets. Besides, we *are* a real family. What are you talking about? Look at us: happy family!" At this moment I spontaneously spread my arms wide apart, gesticulating grandly to suggest the impressive expansiveness of said happy family, when the gin-soaked gyroscope in my inner ear caused me to lose my balance and, as I fell over, snag my hand on the taut laundry cord above me, spilling my icy drink in my crotch while catapulting a pair of boxer shorts, formerly on the line, onto the extended snout of the sleeping Cat, who snuffled loudly.

I looked up at my sweet wife, who looked back in silence at my undoubtedly plaintive expression, and my soaked crotch, and my strewn underwear, and my flatulent dog, and then dropped her pretty forehead into her open palm to hide a smile. She had to be fantasizing about what her life was like before she married me.

"Let me think on it some," I said.

"OK," she replied, looking up with a labored straight face. "Now cut the lime—the round green one, not the long brown one with the fingernail on it. It's your deal, Bubba." I freshened our drinks; removed the boxers from Cat's snout and placed them, officiously, upside-down on my head, waistband-as-headband style; and began to deal a hand of gin and to sing an old Sleepy John Estes song:

When that wind, that chilly breeze,
Come blowin' through your BVDs,
You gotta move, you gotta move child,
You gotta move.

Inspired by my flapping lid, I was belting out the blues with what I took to be the accent of a French chef.

I was pretty sure that adults didn't sit in tents, half-drunk, wearing underwear on their heads, losing repeatedly at gin, and singing the blues in Franco-phony. Adults, I had been led to believe, made mature, considered decisions about things like whether or not to have children. Long after Eryn fell asleep I was still singing mournful old Sleepy John:

> *There's a change in the ocean, a change in the sea,*
> *I declare now, mama, there'll be a change in me,*
> *Everybody, they ought to change sometime,*
> *Sooner or later, you got to go down in that lonesome ground.*

Unlike John, I wasn't sleepy at all. As I lay in my bag listening to the breakers walk up the beach under the pull of the big moon, I thought about change, and love, and water. These are expansive topics, but I tend to sleep about three hours less each night than Eryn, which gives me plenty of extra time for these contemplations—roughly one thousand hours extra each year, the equivalent of around forty days per annum of dangerously abstract and self-absorbed metaphysical musings. In fact, my unique habit of combining strong java, hard liquor, and excessive contemplation makes me an excellent candidate for spontaneous human combustion. I once pointed out to Eryn that thanks to my superhuman frenetic insomnia, I'd get in years more of sentient contemplations than she would before they threw the dirt on the box. Her reply, without hesitation: "What if you're only given a certain number of waking hours in your mortality allowance? You're squandering time thinking about the shape of the universe, while I'm having wonderful dreams about being a kid again." As usual, she had the more gracious and intelligent side of the argument. But I couldn't sleep anyway, so I lay there singing Sleepy John, listening to my snoring dog, and picturing that sleepless ocean rocking on the far side of the dune.

Water. We're made of it, it surrounds us, and we buy the farm if we go more than a few days without taking some of it in or even without squirting some of it out. Mark Twain said that in the West, "whiskey is for drinking and water is for fighting over," and W. C. Fields, pontificating about water while drinking rye, claimed he "never touched the stuff" because, as he put it so memorably, "fish fuck in it." But there's a good reason why a guy with a name like McKinley Morganfield would call himself Muddy Waters. You wouldn't see a guy named Muddy Waters changing his name to McKinley Morganfield, because he'd end up being an accountant rather than wailing the blues. We wouldn't get far—physically or imaginatively—without water. Newborns must revisit the hydrant of their mother's breast ten times a day, and old men must make pilgrimages to the places where they swam and fished and paddled in their youth before they can die well. *Well* . . . another place from which life-giving water flows.

I fell asleep thinking of old friends who were pulled to water. Not just Herman in the South Pacific and Henry at the pond and Walt crossing Brooklyn Ferry, but also Mister Jefferson admiring the dramatic confluence of the Potomac and Shenandoah, Lewis and Clark portaging around the sublime falls of the Missouri, Twain dodging snags in deep fog on the moonlit Mississippi. One-armed John Wesley Powell lashed in his straight-backed chair to the deck of a wooden boat, shooting the gorges of the unknown Colorado.

Obsessed Hemingway cruising the Caribbean in a fishing boat he had outfitted to attack German U-boats. John Muir trying in vain to explain the sacredness of Hetch Hetchy water to folks who believed that water comes from a tap. Cactus Ed Abbey floating in the unspeakable beauty of Glen Canyon before it was buried beneath sunburned water skiers. Ellen Meloy, one of the very finest of our desert writers, running the graceful bows of the Green River year after year. Norman Maclean reaching with the tip of a fly rod to touch the heart of his lost brother on the Big Blackfoot River. I think especially of young Nathaniel Hawthorne, sitting in the upper window of the Old Manse in Concord, looking up from his manuscript and out to the sweeping bend of the Concord River as it glides through swollen spring meadows and under the wooden arch of the historic Old North Bridge. He had just become a father, and he was ecstatic with joy and creative energy.

"Rise and whine, Bubba," said my wife, through the sound of the ocean beyond her. I wriggled from my mummy bag, crawled out of the tent, and stood up, bleary but proud in my American-flag boxer shorts, out of which fell a desiccated slice of lime. "Eeeew," Eryn said, exaggerating for effect as she handed me a cup of cowboy coffee. Cat sniffed the leathery lime, licked it up off the sand, and then spat it out again, shaking his head a little. I pulled on some clothes and scaled the dune to have a look out over the sea. The breeze was up, and the surf was booming. Three gulls circled above me on the spokes of an invisible wheel, and a few light clouds on the horizon said good weather. It was chilly, but not nearly as cold as I had expected it to be.

After breakfast Eryn instructed me to go fishing, which is another of her many fine qualities. "Take your gear and your limes and whatever nastiness you use for bait and go stare at the sea. That's why you came, right? I'm going to read and discuss current events with Cat, the boy genius. Come back whenever." So off I went, shuffling along the shore with my sand spike and rod in one hand, my little cooler in the other, and my libational day pack on my back. Because I was raised as a fisherman and also as a slave to a puritanical work ethic, I must fish in order to think—or to think about something other than how lazy I'm being by just thinking instead of doing something productive, like fishing. So I was following a comfortable routine, except that now I had the burdensome assignment of contemplating progeny, which seemed intimidating. Setting up by the deserted seashore, I sat in the sand and stared at the world, as planned, and I fished and thought, as usual. Although I had pleasant solitary meditations on the important subjects of water and baseball and evolution, I ultimately began to envision the vulnerable, belching, defecating, grinning underwater ape baby I've already described. Unable to shake this vision, I decided to forego the pleasures of angling—old Izaak Walton would have been scandalized—and instead trudged back to camp by early afternoon. I had decided that procreation is a subject more fit for lively discussion than solipsistic meditation—and so I reckoned that, given her central role in the would-be plan, it might be best if Eryn had an opportunity to weigh in on the subject.

Despite my disturbing vision and unproductive musings, I had struck upon one brilliant idea: if I could imagine a name for the child that we might, perhaps, possibly someday have at some unspecified time in the future, I could humanize, personalize, the thing, thus making it easier to imagine without having weird visions. *Baby, infant, toddler:* these words cause mild discomfort and sound like they would trigger the need for substantial responsibility. But somehow it didn't sound so bad to imagine hanging around and listening to a ball game with *Joe* or *Jane*. No big deal. Then Joe or Jane mows the lawn a couple times and goes off to college, right? So I entered camp with what I took to be a superb conversation starter: baby names.

"Honey," I asked, setting my rod and spike aside by the tent, "if we did have a kid, what would you want to name it?" She stared at me blankly.

"That's what you came up with after contemplating the great sea?"

"No, really. You know how when you give a name to something that's nameless, you know, anonymous, like a disease that you have, or somebody faceless like a criminal, it really humanizes the whole thing?" I urged.

"A disease or a criminal?"

"OK, bad examples. But just for fun, come on, let's talk about what names you like. Let's sit in the sand and work on this a little. I'll mix the G and Ts, you start tossing out some names. Let's say it's a girl. Whatcha got?" She paused, looking at me suspiciously, but she couldn't resist, which was when I first realized she had already been thinking about the dangerous subject of kid names. So we sat facing each other, a light breeze easing down the dune and the rocking ocean stretching out beyond us to the western horizon.

"Well, I had a wonderful great-aunt on my mother's side who I really loved, Aunt Mabel," she said, with inexplicable seriousness.

"Mabel," I choked. "Thou shittest me, yes?"

"OK, how about Phyllis—it means 'leafy bow' in Greek. I think that's pretty."

"Don't you think somebody would call her *Sy*-phyllis? We don't need that."

"Well, what about something fun, like Jasmine?" she suggested in frustration.

"Perfect! That is, if you want your daughter to major in pole dancing. Hey, we could just name her Jasmine Syphyllis. Of course, we'd never get affordable health insurance on somebody with a name like that." Eryn was enjoying this exchange, though she also enjoyed pretending that she wasn't.

"Bubba, you're appalling. OK, what girl names do you like?" she asked.

This was a predictable turn in the discussion, but, as usual, I was unprepared for it anyway. I tried to buy some time: "Did I ever tell you about the time I went to Sleepy Hollow Cemetery in Concord to visit the graves of Emerson and Thoreau? No? Well, I made a pilgrimage to the holy burying place, called Author's Ridge, a beautiful, breezy knoll, covered with big white pines and, well, dead writers. It was a beautiful day, midsummer, and I had just come from skinny-dipping in Walden Pond. Emerson's headstone is this big-ass rock—just a giant, unhewn granite boulder. Thoreau, on the other hand, is napping under this dinky little stone that just says Henry. Tasteful, you know. Modest, restrained, not too showy. Still, you'd think they could have taken up a collection or something. Even Hawthorne and Alcott had better stones than Henry."

"So you want to name our daughter Henrietta?"

"*As I was saying*, once I checked out the big boys up on the ridge, I decided to wander around the graveyard looking for the oddest name I could find. Believe me, there were some pretty funkified old-fashioned names there. But when I found what I was looking for, I knew I couldn't possibly do better, and to this day I've never forgotten her name." I paused. "Are you ready for this?" Again, dramatic pause. "Fucius Barzilla Holdenbum."

She rolled her eyes. "First, I don't believe you. Second, that's got to be a boy's name. And, third, it wouldn't be pronounced 'Fewshus'—it would be 'Fewkaius.'"

"First, I do solemnly swear on the grave of Fucius Barzilla Holdenbum," I said, moving my drink to my left hand so I could raise my right in a solemn pledge, "that I have spoken the gospel truth. Second, I don't know how you could think Barzilla is a guy's name. And, third, only an Okie with strong Old Testament leanings could get 'Fewkaius' out of 'Fewshus.'"

"Well, which of these delightful names are you proposing for your poor daughter? Not Holdenbum, certainly?"

"Witty," I said with fake condescension. "I had to marry the witty one." She smiled, a little proudly. "How about Melissa," I offered spontaneously. I had been humming Allman Brothers tunes while fishing, and it was all I could think of besides Fucius Barzilla Holdenbum, which had clearly played out.

"No good. People will call her Mel, and then everybody will think she's a boy—and a truck driver or a short-order cook."

I hesitated, thinking about the fact that two of my best friends were engaged in these noble occupations. But I had already thought of a good follow-up name. Then Eryn continued: "Besides, Melissa is like Jessica—it just sounds kind of trashy." She had an uncanny way of anticipating and blocking my next move, though I suppose I shouldn't have stuck inflexibly with Allman Brothers song titles. But I loved those smooth, sonorous, sibilant southern names.

"Well, how about Althea?" I blurted.

"Althea? That's what you named your guitar!"

"Well, yeah, but it's a great name. From the Greek. Means 'healing herb.' What's not to like?" She stared me down with that great fake-serious look of hers.

"I could rename my ax. No, never mind." I really didn't want to rename that old Martin D-18. It would be like renaming my dog—which I obviously would have done long ago if I could have. I'd just have to figure out the girl's name without borrowing from any of my instruments, pets, or nicknames for body parts.

The longer this went on, the more I realized that if I were to become the father of a daughter I would be compelled, about seventeen years from now, to kick the ass of somebody who would probably look and act a lot like me. I quickly retrieved and refiled for future use the first line my father-in-law had used in welcoming me into his home: "Son, let me show you my gun collection." But beneath the laughter of the name game I felt a real fear, some impossible-to-describe sense that I wasn't ready, that I somehow just wouldn't know what to do—that I'd be a bumbling father to a baby girl, a flawed, obsessive father to a girl kid, an alien species to a teenaged woman. Now I could feel the limey G and T, which I had ingested with a fair amount of sand, begin to roil in my gut. Maybe the escape hatch was to imagine being a father to a son instead. I knew this wasn't something you could count on, but I figured the odds weren't any worse than the ones people wager on at the roulette table—though I also realized that the simple choice of red or black didn't involve changing diapers or saving for college and would, at least, come with free drinks. Still, it seemed worth a try.

"This ain't workin,'" I said. "How about boys' names? Whatcha got?"

"Well, what about Jeremiah? You've always liked strong names," she said.

"Strong, yes; apocalyptic, no. I'd feel like it was the Last Supper every time I called the kid for dinner: 'Oh, Jeremiah, boy, on the way home from school, could you ask the Lord to have mercy on Daddy's soul? Now put down your flaming cross and go mow the lawn, then get washed up for your loaves and fishes.' On the other hand," and now I leaned over toward her, half-turned for dramatic effect, and sang loudly: "'*Jeremiah was a bullfrog!*' A lot of people wouldn't want to have a son who is a bullfrog," I said, "but I'm very accepting. To *Rana catesbeiana*. Long may he jump!" We raised our plastic glasses in a silent toast.

"So, Bubba McBluffer, you don't have a decent boy name, do you?" she asked, starting the next round.

"Nope. I've got three: Diogenes Asclepiades Themistocles. Real name. Means 'fat man with healthy testicles.' Believe me, you could do worse—with those fine testes you'd have good prospects for grandchildren."

"I had to marry the witty one," she said, smiling. "Let's eat. Maybe we're too famished to think clearly."

"Impossible! We're drinking the juice of junipers and limes here—vegetables and fruits, very nutritious. Come on, one last shot at naming the poor boy. Let's use the trusty blues naming formula—works especially well for boys."

Eryn knew this was a trap, but she didn't care. We were by the great ocean, our ancestral home, and we were with our dog, such as he was, and we were drinking G and Ts with fresh lime and sitting in the soft sand. And in our own laughing, indirect way, we were discussing the idea of starting a family.

"Whatcha got?" she asked, knowing how much I would enjoy this. It was like hitting a homer off a tee, but it still felt great.

"Here's the formula: disability plus fruit or vegetable plus last name of US president. Works every time—you know, as in haunted Texas bluesman Blind Lemon Jefferson." This was an example Eryn could appreciate, since my own blues nickname, given to me by bandmates who wanted to encourage my blues harp playing while also forcing me to maintain absolute humility, was a riff on this one: Blind Lemon Pledge.

"Give it a try," I said, with sincere encouragement in my voice.

"Deaf . . . Watermelon . . . Washington." She grinned.

"Perfect! Deef Melon, get in this house and eat your macaroni and cheese! Deef Melon, you damned rounder, you be in by ten!" We toasted again, our plastic cups coming together silently. Cat, disturbed by our laughter, opened one eye briefly before he resumed snoozing.

"How about Bald Pineapple Wilson?" she offered. "Bald Pineapple, you get out there and mow the lawn this minute! Bald Pineapple, put a little elbow grease into those dirty dishes!"

"Bald Pineapple," I continued, sternly, "if I catch you hangin' round the crossroads 7-Eleven I'll slice your noggin and stick toothpicks in the pieces! Why, now, Bald Pineapple, I can't believe you swung a D in math. Way to go, son!" I could hardly speak for laughing. I truly think if we had given birth to a child that moment I would have insisted on naming it Bald Pineapple. It somehow seemed perfect. Then again, everything seemed perfect.

"Bowlegged Broccoli Adams!" Eryn said.

"Specify Adams," I insisted, sounding serious.

"John, of course. The other one is Crippled Quince Adams," she replied instantly.

"I remember now, he ended up in a jam."

"Pigeon-toed Asparagus Taft," she continued.

"Is that the one they used to call Stinky Pee?" I asked.

"The very same. And they said he'd never amount to anything. He was in office just after Rheumatoid Brussels Sprout Roosevelt."

"Teddy, then?" I said, again calling for clarification.

"Of course. FDR was much later—you know, Flatulent Dewberry Roosevelt." We both looked at Cat and laughed.

"Of course. He filled the power vacuum created by Hoover," I said. She smiled.

"Right. Psychotic Carrot Hoover. He was quite unstable, but he had great vision in a dark time, may he rest in peace," she said, momentarily grieving his loss until she broke out laughing again. Now neither of us could stop laughing at the fact that the other was laughing so hard at something so ridiculous. We knew that none of this was really funny, but we didn't care, which made us laugh even more. That is the irrational, liberating nature of joy.

"Wife," I heard myself say unexpectedly. "Do you think I'd be a good father?"

"Yes, Bubba, I do." She smiled. I paused, laughed quietly, and then lowered my head and nodded it left to right—but I meant yes, the way you shake your head and raise your eyebrows and laugh before you start skiing down or climbing up the biggest, most beautiful mountain you've ever seen in your life.

I sat silently now, washed over by a feeling of quiet certainty. Eryn's face was glowing as it must have when she was a curly-headed little baby girl, and the woman who calls me her husband had never looked so beautiful before. I could see in her face a child, and I could also see a mother and an old woman. I heard the swaying ocean and felt the evening breeze and witnessed the bone moon lifting slowly out of the dunes. I was immersed in the moment and yet also somehow already looking back at it with deep satisfaction, as if I was seeing this place and time from an old wicker rocker, rocking with my old wife, endlessly rocking, on some crooked porch—ninety years old, maybe toothless and incontinent, but somehow happy anyway, and happier still to have the great gift of one clear memory of the moment I was now living. It was like sitting backward on a bale of hay in the bed of a speeding pickup: the first moment you see what's around you it's already racing away toward the receding horizon. Only in such a moment can we wrinkle up our lives to make the best parts touch— fold the cascading narrative of days to see ourselves being told by a larger story that, however haltingly, is still being written.

Chapter 2

The Nature
within Us

During the first trimester of Eryn's pregnancy strange things began to happen to me. As Eryn started to experience nausea in the mornings, my own appetite, usually reliable as a plow horse, began to falter. My back started to ache, and I was so fitful at night and so bleary in the morning that I despaired of ever feeling rested again. At the time I supplied a litany of possible explanations: fatigue, old sports injuries, hassles at work. But as Eryn's pregnancy progressed, these things became harder to explain. I began to have headaches and to feel bloated, and I developed disconcerting cravings for foods I had always disliked. I felt as if my body were being taken over by an alien force that I didn't understand and couldn't name. As I treated my ailments with midnight doses of dill pickles, hot and sour soup, and tequila, I wondered if I could have contracted Lyme disease or be suffering from chronic fatigue syndrome. In a desperate moment I even enumerated the karmic missteps by which my health could possibly have been compromised in such a systemic way. I complained little to Eryn, though, and there was a good reason for my reticence: I felt awkward bemoaning my nausea, bloating, appetite loss, cravings, insomnia, fatigue, and headaches when she was so uncomfortable because of her nausea, bloating, appetite loss, cravings, insomnia, fatigue, and headaches.

Strange as it now seems, at the time I simply didn't realize how completely my own physical discomfort mirrored Eryn's. But then one morning I experienced something I had never felt before: my teeth began to hurt—not one or two, but every one of them—with a dull, throbbing pain. Along with this perplexing face ache came a more humiliating and inexplicable symptom: I was salivating excessively, which was easily the grossest of the bizarre tricks my insubordinate body had lately pulled on me. I recall staring at my own incredulous, drooling face in the bathroom mirror, the way the Wolf Man does in that helpless moment when the hair begins to sprout from his once-human forehead. Just as my disgust and confusion reached their heights, Eryn called out from the bedroom: "Ugh, my teeth hurt, and my mouth is so watery. The books say it's pretty common for this stage of pregnancy, though." That was the breakthrough moment. I went to Eryn and, drooling like a rabid coyote, expressed my deep sympathy with her discomfort. Then I confessed my own strange symptoms and swore that I'd figure out what was going on. Eryn was pregnant, but what was I?

Couvade syndrome, sometimes called sympathetic pregnancy, refers to the experiencing by men of some of the physical symptoms of pregnancy during their partner's forty-week journey to delivery. The term comes from the French *couver*, "to hatch." The phenomenon is poorly understood but widespread and has been observed since antiquity in various cultures in Africa, China, Japan, and India, as well as among Native peoples in North and South America and the Basques of France and Spain. The ancient Greek geographer Strabo recorded sympathetic pregnancies, as did the thirteenth-century Venetian traveler Marco Polo, who observed the strange phenomenon around the globe.

Among the first Westerners to offer detailed descriptions of male responses to pregnancy were the twentieth-century anthropologists Margaret Mead, working in the South Pacific, and George Gorer, up in the Himalayas. It turns out that many non-Western native cultures practice rituals that mimic couvade in fascinating ways. In many of these cultures, the husband of a woman in labor will occupy a kind of maternity bed of his own during the time the woman is in childbirth, as if he were the one bearing the child. Such cultural practices, which involve imitation by the man of the experiences of the pregnant or laboring woman, have been explained in a number of ways. Some believe that the practices are purely superstitious and are intended to ward off evil that might otherwise be visited upon the new baby through supernatural means.

A related theory is that the man, by occupying his own birthing bed, attracts the evil spirits toward himself and away from the newborn. It appears that all of these practices involve some ritualized assertion of paternity—a symbolic participation by the man in the birth of his son or daughter.

Perhaps the most dramatic example of this odd ritual occurs among descendants of the mighty Aztecs: the native Huichol people, who still inhabit the mountainous wilderness of the Sierra Madre Occidental in western Mexico. During childbirth, the Huichol father goes not to his own bed but rather into the rafters of the family hut, where he positions himself directly above his laboring wife. Once perched there, he ties one end of a rope around his testicles and lowers the other end to the point where it is within reach of his wife. During labor the wife grasps her end of the rope, yanking it each time she experiences a painful contraction. In this amazing way the husband is made to experience his wife's pain during labor, thus sharing the physical discomfort associated with his child's entry into the world. It is a participatory gesture I suspect few would-be fathers would consent to. If you are unlucky enough to have a female partner who insists that you wear one of those ridiculous artificial pregnancy simulators called Empathy Bellies, you might want to pour yourself a glass of whiskey, recall what is required of the Huichol man, and then silently strap it on.

While most of these practices involve the man's ritual *imitation* of pregnancy and childbirth, couvade syndrome is instead a *physical* response by the man to the pregnancy and childbirth experiences of his partner. Modern scientific studies have found that couvade is surprisingly common among expectant fathers in the United States, Europe, Thailand, and elsewhere. Somewhere between 10 and 60 percent of expectant fathers experience at least some physical symptoms of pregnancy, which run the gamut from changes in appetite, food cravings, nausea, insomnia, weight gain, indigestion, diarrhea, and constipation to headaches, toothaches, nosebleeds, itchy skin, backaches, mood swings, and, in acute cases, even abdominal cramps during the woman's delivery. Symptoms tend to be more intense during the first and third trimesters, and they are more common among men who have a strong emotional involvement with the pregnancy.

Couvade may be related to false pregnancy among women, which has been documented since the time of Hippocrates in 300 B.C. Called pseudocyesis—the word comes from the Greek *pseudes* (false) and *kyesis* (pregnancy)—false pregnancy occurs when a woman manifests objective signs of pregnancy but is not in fact pregnant. Perhaps the most famous victim of pseudocyesis was Mary Tudor, queen of England, but this odd response is surprisingly common, especially among the female relatives and close friends of the pregnant woman. But if the physical effects of false pregnancy in women are strange, couvade syndrome—the experiencing of those same physical symptoms of pregnancy in men—is stranger still.

While couvade syndrome is well documented, it is not easily explained. Some researchers believe couvade is the man's physical reaction to a feeling of marginalization in the processes of pregnancy and parturition. Some argue that the symptoms are instead triggered by the man's sympathy for the woman's discomfort. Others consider couvade an expression of generalized anxiety about the substantial life change parenthood represents. Yet others, drawing upon psychoanalytic principles, propose that the response is a form of "womb envy" triggered by the man's jealousy that he is unable to be the bearer of his own child.

The etiology of couvade is likewise mysterious. Most scientists believe it is a psychosomatic syndrome, but others claim that it cannot be purely psychosomatic since it includes symptoms like nosebleeds, which have mechanical triggers. Others consider couvade a form of Munchausen syndrome, in which individuals feign or imagine symptoms in order to draw attention to themselves. Still others argue that couvade is hormonal, as studies have shown substantial hormonal fluctuations in expectant fathers as well as in expectant mothers. For example, the male partners of pregnant women experience changes in their levels of estradiol (a form of estrogen), prolactin (a female hormone associated with milk production), and cortisol (a hormone related to stress responsiveness). New fathers also have higher levels of estrogen and lower levels of testosterone than do other men. The scientific evidence makes clear that pregnancy has biological and physical—not to mention psychological and emotional—effects on men as well as on women.

As it turned out, the unnatural symptoms I was experiencing were perfectly natural after all. That said, nobody wants to have a syndrome, and being able to name my bizarre symptoms didn't make me feel much better about them—even if confused men have been drooling prodigiously since old Strabo's day. In fact, the choice of explanations for my condition seemed vaguely threatening. I imagined trying to enlighten my male friends: "Look, man, it's not as weird as it sounds," I'd say. "It's just a psychosomatic syndrome with a French name that's triggered by my selfishness, angst, womb envy, and skyrocketing estrogen levels." While the caveman in me felt that my impending fatherhood should make me more of a man, my body was instead being hijacked by an inscrutable second-order pregnancy characterized by a disturbing influx of lady hormones.

My couvade symptoms also highlighted the awkward hitch that only half of us are anatomically equipped to experience pregnancy. For the rest of us, pregnancy is mysterious and also strangely alienating, and if men were entirely candid about this, many of us would confess that the pregnancy of our other half seems by turns terrifying, comical, and bizarre. However much we may want to be a full partner in the experience of pregnancy and birth—a longing revealed by our odd use of the locution "*We* are going to have a baby"—we simply can't be. It is a fact of nature—though one we resist admitting—that it isn't *our* body that is miraculously transformed, and so there are limits to how informed our sympathies can ultimately be. Despite a good deal of hype to the contrary, the male role in the proverbial miracle of birth is marginal. We're the sidekick, supporter, witness, cheerleader, coach, observer, assistant, and though we have box seats we'll never have a chance to step up to the plate. This marginalized status of men is affirmed by every book ever written for prospective parents—books in which countless pages of fascinating descriptions of the development of the fetus are only occasionally broken by small, shaded boxes containing "Dad Tips," which helpfully instruct men to do things like save the toxic outgassing fumes of the newly painted nursery for ourselves.

While men aren't sea horses, many of us secretly wish to be. We want desperately to experience this celebrated miracle of gestation and birth, to feel it rather than simply have it reported to us, to be able to tell our children that we held them before they were born as well as after—to assert that we were more than sperm donors, foot masseurs, nursery painters, and breathing coaches. It is precisely this longing that sympathetic pregnancy expresses and addresses. Mysterious as it may be, couvade syndrome helps to narrow the inevitable gap that exists between the sexes when it comes to the experience of pregnancy and childbirth. In the odd misery of my couvade symptoms, I registered the depth of my connection to Eryn and to our unborn child. And my responses to this wonderful impending change in my life were physical, which made all the difference. What I was experiencing was the product of biology, even if the hormonal wheels inside me were turning magically on the axle of emotion.

If no egg was implanted in me, something was. As it grew, I caught my first glimpse of what all parents must eventually come to see: that their connection to their children is not only deeper than they know but deeper than they *can* know. It is an ancient connection that has been in preparation throughout the long journey of hominid evolution, and not only through the sprint of a flailing spermatozoon. My symptoms provided the first hint that parenthood is a form of love magnified by the deep forces of biology, a double mystery that involves both the wonderful machine of our body and the most beautiful of the ghosts that inhabit it.

My weird symptoms continued apace until the night Eryn's water broke. We rushed to the hospital at 4:00 A.M., where we would begin a marathon that exhausted three shifts of doctors and nurses. Nearly spent after twenty hours of labor, Eryn decided to give pushing one last try before resorting to a C-section—an eventuality I had already prepared for by signing paperwork and snapping on one of those poofy green plastic hair restraints used by old ladies in the shower. When the baby finally crowned, the doctor donned a costume that looked very like police riot gear, complete with a giant Plexiglas face shield, which made me wonder if he was as scared of what was about to happen as I was. Next he attached to our yet unborn daughter's bald scalp a suction device that looked a little too much like a common bathroom plunger, and he pulled as Eryn pushed. Under the pressure of the suction the baby's skull distended so as to resemble the attenuated, aerodynamic teardrop shape of a bicycle racer's helmet, and I confess that in that moment I was more frightened than ecstatic. I'm not squeamish, but a close inspection of the scene from my necessarily limited male point of view had momentarily convinced me that the much vaunted miracle of birth was in fact a terrifying mess. The sheer animal physicality of human birth was unexpected and startling, thrilling but also deeply disconcerting.

When our daughter, who in that moment of nativity and grace had not yet found her name, was finally born, she was whisked away to the neonatal intensive care unit. It would turn out that even after her ordeal the baby was perfectly healthy. As I stood exhausted, with my forehead pressed against the window of the infant ICU, looking down at her weird, bald, beautiful head—which now, unaccountably, had a pink plastic bow glued to it—I wondered where her energy, and Eryn's, had come from during those twenty-two hours.

In some way that I have yet to fully understand, my couvade experience helped prepare me for the challenge and blessing of my daughter's birth. Couvade was a narrow bridge that connected the nature of Eryn's pregnant body and of our baby's tiny, hidden body to the nature of my own body. If I was a bloated, drooling insomniac I was also a father in training, and couvade was a kind of physically enforced education in sensitivity and sympathy. I now know that this capacity for sensitivity is precisely what fathers need most. My symptoms may have been psychosomatic, but they were also an adaptive response to the growth and development of my unborn child. Parenting is physically and emotionally demanding, and while my symptoms disappeared with the birth of our first daughter, other challenges requiring sensitivity, compassion, and empathy emerged with her.

Pregnancy and childbirth are among the most natural events humans experience, and in them we recognize the naturalness of our own bodies—a naturalness that everything from clothes to makeup to plastic surgery is designed to help us forget. While I tend to think of owls' nests and desert springs as "nearby nature," there is no nature so close to us as the nature of our own bodies—and there is nothing that connects us so directly to the nature outside ourselves as the gestation of a child within us. To be pregnant is to hold and grow a world inside yourself, to be joined to elemental natural forces that turn the invisible wheels within wheels throughout nature. We are always in nature, but when we carry a child we are reminded in a profound way that nature is also always in us.

How then are we to distinguish between nature and the self, between physical and emotional experience, between the machine and the ghosts that inhabit it? When our body is gripped by disease we know that our anguish is real, but how should we understand the physical suffering caused by the emotional trauma of grief or the visceral feelings of pleasure sometimes produced by aesthetic experiences? For example, we wouldn't tell an injured war veteran that he doesn't *really* feel the pain in the limb that has been amputated, because this "ghost" pain is ghostly only to us; to the sufferer, it is excruciatingly real. When you feel a pleasant tingle or chill while listening to a song you love, you're actually experiencing increased mood-enhancing endogenous dopamine transmission. When you laugh at a stand-up comic whose work you enjoy, her humor is also raising your heart rate and pulmonary ventilation, increasing your brain activity and alertness, stimulating the production of endorphins in your ventromedial prefrontal cortex, and even reducing your perception of pain.

Pregnancy's effects on the body—even, as in my own case, its effects on the male body—remind us of the deep reciprocity between our bodies and the body of nature. In her 1903 classic *The Land of Little Rain*, Mary Austin wrote of the desert that "there are hints to be had here of the way in which a land forces new habits on its dwellers." Consider something as simple as the effects of this landscape on Great Basin flora. The high winds showed these desert flowers how to keep a low profile, while the sun taught their seeds the patience necessary to lay dormant for years, even decades, waiting for a rare wet spring. The drought-sculpted steppe shrubs learned to give one another space, while the gnarled junipers mastered the enviable trick of allowing parts of themselves to die off in order to keep their core alive during stressful times. Balsamroot and mule's ears, those wild relatives of the sunflower, perfected the art of lifting their hairy, palm-shaped leaves and slowly rotating them on edge, tracking the desert sun throughout the day so as to minimize exposure to its desiccating rays. Many desert plants have allowed fire to prove the value of keeping their true hearts underground, the lovely part we humans see being little more than the replaceable efflorescence of a life whose endurance remains secure beneath the sand. We too are like these desert plants: the landscape we inhabit shapes who we are and who we may become. As Austin wrote, "not the law, but the land sets the limit."

Because the intense emotional feelings we often experience with one another or while we are immersed in a remarkable landscape—like this high desert—are accompanied by very real chemical changes in our bodies, it is a tricky business to say where the nature of our body ends and the nature outside it begins. Derived from the Greek *soma*, which means "body," the *somatic* in *psychoso-matic* reminds us that even imagined pleasure and pain register in our bodies. The word *compassion*, after all, means "to suffer together with another," and *sympathy* has at its etymological root the experi-ence by which our own state of being mirrors that of another with whom we feel a deep connection. And isn't this sympathetic mirror-ing at the heart of our deepest connections to one another and to the natural world? Perhaps I should not have been surprised to discover that, much like my journeys through this wild landscape, the growth of my unborn daughter was altering my body as well as my mind. In the inner and outer landscapes of nature, something invisible is always being born.

We later named our little daughter Hannah Virginia. Hannah, an ancient name meaning "grace," and a name that makes sense both forward and backward, as she races into the unknown future and then returns in her own growing memories of the past. Virginia, the name of the homeland I carried with me so long ago when I came west, as I hope she too will have a homeland within her always. The body that nurtured and shaped Hannah was Eryn's, but that home body was embodied within the larger, visceral body of this open desert. Who can know whether some unique quality of Hannah's body or spirit will be the product of high-elevation sunlight or intense aridity, of this desert that shapes us suddenly, like a flash flood cutting an arroyo, and also incrementally, like wind sculpting sandstone?

Both before and after her birth, Hannah helped connect me to my own body, to Eryn, to this desert place, and to the future. When Hannah hurts, I hurt with her. When she laughs, so do I. When we watch the big moon rise together, we feel something rising within us also, calibrating our small, vulnerable bodies to the body of this vast landscape. For me, couvade was not a disease but rather a cure: a preparation for the remarkable changes that becoming a father would bring. There is no wall but only a permeable membrane between physical and emotional experience—between nature and self, body and mind, ourselves and those we love. The strange mystery of my couvade experience taught me that nature is not only the machine but also its resident ghosts. Look hard at the strange beauty of a child, the lines and curves of her little body repeated in the ridgelines and hilltops of the cold, bright desert that surrounds us. It's a fool's game to try to name the place where nature isn't.

Chapter 3

Tracking Stories

Little Hannah Virginia witnessed her first pronghorn antelope the week before her second birthday. It was early April, and the wind swept light snow around the sage and rabbitbrush as I shoved her three-wheeled stroller up a sandy wash a few miles from our house. Although I was going overland through the high desert, I had customized the stroller for off-road travel, complete with knobby tires, slimed to protect against puncture by desert peach thorns. The sky was cloudless, that shimmering azure that distinguishes winter days in the high desert, and we were surrounded by the dry rattling of last season's balsamroot finning stiffly in the wind. As I dug the toes of my boots into the snow to get traction enough to push Hannah uphill through a thick stand of desert peach, she suddenly took the pacifier out of her mouth with her left hand, pointed to the southern horizon with her right, and said, "Moon." At that age she loved to find the moon, and she often spotted the thinnest crescent even in the brightest sky.

"Good job, honey," I said routinely, keeping my eyes on the terrain ahead and pushing hard.

"Daddy, *moon!*" Her tone was so urgent that I stopped pushing, knelt next to the stroller, and looked with her into the southern sky, where I saw nothing but blue depth and distant snowcapped mountains. Then I noticed that beneath the sky, where no moon hung, two pronghorn does stood on a ridgeline several hundred yards away, staring directly at us. Hannah was not saying "moon" but rather "moo," a sound whose association with cows had made it her shorthand for "big, nonhuman mammal."

What happened next was as memorable as an encounter with wildlife could be. Hannah again said, "*Moo!*" and one of the does responded with a breathy snort, "Cha-oo." Hannah's extended arm shot down into her lap, and she whipped her head toward me with eyes as big as a fawn's. This was the look of alarmed joy that she shot me every time we saw a strange miracle in the desert, which was often. When I smiled, Hannah turned back toward the pronghorn, leaned forward in her stroller, and yelled, "*Moo!*" again into the wind. The second doe replied: "*Cha-oo!*" Now Hannah was thrilled, and she began flapping her arms like a magpie, shouting "*Moo! Moo! Moo!*" at the pronghorn as they stood frozen against the moonless sky. Then she stopped and held absolutely still, listening intently. The sound of the wind seemed more textured than before, surging and lilting like invisible surf. The desiccated balsamroot leaves scraped as if we were hearing them through a stethoscope. Again: "Cha-oo. Cha. *Cha-oo*." Hannah grinned, wide-eyed. And then the two does eased a few steps back and were out of sight on the other side of the ridge. In another five weeks they would each give birth to twin fawns, somewhere out there.

We live on a wind-ripped hilltop on the eastern slope of the Sierra Nevada mountains, in the broken sagebrush steppe hills and high valleys on the northern Nevada-California borderlands. It is a land of lizards and eagles, pack rats and ravens, jackrabbits and mountain bluebirds. Our home mountain, which is three miles to our west and looms 2,000 feet above us, has California on its summit crest. Much of the country around us is managed by the Bureau of Land Management (BLM). And while the BLM is so politicized and under-funded that its ability to manage much of anything remains ever in question, these public lands have made it possible for big mammals to live here too. We're fortunate that our valley and mountain remain wild enough to support not only Old Man Coyote but also mule deer, bobcat, mountain lion, and pronghorn.

Although I am admittedly lococentric and thus strongly biased in favor of my own neighbors, to my mind the pronghorn is the most charismatic of megafauna. It is very unlike any other species on earth, and that is because it is—among the many antelope-like ungulates that once inhabited the prairies of prehistoric North America—the sole survivor of the Pleistocene extinctions that erased three-quarters of this continent's large mammals around eleven thousand years ago. *Antilocapra americana* is alone in its genus because it is a living relic of the late Cenozoic savannah and in fact has no kinship with present-day antelope—nor is it related to goats, despite the *capra* in its name. The pronghorn is a true North American native, having evolved here over the past twenty million years. Sometimes called the "prairie ghost" for its elusiveness and speed, the pronghorn is also the ghost of evolution itself. It is all that remains of at least twelve distinct pronghorn-like genera of animals that once inhabited the ancient North American prairies—some species with two horns, some with four, some with six, some with branching horns, others with horns that spiraled fantastically to a point. Of what were probably dozens of species of antilocaprids, only the pronghorn has survived the crucible of evolution. *Survived* may be too grim a word for so beautiful a product of so beautiful a process. Say instead that pronghorn have been turned on the lathe of evolution for twenty million years, sculpted by predator and place, fired in evolution's prairie and desert furnace. Seen in the light of its evolutionary history, pronghorn is not a thing but rather an outcome—one as inevitable as it was unlikely.

The evolutionary adaptations of these living Paleolithic ghosts to prairie and desert environments are many and remarkable. Their coloration is tawny as dust, and their tan necks are garlanded at the throat with a white shield and higher up with a crescent ring, creating a broken tan-white pattern of camouflaging so effective that when a pronghorn turns to look at you it often seems to magically disappear. Bucks have elegant black patches from the ears downward to beneath the chin, and older, stronger males have intimidating black masks that sometimes cover their eyes. Pronghorn hair, whatever color it may be, is adapted to allow the animal to endure almost inconceivable extremes of heat and cold, from 50 below zero in winter on the northern part of its range, on the windswept Canadian prairies, to summer temperatures of 120 degrees or more on its southern range, in the scorching deserts of the Southwest and Mexico. Each hair is perfectly insulated, spongy and air filled, and can be flattened to create a waterproof and windproof shield in winter or lifted up to allow heat dissipation in summer. The bright white hairs on the rump are controlled by an extreme version of the same process of piloerection that makes the hair on the back of your neck stand up when you're hiking in grizzly country. These three-inch-long hairs, when flared, make the rump appear larger and brighter than usual and so function as a warning signal to other pronghorn, especially in flight. Illuminated in the brittle glare of the high desert sun, these distinctive white patches are often visible from miles away, and I have seen them glide across a distant hillside even when the rest of the animal had vanished into the sage-dotted land.

While pronghorn females sometimes grow short horns, males carry the distinctive pronged horns, which may grow to twenty inches in length and are used as weapons against competing bucks during the autumn rut. These cranial meat hooks are so powerful and sharp that the mortality rate in buck fights sometimes runs to 10 percent or even higher. The horn of the pronghorn is not an antler; while antlers are shed each year and are made of bone, horns are kept for life and consist of keratin—the same material used to build hair and hooves. Yet even here the pronghorn is anomalous. Not only is it the only animal in the world with horns that branch, but it is also the only animal that sheds its horns annually—or, to be more precise, sheds the keratinous sheath that covers the horn's bony core. Although this odd combination of antler and horn qualities has resulted in the pronghorn's notoriously imprecise genus name, *Antilocapra*, which means "antelope goat," the pronghorn is neither antelope nor goat. Most of the several hundred recorded Native American names for pronghorn are more elegant and accurate. Many, including those of the Indian peoples who have long inhabited this region, mimic the pronghorn's breathy snorts. The Northern Paiute of nearby Honey Lake and Surprise Valley call the pronghorn *dü'ná*; to the Western Shoshone of central Nevada, *Antilocapra americana* is *wahn'-ze*; it is called *á-yĭs* by the Washoe people of the eastern Sierra.

Considering that pronghorn are fairly small bodied, with adults typically weighing not much more than a hundred pounds, their eyes are unusually large, almost as large as an elephant's—an adaptation that allows them to see great distances across open landscapes. While they have good hearing and a decent sense of smell, it is their superb vision that they depend upon most, a fact that became clear to me the first time I spooked pronghorn from more than a mile away. The animal's large black eyes are set unusually high in the head and far apart, socketed in bony turrets that allow for nearly panoramic vision. Because pronghorn are native to shortgrass prairie and desert, where cover is low, the high placement of their eyes allows them to scan for cruising predators even as they forage.

Pronghorn are such choosy and itinerant browsers that you can approach an area where they have just been grazing and yet search in vain for any sign of cropped plants. Far from being the rototillers or Weedwackers so common among their fellow ungulates, pronghorn snip individual leaves and stems so selectively that their presence on the range is barely discernible. This discriminating browsing for vascular forbs is also related to their ability to survive with so little water, even in conditions that immediately threaten dehydration for other desert mammals. While pronghorn prefer to drink some free water during most times of the year, they can manage to derive most—or, under extreme conditions, all—of their water from the plants they so carefully select. Pronghorn have a four-chambered stomach, the second chamber of which is loaded with bacteria, protozoa, and fungi that digest cellulose and other plant material the standard-issue mammalian gastric system can't handle. They have coevolved with the microorganisms in their gut, creating an ecosystem-within-an-ecosystem without which they would starve. All of these formidable adaptations to the often fatal extremes of their home environments have been crafted by twenty million years of trial and error in which error soundly dominated. Nevertheless, only a few successes are necessary if you have twenty million years to perfect them. The pronghorn we see today are what remain after twenty million years of errors have been culled from the gene pool, each weakness chipped away until the sculpted form of this evolutionary ghost emerged from the unhewn rock of ages.

Over the past thirty million years, hoofed mammals have evolved to become faster, an acceleration driven by an evolutionary increase in the speed of their predators. That said, pronghorn speed remains in a class of its own. Pronghorn can run thirty miles per hour almost indefinitely, in an effortless trot that barely resembles running. They can run for many miles at forty-five miles per hour, and even their incredible top speed of around sixty miles per hour is sustainable for surprisingly long distances. While their bodies appear much like sausages, an improbable form for a speedster, their stilt-like legs are unusually strong and fast, and their stride, almost inconceivably long. It is this unique combination of stride turnover rate and stride length that propels pronghorn forward at such unbelievable speeds. They complete a full stride in a third of a second, a motion so fast that John James Audubon aptly described running pronghorn as appearing to float above the spokes of a wheel turning so quickly that he could see only a gauzy blur where the legs should be. The stride of a pronghorn running at full speed is about twenty-nine feet, which is almost identical to the world record long jump—only a pronghorn does it stride after stride for mile after mile, and never foot faults, wears goofy shorts, or falls on its ass in the sand. I've watched pronghorn glide effortlessly across our nearby high desert basin in what looked like a relaxed canter, only to find their track sets separated by eighteen or twenty feet. When tracking them I can't help doubling back on the assumption that I've missed a set of hoof prints, as the tracks seem impossibly far apart. No wonder that Meriwether Lewis, when he first saw pronghorn on the western plains, wrote that their running "appeared rather the rapid flight of birds than the motion of quadrupeds."

Flight is an apt metaphor for pronghorn speed. It is difficult to describe how strangely beautiful these animals look simply drifting across the hills at forty or forty-five miles per hour. They don't appear to be straining in the least, and their effortless gait combined with the ridiculous amount of ground they cover makes them seem, by the laws of physics, uncalibrated—magically unmoored from any sense of motion our eyes are equipped to register. Pronghorn are more than twice as fast as white-tailed deer, and even a five-week-old fawn can outrun any Kentucky Derby winner. And pronghorn do their speeding through sagebrush and bitterbrush, over sandy and rocky terrain, upslope and downslope, in conditions of extreme heat and cold. Not only can a pronghorn run the length of a football field in about three seconds, but if you could somehow lean that field up on the shoulder of a desert mountain, fill it with sage and boulders and ground squirrel holes and rattlesnakes, and then crank the temperature up to 100 degrees, a pronghorn would still go end zone to end zone in about three seconds—and would take fewer than a dozen strides to do it.

So how do pronghorn run so fast and so far under such inhospitable environmental circumstances? Practice. Twenty million years of practice. There is no evolutionary paradigm shift at work here, no genetic equivalent of a hydrogen fuel cell, no revolution but evolution. The pronghorn has simply refined traits that are common to most mammals, including ourselves. Where we have five fingers on our hands, pronghorn have fused the third and fourth digits into their perfectly engineered padded cloven hooves. Where we have a wrist with squarish bones a few inches long, the pronghorn has elongated its hand bones until they are almost as long as your forearm. This marvelous cannon bone, nine inches in length but only as thick as your finger, is what allows pronghorn to achieve the stride length necessary for their remarkable speed. I once found one of these impossibly attenuated cannon bones beneath a bitter cherry bush out in the desert scrub, and I now keep it on my writing desk to remind me that even in this broken world, refinement and delicacy, rather than brute strength, can still translate into power.

The downside of this skeletal refinement is that pronghorn find jumping dangerous, as an unstable landing on these delicate, elongated wrist bones can shatter them and thus prove fatal. Pronghorn consider jumping so disconcerting that they rarely attempt to clear anything higher than a few feet, and as a result they often find their movement to winter range or calving grounds blocked by fencing, which proves no significant obstacle to woodland-evolved leapers like deer. Unlike deer, pronghorn have spent millions of years matching themselves to the demands of shortgrass prairie and sagebrush steppe, where running fast is much more important than jumping high. Taking advantage of this reluctance to jump, at one time some Native peoples drove pronghorn into improvised corrals, building immense V-shaped drift fences that were often several miles apart at the mouth but funneled to a chute where pronghorn were killed or captured. The long walls that kept the animals within the V were constructed of rocks, juniper snags, or, more often, sagebrush. If the barrier was even a few feet high, pronghorn would continue to run alongside it rather than jump over it to freedom. About fifteen miles north of where Hannah spotted the two pregnant does is a pronghorn funnel called the Fort Sage Drift Fence, a thousand-year-old Paleo-Indian rock structure, thirty inches high and more than a mile long on each side. In more recent times, the Paiute people of Honey Lake Valley—whose country is visible from the top of our home mountain—wove thick sagebrush-bark ropes more than a mile long, which they shook in order to keep spooked pronghorn running forward rather than attempting to escape by jumping laterally.

Several other pronghorn adaptations for speed are specific to does and fawns. The first has to do with the pronghorn's distinctive reproductive strategy of birthing twins. While a doe breeding for the first time usually calves a single fawn, nearly all her subsequent births—and every healthy doe will be pregnant every year for the rest of her life—will result in twin fawns weighing about eight pounds each. This twinning is ensured not only by a complex process of intrauterine competition among embryos, but also by the fact that the pronghorn uterus, unlike that of a human, is twin horned, thus virtually ensuring that an embryo will develop in each uterine horn. The pronghorn's primary defense against predators is speed, so the development of twins ensures that the doe's body will remain balanced and fast, even as she becomes heavier. Because Eryn is an identical twin, as were my uncles (who were named Robert and Bruce after Robert the Bruce, the warrior who led Scotland to independence during the early fourteenth century), I'm enamored of the idea that for pronghorn twinning is not an anomaly but rather an essential means of bringing a new generation of children into this world.

A related adaptation is the pronghorn's exceptionally long gestation period, which, at about 252 days, is much longer than that of larger ungulates, such as bighorn sheep (about 180 days) or mule deer (about 200 days). This protracted gestation is an evolutionary adaptation that reduces the window of vulnerability for fawns. Because fawns stay in the oven so long, they remain protected from predation longer and are more fully developed at birth. Pronghorn fawns can stand up just thirty minutes after they are born, and four days later they can outrun you or me. Although many fawns fall prey to coyotes, the fact that pronghorn gain size and speed so quickly allows many more to survive than would otherwise be possible. Because I am now a father, it is impossible for me not to see compelling correspondences between pronghorn fawns and human kids. The pronghorn's extended gestation of about thirty-six weeks is remarkably close to the human gestation period of forty weeks, and I too have a fawn who weighed not much less than eight pounds when she entered the world. Whenever I find fawn bones in the desert hills I struggle to negotiate my own allegiances, for both the pronghorn and coyote, like me, have children to feed.

The primary fuel of a pronghorn's speed is oxygen, and it is here that the animal's evolutionary adaptations are most impressive. Where you and I do a respectable job metabolizing oxygen so we can have muscular strength sufficient to thumb text messages and hoist pints, the pronghorn consumes three times the oxygen we do. Its heart is enormous, and its lungs are triple the size of those found in comparably sized mammals. In fact, all the organs and processes associated with burning oxygen are radically developed in pronghorn. Compared with other mammals their size they have a third more blood cells, half again as much blood, and two-thirds more hemoglobin; their muscle cells are loaded with the mitochondria necessary to process all this oxygen. Unlike the three-quarter-inch tube through which we pathetically slow bipeds suck wind when we're out for a jog, the pronghorn has a two-inch windpipe that allows it to shotgun air while running. In fact, the minute it takes off sprinting it lolls its tongue out and opens its mouth to clear the tracheal opening for a full blast. If you don't think this form of air gathering works, try sticking your open-mouthed noggin out the window of your car while going sixty miles per hour. One unfortunate by-product of all this oxygen-stoked muscular performance is tremendous heat, which is especially threatening to the animal's brain. But pronghorn have developed a number of novel thermoregulation strategies, among which is a fascinating circulatory system that shunts overheated blood through a network of superficial arteries and veins that cool the blood before it is redirected to the brain.

Although these and many other adaptations for speed have been sculpted by the pressures of natural selection, the creation of the amazing feat of form and function that we call the pronghorn has required eons. When I despair at how shortsighted we humans often are, I find it comforting to remember that *Homo not-so-sapiens* has had only a quarter of a million years or so of practice. Even the aches in our backs and knees remind us that our ancestors haven't been standing upright for very long—and, in fact, that the evolutionary jury is still out on whether this bold uprising to verticality really pays off for anybody other than NBA players and chiropractors. Pronghorn, by contrast, have been trying to get it right for at least eighty times longer than we have, which provides some hope that in another nineteen and a half million years we might gain wisdom enough to be worthy of our name, *sapiens*. Then again, since we were the ones foolish enough to name ourselves in celebration of our wisdom, it is a good bet that we may lack the humility necessary to survive that long.

To understand something of *how* pronghorn run so fast remains a far cry from understanding *why* they do so, especially in the context of such core evolutionary concepts as selective pressure and speciation. The problem with pronghorn speed is that it is anomalous. No predator in North America can catch an adult pronghorn, and none even comes close. While coyotes exact a heavy toll on each year's crop of pronghorn fawns—and golden eagles and bobcats pick off a few as well—Old Man Coyote can't begin to catch an adult pronghorn. The sophisticated pack-hunting strategies used by wolves gives them a better shot at relay racing a pronghorn to death, but even here predation is minimal. In fact, some studies suggest that the presence of wolves on the range increases pronghorn populations because wolves regularly haze the coyotes that are the major predator of pronghorn fawns. Like every other major predator in North America, coyotes, wolves, and mountain lions are so incredibly slow compared with pronghorn that predation by these animals cannot have provided the selection pressure necessary to create the pronghorn's speed. Where, then, did this amazing speed come from? Evolutionary theory allows only one explanation: pronghorn run so fast because they are being chased by ghosts.

Imagine a lovely, sunny spring day out on the North American prairie, a million years ago. You are one of tens of millions of pronghorn that live on the savannah, which you share with a great many other mammals, most of which will be extinct a million years from now. As you stand eyeing the prairie horizon—or perhaps you are reclined, chewing your cud—you are worried, and it isn't because you have bills to pay or your car is making a funny sound. You have real, urgent, and incessant reasons to be terrified. Of course Old Man Coyote wants to snap your fawns' necks today—just as he will on this day a million years from now—but at least he isn't fast enough to catch you. Wolves are a more serious concern, as they'll separate you from your herd and pack hunt you if they can. Thank goodness the gluttonous plundering dog *Borophagus* finally went extinct after seven million years of crunching your kids' spines in its powerful jaws. Although evolution is busy replacing *Borophagus* with the huge, bone-crushing dire wolf (*Canis dirus*), it will be a few hundred thousand years before you really have to worry about that. In the meantime, you can handle most of these *Canis* types. After all, how scared can you be of a genus that will eventually produce animals that prance along on a leash and wear little sweaters? The hyenas are a bigger problem. Ever since they crossed the Bering land bridge back in the Pliocene, they've been getting better and better at chasing you. In fact, when he's hot on your white rump, the running hyena *Chasmaporthetes* looks more like a jaguar than it does like the slouchy little hyena that will be around a million years from now.

That's just for starters. The short ambush predators can really ruin your day. Of these, the gnarliest is *Arctodus simus*, the giant short-faced bear. Don't try any of your excellent short-face jokes on him, because he weighs eighteen hundred pounds, is seven feet tall at the shoulder and ten feet tall on hind legs, and has a reach of about fourteen feet. He needs to eat thirty-five pounds of meat each day, which is about what you weigh once he picks his teeth with your ribs and gets to the juicy part. What's worse, unlike bears a million years from now—the ones that lumber over to the park dumpster to scavenge from discarded buckets of KFC—his feet are oriented with toes straight forward, which means he can really run. He can't outrun you in a prairie race, of course, but if you spend one second too long daydreaming about the upcoming rut while drinking from the spring, you're a goner.

The stalk-and-ambush crew also includes the scimitar cats (*Homotherium*) and the saber-toothed cats—which aren't named *Smilodon fatalis* for nothing. There are a bunch of species of each, all of them weighing five or six hundred pounds, with six- or seven-inch-long teeth hanging out of their mouths, quiet as a mouse when stalking, and not too shabby running short distances. The "smaller" cats also cause problems. The American lion (*Panthera leo atrox*) is five hundred pounds of bad-tempered nuisance, and the cougar (*Felis concolor*) and jaguar (*Panthera onca*) are always staking out your migration routes. A good rule of thumb with all these cats is that you should just stick with your herd, eat a nutritious diet of succulent forbs, get lots of exercise, and stay out of situations where you can get bushwhacked. Of course they're going to eat most of your children, but as long as you stay out in the open and remain vigilant, you can outrun any of these carnivores in a pinch. Still, I'll bet you can hardly wait for the Pleistocene extinctions to get some of these giant monsters off your back.

But here's the real problem, the one you'd really prefer not to discuss. There's one thing out there that is faster than you are, at least in a short sprint—and if you get taken down in the first hundred yards, then your ability to run fast mile after mile won't help you, will it? What's worse, *you* made that thing fast. You made it fast by being so fast yourself. It is thanks to you that the American cheetah can sprint seventy miles per hour and is thus among the swiftest of terrestrial mammals. His adaptations for speed are numerous, fabulously inventive, and all your fault. Many's the day you pranced around racking your brain for a new way to pick up just a few MPHs. Put your ears back to reduce wind resistance? Stick out your tongue to shotgun air? Find some way to stretch your stride length from twenty-eight to twenty-nine feet? Seems like every time you came up with something, though, he did too; no matter how fast you became, the American cheetah was a little faster, at least in the short run. But if it bothers you that he's faster than you are, remember that you also have him to thank for making you so fast. If you weren't running from him all the time, you'd never have become fast enough to outrace all those other voracious predators, and then where would you be? Your speed and his have coevolved, each causing the other. I know you hate it when he eats you, but he really has made you the best pronghorn you can be.

Nobody knows for certain why most large mammals went extinct around eleven thousand years ago. In North America, roughly thirty-three of forty-five genera of mammals larger than about ninety pounds disappeared in a wave that erased the mastodons, mammoths, dire wolves, giant short-faced bears, saber-toothed cats, and many other mammals—including the American cheetah and all species of antilocaprids except the pronghorn. Some believe that overhunting by the humans who were then on the scene and wielding the new Clovis spearpoint technology was a major factor. Others find it more likely that a changing climate disturbed the ecosystems upon which large carnivores depended for survival. Yet others subscribe to the theory that the late Pleistocene extinctions are attributable to a wave of highly infectious diseases against which few large mammals had adequate defenses.

We do know that the lightning-fast American cheetah (*Miracinonyx trumani*) went extinct about ten thousand years ago, while its prey, the pronghorn, did not. As a result, *Antilocapra americana* has been alone out there for the past ten thousand years, running much faster than anything in North America, though the pronghorn doesn't seem to know that yet. And this is the most fascinating part of the pronghorn's story. Evolutionary theory provides no way to account for *Antilocapra*'s excessive speed except to say that the pronghorn still sees the sleek shadow of the American cheetah over its shoulder. The pronghorn has experienced twenty million years of directional selection for speed: it just kept getting faster and faster in an attempt to outrun its ever speedier predators. For the last ten thousand years, though, that selection pressure has been relaxed. Now you might think that if you had ten thousand years to change your ways you could do so (though my experience with humans suggests this isn't a sure thing), but the pronghorn's speed—and a number of its other adaptations to avoid Pleistocene predators that no longer exist—is inscribed in its body. It can't simply decide that it really doesn't need so large a windpipe or even that it can abandon its vigilance while browsing. If we assume a twenty-million-year evolutionary history for the pronghorn, then the ten-thousand-year period during which directional selection for speed has been relaxed amounts to just 0.0005 percent of that history. The pronghorn is a product of millions of years, not thousands. Pronghorn run fast because evolution hasn't yet had time to slow them down.

Unlike many people, I have a neighbor who has cheetahs. My friend Aaron, who lives just four miles from our place as the kestrel flies, has for more than twenty-five years managed an animal rehabilitation center that cares for injured wild animals and for exotic animals confiscated from traders trafficking illegally in endangered species. Many years ago a pair of orphaned African cheetah cubs found their way to Aaron, who immediately began working to figure out how best to keep them healthy. Veterinarians at zoos had long observed that captive cheetahs developed a wide variety of health problems and that gastrointestinal diseases often claimed their lives. Using the kind of common sense that is as valuable to a human as speed is to a cheetah, Aaron reckoned that animals evolved to run seventy miles per hour would be healthiest if they could run seventy miles per hour. In his early work with the cheetahs, Aaron took them out to a desert playa not far from here, attached a flagged lure to a rope behind his pickup truck, and literally ran the cats across the desert as fast as he could zigzag without rolling his F-150. Aaron tells a wonderful story of once seeing a group of pronghorn lining a ridge above him, watching intently as the cheetahs sprinted across the playa at top speed. I love to imagine what kind of evolutionary ticking must have been going on behind those huge antilocaprid eyes. Were they curious, surprised, terrified? Or had evolution hardwired them so effectively that they simply thought the pronghorn version of "You again, huh?" Indeed, if advocates of the radical idea of "Pleistocene rewilding" ever get their way, African cheetahs (*Acinonyx jubatus*) will be introduced to the pronghorn range as a substitute for the extinct American cheetah. And if that wild day ever comes, pronghorn will be mighty glad they didn't become slackers just because the Pleistocene extinctions wiped out their fastest predator.

It isn't only pronghorn physiology and speed that are vestigial but many pronghorn behaviors as well. These "relict behaviors" are another kind of evolutionary shadow—another indication that it takes tens of thousands of years to unlearn the lessons that millions of years have taught. Among relict behaviors in pronghorn, the most dramatic is the animals' congregation into large herds during winter. Typically, herding is a behavior that increases energy-draining competition for food, but it is worthwhile because it is an effective way to guard against predation. After all, your chances of seeing spring will be much better if a few dozen or a few hundred of your buddies are scanning the ridges while you're pawing away snow to get at forage. And the pronghorn winter herd displays the additional skill of being synchronized to a degree of precision that is incomprehensible to a bumbling biped like me. When the herd moves across the land, it exhibits a 97 percent synchrony of gait, which means that whether there are twenty pronghorn or two hundred, 97 percent of them will put their four hooves on the ground in exactly the same sequence and at exactly the same time. Pronghorn have at least four distinct gaits, or running patterns, but even when they shift from one to another at high speed (which is analogous to your shifting the gears of your bike or car as you increase speed), there remains better than 90 percent synchrony in the herd. Even in the exact instant they change their hoof sequence and timing while running at forty or fifty miles per hour, 93 percent of them will do so at precisely the same time—and the rest will correct within a fraction of a second.

Although I have witnessed the full winter herd only once, there is no possibility that I will ever forget it. The flawless synchronization of the animals' gait makes the herd's movement indescribably graceful. These animals don't appear to run at all but instead seem to flow across the land like a single organism. At first glance I assumed that I was seeing the shadow of a cloud rippling across the desert hills; when I looked again, my home desert had been fantastically transformed into the Serengeti, with graceful herds pouring out beneath a towering sky. As a result of the pronghorn's incredible synchronization, predators find it difficult to single out an individual to attack, and some scientists have even suggested that the weird effect of the perfectly coordinated herd—which looks more like a school of fish than it does a bunch of long-legged mammals—may actually have a hypnotic effect on predators.

Of course the fleet predators this herding instinct evolved to protect against no longer exist. So how long will it take before pronghorn will slow down, before evolutionary pressures will select for something different, like the ability to jump a fence or to recognize the glint of sunlight off gunmetal? Or will they remain incredibly fast, while their slower predators evolve to become as fast as cheetahs? Or will the ongoing biodiversity and climate change crises, which threaten the extinction of numberless species, wipe pronghorn out before evolution can correct for their anomalous speed? Nobody knows. In the meantime, the pronghorn is still out there, calving twins, hanging on, running as fast as it can. It is still out there, a ghost being chased by the ghosts of predators past.

We don't know how many pronghorn inhabited North America before their slaughter began in earnest during the mid-nineteenth century. An educated guess is that a hundred and fifty years ago there were around forty million pronghorn in North America, ranging from the oxbows of the Mississippi west almost to the breakers of the Pacific, and they flourished in numbers comparable to those of the iconic American bison. Then came White Guy with Fire Stick, and pronghorn were shot for meat, for pelts, and often just for fun. To cite a particularly egregious example, in 1859 a single pelt hunter killed five thousand pronghorn at one watering hole without using a pound of the resulting hundred tons of meat. After a venerable twenty-million-year evolutionary history, it took only a century for pronghorn numbers to be reduced from forty million or so to fewer than fifteen thousand by the early twentieth century. Not only was the species in imminent danger of extinction; many conservation biologists felt that the numbers had already fallen too low—that the prairie ghost was doomed, regardless of any efforts that might be made to prevent the curtain of time from being drawn on it forever.

Fortunately, this grim forecast didn't stop some people from trying anyway, and their ultimately successful efforts are the reason pronghorn are still being born on our prairies and in our deserts today. The odd combination of realistic pessimism and idealistic optimism necessary to take up the gauntlet of pronghorn conservation was expressed by Charles Sheldon, after whom the Sheldon National Wildlife Refuge in northern Nevada is named: "I think that the antelope are doomed, yet every attempt should be made to save them." Thanks to Sheldon and many others, most western states imposed moratoriums on hunting pronghorn—prohibitions that here in Nevada gave complete protection to the species from 1917 through 1943. Refuges were created, management guidelines instituted, and trap-and-relocate programs initiated to return pronghorn to parts of the range from which they had been extirpated. In the half century between 1925 and 1975, pronghorn increased from what may have been as few as thirteen thousand animals to a half million, and the population now stands at around one million.

Despite this inspiring conservation success story, the future of the species remains uncertain. It is now development rather than wanton slaughter that impinges on ancient pronghorn migration routes, deprives the animals of winter range, and covers their calving grounds with asphalt or drilling pads. Most of the valley just south of where Hannah saw her first pronghorn was recently proposed for transformation into "Evans Ranch." If you live in the West, you already know that "ranch" is the going euphemism for "massive subdevelopment," and so Evans Ranch will be no ranch at all but rather a dense concentration of more than five thousand houses and apartments in a valley where pronghorn now forage, water, and calve. This valley has remained mostly wild because of our federally protected aquifer: we have so little water here—about seven inches of precipitation each year (most of it snow) and almost no surface water—that anything more than a rural scattering of homes is plainly unsustainable. But that was before trans-basin water importation, the latest in a long line of get-rich-quick schemes to force the intermountain West to bloom and fructify. The plan for Evans Ranch is to drain a desert aquifer someplace else—most likely in the Honey Lake basin, where Paiutes have honored the pronghorn for millennia—and pipe the liquid gold to this valley.

When Evans Ranch was proposed to city government, it was described in a planning document more than a thousand pages in length. That document never mentioned pronghorn. The property to be developed borders public land on two-thirds of its huge perimeter; despite this, the BLM, which represents the public interest, was never even consulted about the negative effects the development would have on public lands. When the project came before the city's planning commission, one commissioner was forced to recuse herself because she is the wife of the developer's lead PR man; another insisted that people who care about wildlife shouldn't try to stop progress but should instead pick up trash in the desert. Then the commissioners voted unanimously to approve the development. When Evans Ranch subsequently went before the Reno City Council, letters opposing the development arrived in a landslide, while statements of support came in a feeble trickle; testimony ran about five to one against the development, with nearly all of those who spoke in favor of the project being the developer's own employees. In advance of the hearing, the developer told the media that in twenty years he had never seen pronghorn in the valley; in response, many citizens who testified showed photographs of pronghorn grazing on or near their properties.

I was the citizen appellant to the Evans Ranch decision, which meant that while Eryn was hosting Hannah's second birthday party I was in city council chambers speaking as best I could for public lands, for sustainable growth, for sparing the pronghorn. On one side was a row of experts on traffic flow, water importation, effluent disposal, and a number of other bleak arts. On the other side were a bunch of my heartbroken neighbors and I trying to explain why an ineffable mystery like the pronghorn might matter—and trying to explain it to people whose minds were already made up. When I rose to offer my rebuttal to the developer's PR man, the mayor of Reno instructed me to sit down and be quiet—until his legal counsel reminded him of his statutory obligation to allow me to speak, at which point he acquiesced and permitted me two minutes to make the case for protecting a species that has lived here for twenty million years. In the end, the arguments made by those of us who value wildlife, open space, and public lands were compelling. One staunchly prodevelopment member of the growth-at-all-costs city council even complimented us on what he characterized as the most passionate and well-reasoned citizen appeal ever heard before council. Then he voted, along with every other council member, to approve the development. It was painfully apparent to everyone in those packed chambers that the vital process of citizen appeal and testimony had been reduced to a form of window dressing intended to superficially legitimate a deal long since struck between local power brokers.

I've seen pronghorn yearlings alone and in pairs, does alone and in groupings, males alone and in bachelor herds, huge bucks herding and hiding harems of as many as fourteen does; and I've witnessed the winter herd of scores of animals together flowing across the land in synchrony. That's here, in our home valley, where the developer apparently hasn't managed to spot a pronghorn in twenty years. Some may be mercenary enough to argue that we humans, developers and environmentalists alike, are just maximizing our opportunity to prosper, to make homes for our children, to ensure that our way of life—or, considered sociobiologically, our genetic heritage—will be borne into future generations. If we erase the astonishing evolutionary phenomenon that is the pronghorn in order to do so, that's simply collateral damage.

But the counterargument comes from the depth of ages: it cannot be evolutionarily adaptive for us to proceed so recto-cranially, with our selfish heads so far up our asses that we can no longer see the beauty of this world. We don't have nineteen and a half million years to come up with intelligent, sustainable practices of inhabitation that will allow the pronghorn miracle to live with us. If we do not evolve ethically, and do so quickly, we will suffer what the ecologist and writer Robert Michael Pyle calls "the extinction of experience." We will deprive ourselves of rich contact with the physical world, which is something evolution has taught us to need. We will replace the textured earth that has literally made us human with an impoverished remnant earth in which our children will no longer have the chance to converse with pronghorn.

In an ancient cave not far from here there is an infant interred with a rattle made from the horn sheaths of the pronghorn. At another Paleo-Indian burial site, the body of an eight-year-old girl is found at repose; she has been laid to rest wearing a necklace made of the hooves of unborn pronghorn fawns, a sacred ornament possessing the power to help her travel swiftly across worlds. As a father, I cannot conceive the species of grief caused by the loss of a daughter—what terrifying ghosts this unspeakable loss might summon. I do not know what kind of necklace I could make. I do know that when unchecked development has erased the unique evolutionary phenomenon that is the pronghorn from our home valley and mountain, something that animates this place will be extinguished. Its loss will ripple through the life of this fragile montane desert ecosystem and through the lives of anyone capable of appreciating what twenty million years of striving for perfection has wrought. There will be a new ghost here, and it will haunt us for a very long time to come.

Chapter 4

Ladder to the Pleiades

Hannah, who recently turned three years old, is teaching me about the stars. Far from being a liability to her, my own profound astronomical ignorance has turned out to be her boon and, through her, a boon to me as well. The most important thing the kid has taught me about the stars is the brilliant open secret that if you don't go outside and look up, you won't see anything. Every night before bedtime she takes my hand and insists that I get my bedraggled ass up and take her outside to look at the stars. If this sounds easy, ask yourself if you can match her record of going out every single night to observe the sky—something she has done without fail for more than a year now. It seems to me that Hannah has accomplished something impressive: she has perfect attendance at the one-room schoolhouse of night. That she has some-how brought her celestially illiterate father along is more amazing still.

Following the inexorable logic that makes a kid's universe so astonishing, Hannah insists on looking for stars no matter the weather. At first I attempted the rational, grown-up answer: "It just isn't clear enough to see anything tonight, honey." But her response, which is always the same, is so emphatic that it is irresistible: "Dad, we can always *check*." And so we check. And it is when we check that the rewards of lifting my head up and out of another long day come into focus. One cold and windy night we stepped out and discovered, through a momentary break in an impossibly thick mat of clouds, a stunning view of Sirius blazing low in the southeast. Another eve-ning we stood in an unusual late winter fog and saw nothing—but then we heard the courtship hooting of a nearby great horned owl, followed immediately by the distant yelping of coyotes up in the hills. At Hannah's insistence we even stand out in snowstorms to stargaze, and while we've never seen any stars on those wild, white nights, we've seen and felt and smelled the crisp shimmering that arrives only on the wings of a big January storm. Snow or no snow, she knows those stars are up there, and so she does easily what is somehow difficult for many of us grown-ups: she looks for them. Whether Hannah actually sees stars or not, in seeking them every evening she has forged an unbreakable relation with the world-within-a-world that is night.

Questions are the waypoints along which Hannah's orbit around things can be plotted, and she has asked so many ques-tions about stars for so many nights in a row that at last I've been compelled to learn enough to answer some of them. In doing so I've stumbled into placing myself, my family, my home on the cosmic map whose points of reference wheel across the sky. We've learned a surprising number of stars and constellations together, and we each have our favorites. Now that we're in our second year of performing this unfailing nightly ritual, we're also having the gratifying experience of seeing our favorite summer stars, long gone in the high desert winter, come round again on the dark face of the year's towering clock of night.

The other evening after supper, Eryn asked Hannah to make a wish. Without hesitating she replied, "I wish I could have a ladder tall enough to reach the stars." As usual, I didn't know what to say. It is impossible to dismiss a three-year-old kid—who, among other things, discovered the cosmos without much help from me—when she articulates a hope that is at once so perfectly reasonable and so beautifully impossible. Before she goes to sleep, Hannah and I look at the six-dollar cardboard star wheel I bought to help us identify constellations. Too tired to make much of it, I toss the disk down on her bed in mild frustration. But she picks it up, holds it upright in front of her with both hands, stares earnestly out beyond the walls of her room, and begins to turn it left and right as if it were a steering wheel.

"Where you going?" I ask.

"Pleiades," she replies. "Want to come?"

Despite its faintness relative to many other celestial objects, the Pleiades—which Hannah still pronounces Tweety Bird style, "Pwee-adeez"—are Hannah's favorite thing in the sky. If you're in the northern hemisphere, this lovely cluster is relatively easy to locate: when looking south in summer, it appears above and to the right of Orion the hunter, the three bright stars of whose belt align to form an unmistakable field mark. To the naked eye, the Pleiades resemble the dipper shape that is better known in the northern sky, where the Big and Little Dippers of Ursa Major and Ursa Minor, the two bears, revolve endlessly around the axle of Polaris, the North Star. Known to myth as the Seven Sisters and to science as Messier object 45 (M45), the Pleiades are an open cluster of stars—not a random constellation but a close grouping of intimately related stars that were born together from a single nebula cradled in the arms of a spiral galaxy. Dominated by hot blue stars, the Pleiades cluster consists of at least five hundred members, which formed together as recently as 100 million years ago. It is a tightly woven nest of baby stars, a galactic brood perhaps only one-fiftieth the age of our own sun. The cluster is expected to survive only another 250 million years or so, after which its individual stars will flee the spiral arms of our home galaxy and its giant molecular clouds and will break their sisterly gravitational bonds, causing them to forget their common origin. They will light out for the territory, wayward, each on its own new path.

Among the nearest to the earth of all open clusters, the Pleiades cluster is 12 light-years in diameter and a mere skip of 440 light-years away from Hannah's upturned face. Despite the tranquillity of their huddled glow, some Pleiades stars are actually spinning at up to three hundred kilometers per second at their surfaces. The

Pleiades are also celebrated for their remarkable nebulosity, which was revealed by the first astrophotographs, taken during the 1880s. Otherworldly pictures capture spectacular blue reflection nebulae, illuminated clouds of interstellar dust attenuated into ghostly, cirrus-shaped wings by the intense stellar radiation emanating from Pleiades stars. The lyricism of Tennyson's 1835 poem "Locksley Hall" reflects this wonderful nebulosity: "Many a night I saw the Pleiads, rising thro' the mellow shade, / Glitter like a swarm of fire-flies tangled in a silver braid."

I still don't know why Hannah loves the Pleiades so much, and I wonder if I'll ever fully understand. She gives different answers on different nights, and though she's patient with me, mostly she seems to think I'm asking the wrong question. What fascinates me most about the Pleiades is not any arcana of astrogeekery but rather the simple fact that they are beautiful yet barely visible. The nine brightest stars in the cluster all have magnitudes hovering just around the limit of sharp human vision under excellent viewing conditions. But how many you actually see depends not only upon your eyesight and the weather and the position and phase of the moon, but also upon altitude, humidity, dust, pollution, and the most critical factor: light levels in the night sky.

"Let there be light" may have sounded good at first, but for there to be Pleiadian light there must first be earthly darkness. Although even the dimmest of the major Pleiades stars is forty times brighter than our own sun would appear at a similar distance (the brightest, Alcyone, is a thousand times brighter than our sun), only six stars are usually visible to the unaided eye. Although some people can see the seventh sister as well, I myself have witnessed it only three nights in thirty years of admiring this cluster—a once-in-a-decade pace that I find perfectly satisfying. Under ideal viewing conditions it is occasionally possible for extremely sharp-sighted people to see nine stars. In 1579, before the invention of the telescope, the astronomer Michael Maestlin accurately drew the positions of eleven of the cluster's stars. In Egyptian tombs archaeologists have found, buried along with mummies, ancient calendars ornamented with a dozen Pleiades stars, and aboriginal cultures in remote desert regions of Australia produced art depicting thirteen Pleiades. There is even some evidence that in the rarefied air of the high Andes some Incan people may once have been able to see fourteen member stars. It was common among Native American peoples in North America—just as it was among stargazers in ancient Greece—to measure the acuity of one's vision by the number of Pleiades stars they could see. Simply by being there, the Pleiades test the limits of our vision. These stars are easy to find but also easy to lose. Like most things that are precious, they are there but barely, and how well we see them—or if we see them at all—matters enormously.

In Greek mythology, the Pleiades are the celebrated Seven Sisters, celestial daughters of the sea nymph Pleione and the Titan Atlas, whose punishment from Zeus was to bear the weight of the heavens upon his shoulders. The Seven Sisters—Alcyone, Celaeno, Electra, Maia, Merope, Sterope, and Taygete—were nymphs in the train of Artemis, and I owe them a deep debt of gratitude because they served as nursemaids to baby Bacchus, the feisty little god of booze. The Pleiades sisters must have been easy on the eyes, as many well-heeled Olympian gods, including Poseidon, Ares, and even Zeus himself, had affairs with ladies from this fine retinue of astral maidens. Only Merope, whose name means "mortal," resisted seduction by the gods, a mistake for which she took a lot of grief. Or perhaps the problem was that the mortal she chose to marry, that old coyote Sisyphus, was a fast-talking con man whose infamous boulder-rolling punishment made Atlas's bad day at the office seem like a moonlight stroll.

So while Daddy Atlas was too busy holding up the cosmos to stand on his crooked porch with the twelve gauge, Orion the great hunter set eyes on the Pleiades gals and decided to follow a new quarry. This turned out to be a bigger challenge than Orion expected, and after seven frustrating years of pursuit his lust remained unsatisfied. In some mythological genealogies Atlas and Orion are related, which suggests that Orion wasn't above cruising for chicks at the family reunion (in most old European languages, the Pleiades were indeed called "the chicks"). Tired of fielding complaints from the harried Pleiades maidens and their kin, Zeus finally agreed to perform an Olympian feat of astromorphosis: he turned the seven sisters into doves and placed them in the sky, where they had good reason to suppose they would be free from sexual harassment. So much for that; later, when Orion was killed, Zeus placed him in the heavens just east of the sisters, where he might pursue them across the wheeling night for all eternity.

The word *Pleiades*, a Greek name lovely to both eye and ear, has a mysterious etymology. A likely origin is *plein*, which means "to sail." Scientifically speaking, because Pleiades is a cluster, its member stars do sail across the wine-dark ocean of space together, as the unrelated stars of most constellations and asterisms do not. The more direct connotation of sailing, though, is hinted at by the ancient Greek nickname for the Pleiades: "Sailors' Stars." The cluster's conjunction with the sun in spring and opposition with the sun in fall marked the opening and closing of the season for safe sailing in the ancient Mediterranean world. Around 700 B.C. the Greek poet Hesiod included this lyrical admonition in his "Works and Days":

> *And if longing seizes you for sailing the stormy seas,*
> *when the Pleiades flee mighty Orion*
> *and plunge into the misty deep*
> *and all the gusty winds are raging,*
> *then do not keep your ship on the wine-dark sea*
> *but, as I bid you, remember to work the land.*

Hesiod well knew the winds of trade and adventure that drove Greek ships and Greek ambition, but he also knew that to sail after the heliacal setting of the Pleiades was to risk a permanent visit to Poseidon's coral caves. Our limits are written in the stars, he seems to say: know the time to plow the earth and not the waves, planting spring's hope in soil and not upon the furrows of the deep.

But the word *Pleiades* may instead be derived from *pleos*, meaning "full," which perhaps alludes to the wind-filled sails of Aegean summer but suggests other meanings as well. The plural of *pleos* means "many," an apt description of the cluster's stars. Or perhaps the name is derived matriarchally, from Pleione, the mythological sea nymph who is mother to the Seven Sisters and whose own name means "to increase in numbers." But the etymology most consistent with the mythic astromorphosis of the sisters comes from *peleiades*, which means "flock of doves." Although some believe this derivation to be merely poetic, having perhaps originated with the ancient Greek poet Pindar, many etymologists maintain that the literal meaning of *Pleiades* is "constellation of the doves." The only certainty is that the origin of this name has vanished into the dark ocean of time. *Pleiades* stands as a lovely marker of a harbor now lost, a lyrical name that remains unmoored and sailing.

I spin for Hannah the yarn of the seven dove sisters, and she performs morphoses of her own, changing them into the ravens and meadowlarks who are her neighbors, and then into girls, and back into stars once more. She also changes the Pleiadian doves into her own sisters, whom she plans to visit up in the sky whenever she pleases. Narratives of sisterly bonds have special appeal for Hannah these days, because she knows that her mommy now carries within her a five-month-old fetus—a little sister who, on the ultrasound's photograph of galactic inner space, appears gently lit and curved, a crescent moon floating in a dark sky of amniotic fluid. The magic of transformation is closer to Hannah's reality than mine, a fact made plain by her fluidity in imagining and describing transformations of all kinds: in herself and her unborn sister, in her nonhuman neighbors, in the night sky. On the mountain behind our house, she tells me, pronghorn drink together at the same springs with a local dinosaur she has imagined and named Braucus. She's certain that pronghorn and plesiosaurs sleep in the same caves, have breakfast together, even go to the same birthday parties wearing homemade garlands of lupine, sidalcea, and balsamroot flowers. The walls of the world—the ones that delineate the boxes within boxes where we grown-ups live and work—are invisible to her. For Hannah, the net of relations that makes the universe cohere is as interstitial as it is connective: strong and flexible, but full of inviting passages between worlds and permeable in ways that have long since been lost to me.

I tell Hannah about the science of the Pleiades as well as their mythology, but to her these two modes of perception offer equally compelling explanations for something she experiences in a relatively unmediated way. Orbital gravity, escape velocity, open cluster, reflection nebulae—that story is fine with her. Seven sisters who, while their daddy tries to hold up the world, become doves in the night sky—that makes perfect sense, too. Hannah loves stories, but behind the stories she sees only the world, just as it is, entirely full of possibility, every night when the light of the sun goes out.

Many ancient Greek temples, including the celebrated Parthenon, were constructed precisely so as to align with the heliacal rising or setting of the Pleiades. By orienting their temples in this way the

Greeks were also orienting themselves within a universe in which this tiny, dipper-shaped net of stars formed the hub. The Seven Sisters are vitally important to ancient Greek culture—they figure in *The Iliad, The Odyssey,* and other foundational Greek texts—and their beauty is also sung by the Romans, including Cicero, Ovid, Varro, Pliny, and Virgil. But the delicate beauty of the cluster, its visibility from both hemispheres, and its importance in marking the seasons of navigation and agriculture have given it prominence in cosmologies and agricultural calendars from around the planet.

In many ancient cultures the Pleiades cluster was considered the *axis mundi*—the hub of the universe, around which all else revolves. In ancient Arabic cultures the cluster was known as Al Na'ir ("the bright one"), and in ancient Egypt the ritual of the dead included speaking the names of the seven Hathors—the Pleiades—to assist the dead on their journey to the distant stars. In Hindu mythology the Pleiades stars were called the Krittika (Sanskrit for "the cutters"), the seven daughters of Brahma who married the Seven Rishis, or Seven Sages. The skilled sailors of ancient Polynesia celebrated these "highborn" stars as crucial navigational guides whose arrival initiated their new year. The Chaldeans called the cluster Chimah, meaning "hinge," because it was thought to be the point upon which the universe pivots. In China this cluster of "Blossom Stars" was recorded in a 2357 B.C. reference, which may be the first in astronomical literature. The indigenous Ainu people of Japan saw not a blossom but instead a great tortoise that they called Subaru, a designation we still see on the six-star logo of the automotive conglomerate that borrowed its name from the Pleiades. To the Maori of New Zealand the Pleiades are Matariki, the beloved "little eyes of heaven." Among the aboriginal peoples of Australia, who believe the Seven Sisters came to earth from the celestial sphere during the ancient Dreamtime, each tribe calls the cluster by its own name: to the Kulin people the Pleiades were Karagurk; to the Adnyamathanha, Magara; to the Bundjalung, Meamai; and to the Walmadjeri, Gungaguranggara.

I can also tell Hannah stories that are closer to home, since most of the indigenous peoples of North America have rich cultural connections to the Pleiades. The Navajo, who called the cluster Dilyehe, claimed that these special stars were placed in the heavens by the Fire God. The Blackfeet have a myth of lost children who eventually find safety in the sky, and the Lakota believed that after death one's soul returns to the Pleiades. The Wyandot tell a story of seven girls who fly up to the star cluster in a big basket, in part to escape an amorous hunter. The Hopi called the Pleiades the Chuhukon ("those who cling together") and considered themselves descended from these stars, while Cree myths claim that protohumans came to earth from the Pleiades in spirit form before becoming corporeal bodies here. The Iroquois performed a prayer to the Seven Sisters, while Dakota myths relate that the home of the ancestors was among the Pleiades.

Hannah's favorite of these many wonderful stories, which is shared by the Arapaho, Crow, Cheyenne, Kiowa, Lakota, and our own local Shoshone peoples, closely links the Pleiades to Devils Tower (in Lakota, Mathó Thípila, which means "Bear Lodge"), a sacred site in present-day northeastern Wyoming that functions as the axis mundi within several Native American cosmographies. Seven Indian girls who were fleeing a great bear climbed to the top of the volcanic tower and prayed to the Great Spirit for help, after which the tower magically soared upward until the girls were delivered into the heavens for their protection. Once her little sister is born, Hannah tells me, she hopes the two of them can visit the top of that tower, just to see how close they can get to the stars.

The Pleiades were also used to calibrate many ancient agricultural and sacred calendars, and festivals devised to honor the Seven Sisters have even survived into our own day. The Aztecs based their famous calendar on the Pleiades, whose heliacal rising, ritually marked by priests, began their calendrical year. At Cusco, the capital of the ancient Incan empire, the 328-night year also began with the celebrated vernal rising of the Sisters. The Mayan sacred calendar, the Tzolk'in, describes a 26,000-year period and is likewise based upon the cycles of the Pleiades. And throughout much of pre-Columbian Mesoamerica there was, every fifty-two years, a monumental celebration when the Pleiades culminated (reached their highest point in the sky) just at midnight. In both spatial and temporal terms, these ancient cultures located themselves in the universe by calculating their relationship to the sacred star cluster.

Because the heliacal rising of the Pleiades in spring coincides with the life-giving season of new growth, many ancient traditions associate the cluster with fertility and plenitude. But the cycles of the Pleiades have also marked the end of seasons and the end of life itself. In old Europe the cluster was powerfully associated with mourning because its acronychal rising (rising in the east just as the sun sets in the west) occurred on the cross-quarter day between the autumnal equinox and the winter solstice and thus marked All Hallows' Eve, the feast of the dead that was later Christianized as All Saints' Day and eventually secularized as Halloween. Traced back far enough, Halloween leads to the ancient Celtic feast of Samhain, which was also calibrated to the midnight culmination of the Pleiades. In fact, the two prominent cross-quarter times in the old Dorian calendar were both marked by the Pleiades, and they evolved into May Day and Halloween, those vital pagan celebrations of life and death. The Pleiades are thus an illuminated bridge between ourselves and our ancestors. When little Hannah dons her Halloween butterfly costume and completes her metamorphosis from girl into butterfly, she is actually participating in an ancient ritual of death and rebirth that has for millennia been marked by the movement of her favorite stars.

Given that astral worship was one of the forms of pagan idolatry against which the ancient Hebrews defined their faith, it is fascinating that the Old Testament—a book not rich in stars—contains explicit references to the Pleiades. Both are in the Book of Job, and both are assertions of God's authority as supreme creator of heaven and earth. Job's problem is that, like Hannah, he asks a lot of questions. In Job 38:31–33, the Old Testament God—who is master of, among other things, the high-stakes rhetorical question—asks Job the sort of question one had better answer correctly: "Canst thou bind the sweet influences of Pleiades, or loose the bands of Orion?" The correct answer, of course, is "No way, boss." Job's inability to govern the stars defines the limit of his mortal gifts, for only omniscient God can penetrate the nebular veil shrouding the Seven Sisters. Like Job, Hannah and I must get along as best we can, asking much but understanding little.

Among the innumerable myths about the Pleiades are many that attempt to account for the "Lost Pleiad"—that missing seventh sister we so seldom see when gazing skyward at night. Some say that Merope, having married the mortal Sisyphus, went dim with shame. Others claim that it is Electra, who in mourning hid her bright face in grief upon the death of her son, Dardanus. Scientists tend to identify the missing Pleiad as Celaeno because it is the dimmest of the seven stars and just at the limit of human vision. But even here there is uncertainty, for the fluctuations in apparent magnitude that occur over time in these stars may mean that the ancients saw a brighter seventh sister than we see today. I do not know which Pleiad is the lost sister. In one story I often tell Hannah, she herself is the seventh sister, now invisible in the sky because she descended to earth to become part of our family. She likes that story, and whenever I tell it she smiles and sings an incisive line of verse: "Twinkle, twinkle, little star, how I wonder what you are."

The myth of the lost Pleiad has more serious implications in our own day, for now all seven sisters are in danger of becoming lost. Because the Pleiades stars are barely visible, even moderate levels of human-generated light in the night sky wash them away as if they had never existed. Insofar as our visceral experience of them is concerned, these stars are critically endangered. If the light of the Pleiadian doves is extinguished, it will not be the same kind of extinction suffered by the passenger pigeon and Carolina parakeet—but it will be extinction nonetheless. When I crest the last dark desert ridge before entering the city, I see in the southern sky the shining stars of Orion's belt. But above and to the right of the hunter I see nothing—the sisters are lost in the hazy glow of city lights, and where there should be beauty there is instead a hole in the sky. I know that beyond the cloud of light generated by the Walmart and its satellites floats a delicate net of exquisite stars that has played a vital role in human culture for millennia, but this abstract knowledge cannot substitute for the experience of seeing the sisters for myself.

When the pagans celebrated feasts to honor the Pleiades, they first extinguished every fire in the land so as to better view the Seven Sisters ignited in the heavens. Our age, too, must find some ritual to honor the stars, for darkness is the only mother from which starlight can be born. Modern connotations of the word *benighted* are strictly pejorative: "to be unenlightened; involved in intellectual or moral darkness." But the word's archaic meaning sings a different tune: "to be overtaken or affected by the darkness of the night." We cannot be enlightened without first becoming benighted. In *Nature* Emerson tried to rekindle in his readers the miraculous wonder of stargazing: "If the stars should appear one night in a thousand years, how would men believe and adore; and preserve for many generations the remembrance." What new myth can inspire us to restore the darkness that now lies hidden beneath the bright map of America?

How long will my little daughter continue to check nightly for the Pleiades if the light spewing from the sprawling city sends the other six stars into exile with their seventh sister? How can we measure what is lost when something that connects us viscerally to the universe simply ceases to be part of our sensory experience? I wonder what will have vanished when the nebulous glow of this celebrated cluster recedes, leaving only a blank spot on Hannah's treasure map of night. I have no way of knowing how the woman she grows to become will have been enriched by the presence of her sisterly stars or, conversely, impoverished by their silent vanishing into the artificially illuminated night. I do know that Hannah cannot bear the thought of her own little sister being born into a world from which the light of the lovely Pleiadian sister doves has been exiled.

PART TWO

Wilding

Life in the wild is not just eating berries in the sunlight. I like to imagine a "depth ecology" that would go to the dark side of nature—the ball of crunched bones in a scat, the feathers in the snow, the tales of insatiable appetite.

—GARY SNYDER, *The Practice of the Wild*

Chapter 5

The Adventures
of Peavine and Charlie

Late one summer afternoon, while out for a walk, Hannah and I
decide to follow some pronghorn tracks, just for practice. Tracks, as
Hannah knows, are story. To follow a track is to pursue a single story
line through a palimpsest landscape, a richly imbricated world of
interlacing narrative possibilities, the ultimate hypertext. How fast is
the animal moving, in what direction, and for what purpose? Where
does it pause to rest or forage? Why is it here at this time of year and
this time of day? Where is it coming from, and where is it going?
The pronghorn's trail intersects with those of jackrabbit and coyote,
kangaroo rat and quail, father and little girl; its story unfolds in a
particular place at a specific time and for certain reasons, only some

of which are discernible by us. We engage with this text because we relish the language of hoofprint and fur tuft and scat in which it is told, but also because, like all readers, we crave narrative resolution.

After we have followed the antelope trail for a few hundred yards, Hannah asks, "Dad, what's at the end of these tracks?"

"A pronghorn," I reply.

"How do you know?" she insists.

"I can't be sure, but that's what I believe."

"OK," she says, "let's keep going until we find it." We follow the dual crescent moons of the socketed hoofprints another hundred yards until they crest a rise, from which we look down and see a large pronghorn buck looking up at us. *"Dad, just like you said!"* Hannah whispers excitedly. It is as if, in turning the pages of an autobiography, we have somehow read our way up to the author as he sits at the desk, writing.

I never figured out how to explain to Hannah that in more than thirty years of following tracks I have never—either before that day or since—walked a track right up to the animal that was making it. It was as if Hannah's question about the outcome of the antelope's trail had somehow called the animal into being—as if by reading the trail's story carefully, she was able to write for herself a satisfying conclusion to it. If a trail is certain evidence of our faith in things unseen, the pronghorn was for Hannah the substance of the thing hoped for.

The exposed hilltop on which we live is desiccated by extreme aridity, raked by howling winds, inundated with deep snowdrifts, rocked by frequent earthquakes, incinerated by raging wildfires, and inhabited by rattlesnakes, scorpions, and vultures. Hannah Virginia and her little sister, Caroline Emerson, have never known another home. To them, living in this place and under these conditions is simply what little girls do. This is the place our stories come from, by which I mean this stark high desert landscape holds and inspires fantastic tales, but also that it profoundly shapes the larger story of our shared lives—our human attempt to structure, articulate, revise, and interpret the narrative of our experience in the world.

When I was Caroline's age, my father told me bedtime stories about Harry the Duck, a character of his own invention. Like my father himself, Harry was a great friend and also a comic figure. He was a resilient creature, always in a little trouble but perpetually able, through resourcefulness, generosity, and good humor, to escape his various predicaments—though I recall worrying that Harry might not survive some of his more harrowing adventures. When, at about two years old, Hannah seemed ready for bedtime stories, I considered making Harry an intergenerational narrative figure in our family. But as I reflected on how attached Hannah was already becoming to her desert home, a duck seemed the narrative equivalent of an invasive species, an alien figure ill suited to the dry hills among which we live. Instead, the very first story I offered to tell Hannah was about a pair of black-tailed jackrabbits that frequented the weedy sand flat that passes for our yard.

"What are their names?" she asked.

"Well, the older one is named . . . Peavine," I said, quickly appropriating the name of the mountain to our south to cover for my lack of preparation.

"And his little brother is Charlie!" she declared, out of nowhere.

"Sure," I said. "That's right. Peavine and Charlie."

From that moment on, Peavine and Charlie became a part of our family, and each evening I'd detail their latest adventure for Hannah before she slipped into slumber. In the early going I wasn't a very resourceful storyteller, and I noticed to my disappointment that Peavine and Charlie, endearing as they were, tended to become dull, especially when I was tired, or when the frustrations of work impinged on the joy the jackrabbits would otherwise have sought and found. Worse still, many of my narratives seemed heavy-handed and didactic, as if the brother rabbits existed only to serve my adult need to foist lessons upon my daughter. I often felt that I had imprisoned poor Peavine and Charlie—who were, after all, wild animals—in a narrative cage fabricated of my own fatigue or anxiety. There were some evenings when I almost sensed the jackrabbits' frustration with me, and they might well have wished they could step out of my bland tales and wrest control of their telling, if only to liberate themselves from the constraints of my tepid imagination.

Over time, though, Peavine and Charlie began to push back, to defy my urge to control them, occasionally rupturing the boundaries within which my stories tried to enclose them. They became less predictable, wilder, at times even irreverent. They would suddenly do or say things I hadn't anticipated, taking my tales in new and sometimes dangerous directions. When the rabbit boys were challenged to a soccer match by Raven and Magpie, they secretly persuaded Pack Rat to piss on the ball, since they suspected—correctly, as it turned out—that their corvid opponents would find the stench intolerable. When Peavine and Charlie were warned by their parents not to venture beyond the rim of their desert basin, they instead persuaded Golden Eagle to fly them all the way to the summit of the highest mountain in our valley. Whereas in earlier stories the boys might have learned a valuable lesson from their disobedience, they now had the time of their lives, returned home before supper, and were never found out. In some stories the jackrabbits even shared adventures with Old Man Coyote, an unsavory companion borrowed from Native trickster tales: a witty, energetic, ingenious, libidinous, transgressive, impertinent outlaw who drinks heavily, has sex frequently, farts lustily, and boasts loudly about it all.

The most important developments in the Peavine and Charlie tales, however, came from Hannah, whose increasing involvement in their telling helped the brother rabbits to grow into three-dimensional characters. When I first began this bedtime ritual I would announce, with unassailable adult authorial intention, the topic of the evening's story: "Tonight I'm going to tell you about the time Peavine and Charlie went to a birthday party with the white pelicans." And that was that. Later, Hannah began asking me to repeat stories, which I soon discovered I could not do to her satisfaction, since her memory of a story's details was so much keener than my own. As a result of this incapacity on my part, Hannah inadvertently became a more active participant, a co-narrator who corrected and inserted details as necessary: "No, Dad, the king of the white pelicans baked a *chocolate* birthday cake, remember?"

As Hannah's role in the evening storytelling grew, a new dimension emerged in our narrative collaboration. She began to ask me if I knew a particular story—but in asking she would refer to an original story rather than one previously told. For example, she might ask, without provocation or precedent, whether I knew the story about the time Peavine and Charlie flew from Nevada to Australia in a hot air balloon—a story I had never dreamed of. Hannah's presumption was that the story existed independently of my ability to create it, and so the question was not whether Peavine and Charlie had actually flown to Australia in a balloon (of course they had!), but instead whether my own limited life experience had made me familiar with that particular story. As our bedtime stories evolved, we no longer told tales of my own imagining, and we ceased repeating tales. Instead, each evening Hannah would ask if I knew the story of the time Peavine and Charlie took a nap on top of a thundercloud, or the time the jackrabbits ate a bunch of fence lizards just to see if they would get a tummy ache, or the time they saw Old Man Coyote drink up the whole ocean, or the time they helped Kestrel fly so fast that it made the sun dizzy to watch.

What came of this new phase in our evening storytelling was as remarkable as it was simple, as illuminating as it was obvious: it turned out that I *did* know the stories. All of them. While Hannah expressed amazement each night that I knew every tale she suggested (asking once, "Dad, when did you have time to learn all these stories?"), I too was amazed. I was astonished at the elasticity and power of narrative to spontaneously express any set of experiences that two jackrabbits—or, by extension, a father and his daughter—might have, and in that amazement I was liberated, along with Peavine and Charlie, from the repetitive plots and moralistic conclusions that had previously constrained me. Instead of forcing my furry protagonists forward at narrative gunpoint toward a preconceived and didactic conclusion, the jackrabbits now led us into fields of story we had never imagined. While the new stories were fragmented, often implausible, sometimes even unfathomable, they were utterly spontaneous and fresh. They were also funnier and more engaging, though less conclusive. Telling Peavine and Charlie stories was now like following tracks: the more attention we paid to each meandering narrative hoofprint, the more certain we were that a big buck was out there, even if it remained invisible from where we stood or lay while telling the tale.

Soon enough Hannah was no longer simply suggesting the stories but actively helping me to tell them. I'd ramble up to a particular plot point and then ask her if she "remembered" what happened next—even though the story was being told for the first time. So if Peavine and Charlie were swimming across Pyramid Lake on the back of Lahontan Cutthroat Trout, I'd ask if she remembered where they swam to.

"Oh, sure!" Hannah would always say at first, perhaps to give herself a moment to formulate the next passage of the story. "They swam all the way to Anaho Island so they could eat rattlesnake eggs and visit the magic well near where the white pelicans live!"

"Exactly," I'd reply, affirming her acts of imagination. "And do you remember how they got the water out of the magic well?"

"Oh, sure! They drank it up with a really, really long straw!"

On we'd go like this, taking turns telling, stitching together stories off the cuff and on the fly, without the slightest idea where we were headed, enjoying the experience immensely. We never corrected each other or felt that one person's story had been stifled by some outrageous turn the other person had interjected into the narrative. On the contrary, the delight for me came from the way the collaborative dynamic prevented the narrative from conforming to my own narrow, linear adult expectations for how a story should proceed. Because I'm a grown-up—which I can't help and for which I might well be pitied—I would have thought Peavine and Charlie would retrieve Anaho Island's well water using a bucket. But, of course, I was wrong. Since they had instead used a really, really long straw, that magical water was now inside them, and it would be up to me to discern what wonderful effects it might produce. The godlike omniscient narrator was at last dead and gone; what remained was a world of uncertainty and flux, which is to say a world where it is easy to become lost and where everything you experience feels inimitable and enchanted.

During this phase of our collaborative bedtime storytelling, Hannah never once implied that she viewed our stories as the product of invention or imagination. Instead, she continued to speak of the tales as if they preceded both the tellers and the telling. As far as she was concerned, all possible stories existed, and all existed independently of our speaking them. Even in their most unexpected and peculiar details, the tales were to Hannah an infinite number of tracks that we had not made but could always follow. To her, the stories of the nonhuman beings whose lives we narrated already possessed an uneditable fullness and integrity of their own—a fantastic, preexistent logic we could never contain or control but were free to discover and express. As our collaborative storytelling progressed, I began to wonder if Hannah wasn't somehow correct that even our wildest and most improbable narrative imaginings simply describe the world as it is. Because the world was there before us, maybe she's right that the stories were there before us too.

Hannah, who was three years old at the time, began telling stories to baby Caroline on the day Caroline was born. This introduced yet another phase in the lives of Peavine and Charlie, one that positioned Hannah as the primary teller of tales in our family. Many of the stories Hannah told her sister in that first year seemed designed to convey practical information about our home landscape. There were stories about how Peavine and Charlie learned to recognize and avoid the buzz of the rattler, and how they used snowshoes to keep from becoming trapped in the drifts, and what precautions they took when wildfire scoured the hills behind our house. In one tale, Peavine and Charlie strayed too far from home one evening but navigated back by walking toward Polaris, the North Star, which Hannah explained could be found by drawing an imaginary line through the Big Dipper's bowl. In another, the jackrabbits wisely avoided going out after dark, since Mountain Lion had been hunting the area. In yet another, the rabbit brothers failed to carry enough water on a hike up our home mountain and so would have become dehydrated had not Raven flown to their rescue from Summit Spring carrying water in a bag of balsamroot leaves woven together with strips of sage bark.

In addition to being dramatic admonitions about scorpions and rattlers, Hannah's stories for Caroline also functioned as an introduction to the natural history of this high desert environment. In the single story of "Peavine and Charlie's Bird World Series," for example, Caroline was introduced to most of the avian species that live here in summer. In the tale of the rabbit boys' long walk to Lone Tree, Caroline was offered a clear overview of kid's-eye geomorphology: the best climbing rock, the canyon where the snow stays deep, the ridge where the stars look *so* bright. The story of the jackrabbits' "Great Water Race" identified the general locations of the two natural springs within hiking distance of our home, while the account of how Peavine and Charlie enjoyed a midday nap in the shade of some boulders seemed calculated to instill a potentially life-saving respect for the intensity of the desert sun at high elevation.

I listened to these stories but never interfered with their telling, except when I was asked to help—as when Hannah couldn't quite fill out the rosters of Peavine and Charlie's bird baseball teams without me suggesting Juniper Titmouse, Say's Phoebe, and Western Tanager. As I listened, I was amazed not only at how much Hannah had learned about her local environment but also at how clearly she could convey information through the vehicle of her Peavine and Charlie narratives. It was telling, too, that while Hannah's stories were replete with joy and humor, they also seemed crafted to convey lessons that one's little sister, if she intended to become a permanent inhabitant of the sagebrush steppe, would need to learn. In this sense, Hannah's stories adopted a touch of Dad's earlier didacticism, the key difference being that her jackrabbit tales were not contrived morality plays, as my stories had so often been, but instead were engaging, detailed, informed local narratives that used nonhuman lives to convey valuable information about how to live well in this place. And this, it seemed to me, must be very close to the root of all stories, which from time immemorial must have sprung from the desire of one person to teach someone they love how to feel at home in the world.

If Hannah had in some senses taken on the adult role of storyteller, it was interesting how quickly Caroline consequently grew into the role that Hannah had once played. Not content with only listening to and learning from the tales, Caroline by age three wanted to help shape and guide the narratives, often blurting out suggestions that Hannah was challenged to accommodate. So, for example, Hannah would announce that she was about to tell the story of the time Peavine and Charlie discovered the buried treasure, when Caroline would stubbornly insist that the treasure was not buried but instead hidden in the crown of a cottonwood tree. Or Hannah would prepare to tell of how the jackrabbits helped California Ground Squirrel and Antelope Ground Squirrel get married, when Caroline would instead demand to hear how the rabbit boys taught the ground squirrels to play blues harmonica. I confess that it was amusing to see Hannah's exasperation in these moments; each time Caroline shouted out a suggestion, Hannah was compelled to relinquish her own narrative intentions and expectations and instead follow the tracks that Caroline's imagination was laying down. Hannah had to learn to share the stories: to view them as the fruit of collaboration with her sister rather than as the product of her own unmediated authorial intent.

Then another wonderful thing happened. Caroline began to ask Hannah, just as Hannah had once asked me, if she "remembered the story about the time" the jackrabbits had this or that adventure—referring, as Hannah once had, to entirely new stories of her own invention. Hannah, for her part, fell naturally into the role I had formerly played, which was to reply joyfully that yes, in fact, she did remember that particular story. Although little sister was duly amazed at big sister's wonderful capacity to "remember" all the stories she requested, Caroline nevertheless participated actively in their telling. Rather than seeing her involvement as a disruption of a stable or proprietary text, Caroline instead assumed, precisely as Hannah once had, that all the stories were simply out there in the world, preexistent and waiting to be recalled by their tellers. To listen to the girls tell Peavine and Charlie stories was not only to marvel at their imaginative capacity to empathize with the lives of jackrabbits and their other nonhuman neighbors; it was also to realize that in the girls' world no story's path was ever blocked, no detail unchangeable, no conclusion assumed, no possibility foreclosed. For Hannah and Caroline, the tracks of a story could lead anywhere, and did.

We are each the hero of our own life story, which we write daily with our actions and ambitions, failings and fantasies. If we're fortunate, we may be able to construct ourselves as comic rather than tragic heroes, but our attempt to write our lives ultimately remains embattled. We struggle to control a recalcitrant protagonist, to impose narrative structure on a disorderly reality, to extract meaning from a personal story that is by turns fragmented, unfathomable, or mundane. And we often adhere obsessively to a preconceived story line, even when our lived experience is painfully incongruous with it. I'm certain, for example, that those of us who are parents remain bound by a story line within which we teach and inspire our children, helping them to mature into truly good people while also demonstrating our wisdom and affirming our values. But even as we wish our lives to proceed according to the stories we tell about them, we also struggle with the obdurate tensions those lives invariably present: their fractured narrative arcs and rough transitions, glaring stylistic flaws and troubling ambiguities, undesirable settings and underdeveloped characters, tediously predictable plot points and frustrating lack of closure. Rather than embrace the inevitability of this uncertainty, difficulty, and flux, we instead stubbornly pretend that we possess infallible authorial control. As a consequence, the writing of our lives reflects an impoverishment of narrative possibility—an overreliance upon a limited set of plot lines designed to force our story toward the denouement we most desire.

I try to remember how the world looks to a kid, but I find this imaginative leap increasingly difficult to make. There is something about adult perception, however finely honed it might be, that struggles to attain the sense of possibility that is instinctive to children. While I reject sentimental rhapsodies about the angelic nature of children—romantic propositions that the odor of a single diaper plainly refutes—it does seem to me that children possess the enviable capacity to imagine and thus inhabit a world in which all stories remain possible and in which any story may be told by any person at any time. The fluidity with which Hannah and Caroline's spontaneous tales narrated imaginative voyages across the permeable boundary between themselves and their nonhuman neighbors showed me how wild are the stories that link our domestic sphere to the natural world that is our widest home. Even here, by the wood stove's hearth, the girls discovered a wilderness of possibility in the expansive relations those words helped them to imagine.

What if adults lived in a world of comparable imaginative richness? What if, instead of choosing desperately from among the half-dozen threadbare plots our popular culture sells, we asked a broader range of questions about our stories? "Do you know the one about the man who learned to love his wife?" "Will you tell about how the lady in the cubicle discovered that her work really mattered in the world?" "Do you remember the tale about the old man who played guitar for the very first time?" "Please spin the yarn of that father who, while splitting a bucked juniper stump just at dusk, suddenly remembered his daughters' coyote story and so looked beyond himself and witnessed alpenglow igniting the snowy flanks of his home mountain." Who knows what new questions we might ask, what new language we might ask them in, what new answers our stories might inspire? After all, no fine story unfolds without surprising plot twists, and no real story can know its own conclusion. Perhaps our lives may only be fully written once we relinquish narrative control, allowing the tale to tell the teller—once we renew our belief in a world in which a little girl reading the trail of a pronghorn can imagine the animal and, in that imagining, can summon a breathing ungulate on a dusty desert mountainside.

Chapter 6

The Wild within Our Walls

"Honey, get the camera!" I've just peeled back the tarp covering a half-used pallet of quartzite flagstone to reveal the cutest thing I've ever seen. From between the slats of the empty part of the pallet pokes a furry little head with large, dark, shining eyes, a tiny, sniffing nose, and twitching whiskers. Its big, rounded ears are backlit in the early morning summer sun, and its bushy tail is partially visible through the slats just behind its body. Then a second curious little head appears, and a third, and a fourth! By now Eryn has arrived with Hannah and Caroline, and with each furry noggin that pops up the girls' eyes open wider with surprise and joy.

"They're so cute!" Eryn exclaims, snapping away with her camera.

"What are their names?" Hannah asks, as she holds the hand of little Caroline, who is squealing with delight.

"Pack rats." It is the gravelly voice of my mason and surly neighbor, Charlie, who is coming around the corner of the house, finishing his third beer and getting ready to lay stone. In building this passive solar house of our own design here at 6,000 feet in the remote high desert, we've employed mostly rural neighbors, and there have been some hardpan characters among them. Charlie the mason—whom Eryn refers to as Charlie Manson—is an irredeemable desert rat, and though he's wild-eyed and sullen, I like him very much. He knows stone and he knows the desert, which is good enough for me.

"Pack rats?" Eryn asks. "Is that really a kind of rat? It looks more like a baby squirrel."

"Pack rat," Charlie repeats, scowling a little from behind his beer. "Wood rat. Trade rat. Pack rat. Rat. Deal with him." He's looking straight at me. My daughters are still smiling, but my wife is now frowning. I reach over and slowly slide the glass door closed in front of them. I can see the girls' lips moving but can no longer hear their voices.

I turn to Charlie. "What do you mean, 'Deal with him'?"

Charlie takes a big step closer to me, crushing and dropping his beer can as he does. "You don't know him like I know him, Nature Boy." I hated when he called me that, but I tried never to show it. "One day you'll step out of your house to take a piss behind that woodpile, and when you come back inside you'll find your bottle of single-barrel empty and that rat bastard sitting up in bed with your wife, smoking a Marlboro." Charlie is as earnest as a shark hunter, and he's in my face, reeking and squinting as he growls out his apocalyptic warning.

"Come on, Charlie, it's just a little squirrely thing." I gesture toward the pallet, where one of the wee, timorous beasties is still peeping up at us, cute as can be.

"Deal with him," he says over his shoulder as he walks back to his pickup to fetch another beer.

That night I heard no hooting from the resident great horned owls, no yelping from the upcanyon band of coyotes. Instead, strange scurrying sounds filled the darkness, unmistakably the acoustic trail of rodents, though the sounds were as loud as the jackrabbits out here are big. Scurrying on the deck, the walls, even the sill of the window just behind the headboard of our bed—the scratching and scrabbling sounds of claws, so loud that they kept me awake most of the night. In the morning I found small, sausage-shaped lumps of poop on the stoops of the house, with the greatest concentration on the doormats, as if the calling card had been left intentionally. Brownish-yellow streaks ran down our stucco walls, as if pints of porter had been spilled from the window ledges. The flowers in the pots on our porch had been clear-cut, leaving sheared stems where their colorful stalks had recently stood.

By breakfast I was already hunched over my field guides, reciting preliminary findings to Eryn. "Got to be *Neotoma cinerea,* the bushy-tailed wood rat," I concluded. "There are twenty-one species of wood rats, spread out across the United States and from Arctic Canada south to the jungles of Nicaragua, but this is the only one that fits: fairly boreal, widely distributed in the Great Basin, and has that big, fluffy tail. Nocturnal, good climber, likes to hole up in crevices in rock faces but also builds stick houses in juniper country like this. Will carry stuff off and pack it into its house. Generalist herbivore, but relishes succulent plants like, say, your snapdragons. *Neotoma cinerea.* That's our boy." Now I can answer Hannah's question. "He's named 'bushy tail,'" I tell her. Caroline likes that.

In the days that followed, the signs of a rodent invasion became increasingly evident. Each night brought the Mardi Gras of scurrying, and every morning, a new harvest of the signature butt pellets and the proliferation of nasty yellow streaks down the walls of the house. The potted plants were soon completely gone, and their stems invariably showed the distinctive angular cut of rodent teeth, which got the maligned desert cottontails off the hook. Bugs Bunny just chomps and gnaws, while rodents slash stems on a perfect angle, like a carrot julienned with the precision of a sous chef's blade.

One morning I went to fetch our hidden house key to loan it to Charlie, and it was unaccountably missing from its secret hiding place. Then in the afternoon I opened the hood of my truck to add windshield wiper fluid and discovered that over a single night the bushy tails had built a respectable nest atop my battery, one that was not only well wrought but also colorful. As I removed the nest I called out to Eryn: "Honey, I found your snapdragons." Then the inevitable happened. Evolutionary programming told the pack rats that our stucco house was the sheer face of a rock cliff and the cement roof tiles were the innumerable doorways to a honeycomb of crevices and cavities. Once under the tiles, they had the run of the joint and could enter the soffits and at their leisure chew their way into the attic space, where they proceeded to gnaw insulation off pipes and coating off wiring. Now we had a critter issue that no amount of cute was going to fix. Despite the girls' enthusiasm for these furry visitors, if something wasn't done soon we'd be driven from our home by an army of furry little *Neotoma*. I had to "deal with him" and without delay.

But in a matter of twenty-four hours, before I could even formulate a strategy, something happened that should happen only in tales born in the dark imagination of Edgar Allan Poe: scratching, scrabbling, clawing sounds came from *within* the interior walls of the house. Even Nature Boy was forced to admit that things were now out of hand. I winced, steeling myself for what I knew was necessary: a belly wriggle through the dark, claustrophobic crawl space beneath the house. If the rats were down there (at some point I had stopped calling them "bushy tails" and started calling them "rats"), then the levee was breached, and they would not only be under the roof and in the walls but would also have access to a labyrinth of ducts.

I drained a glass of single-barrel sour mash before strapping on my headlamp and dropping through the trap hole in the floor as the girls held Eryn's hands and watched me vanish into the darkness. It was immediately clear from the acrid smell that something was down there, and the stench wasn't coming from the glossy, bulbous black widow spider whose orange hourglass tattoo was the first thing illuminated in the beam of my small headlamp. With less than two feet of clearance I commando crawled across the vapor barrier on the ground, where I soon discovered that the plastic sheeting was littered with turds and sticky with the same Grey Poupon that streaked the walls of the house. They were down here, all right, but I didn't know where, or what I'd do if I found them. How many would there be? What diseases would they carry? Would they julienne my fingers with their razor-sharp choppers, leaving me with ten precisely angled stumps?

As I pulled myself forward with my forearms, I began to identify trash that had been collected from around our property: bottle cap, tinfoil, coyote scat, wood screw, tuft of dog hair, flagging tape, masonry nail, owl pellet, snapdragon stalk, tabs from Charlie's beer cans, even my spare house key. There were clipped juniper twigs lying all around, most of them still fresh and green. It was immediately clear that here, within the very foundation of our home, something quite wild had been going on. This was my house but their territory, and since they were accustomed to crawling around the dark in the choking ammonia stench of urine, they had an immediate advantage over me. Continuing my commando crawl, in the dusty beam of my headlamp, I noticed a pile of sticks a few yards ahead, tucked against a foundation wall and behind the elbow of a large duct. Nudging forward in the dark, I expected at any moment to feel a rat run across my back or tangle itself in my hair.

At last I eased up close to the duct behind which the stick nest was concealed and then slowly craned my neck down and around the duct, turning my head to allow the beam of my headlamp to fall onto the bundle of sticks. There he was, a foot from my face and exactly at eye level, and he was all attitude, standing straight up on his hind legs and glaring at me as if ready to rumble. I had somehow assumed that if I found the little beast he would simply scurry away, but clearly this bruiser had no intention of stepping off. Which of us would blink first? In the next moment I reached the turning point in my increasingly troubled relationship with *Neotoma cinerea*. As I tilted my head a little, the lamp revealed the treasures he was defending in his nest. Nestled among juniper berries and beer can tabs rested Caroline's pink pacifier. Now I could feel my jaws clench. "Listen here, you wife-stealing rat bastard," I said aloud, "you are *not* going to drink my good bourbon." He didn't move a whisker, and he didn't look at all scared.

Since moving out to this remote hilltop in the western Great Basin I've dealt with plenty of critters. A great horned owl once swooped in front of us in an attempt to airlift our cat in its talons. On another occasion I intercepted a scorpion crawling along the baseboard beneath Caroline's crib. Then there was the time the big bobcat walked coolly beneath the girls' swing set on his way to raid our chicken coop. I'd even had my truck towed to the shop only to have the mechanic call to say he couldn't work on it because there was a four-foot gopher snake snoozing on the engine block. But it was Caroline's pilfered pacifier that finally pushed me over the edge. In a way that perhaps only a father can understand, that was going too far. Nature Boy was on the warpath.

I started by doing a lot of research quickly. I reckoned that to defeat an enemy you must first understand his strengths and weaknesses and compare them to your own. What would make my adversary hungry, thirsty, tired, cold, worried, existentially despondent? What might a bad day for a pack rat look like? I read what I could find on wood rat social biology and then made a two-column list documenting a point-by-point comparison of the relative strengths of Rat Bastard and Nature Boy. I expected, given my status as a member of the species widely celebrated as the pinnacle of evolution (albeit only among ourselves), that I'd have impressive advantages over my foe. As the two-columned list shaped up, I soon discovered that the opposite was true. Rat Bastard was such a dietary generalist that I could never stop him by cutting off his food supply—he'd eat almost anything, from plants, berries, seeds, twigs, and bark to small invertebrates, fungi, and even his own feces. I couldn't chase him down, as he could climb like lightning up vertical and even inverted faces, and I couldn't shoot him because he was nocturnal and, besides, he was always crawling across my damned house. I couldn't track him, as he could navigate by kinesthetic memory and scent markings—detailed maps I couldn't even see to take away. Because he was hydrated by the plant matter he ate, he could go his whole life without taking a drink, while I, by contrast, couldn't go a day without whiskey, let alone water. When I was roasting in summer he'd be chillin' in a cool rock crevice, and when I was freezing in winter the master of thermoregulation would be toasty in the heart of his insulated den, curled into a ball and wrapped snugly in a long, furry tail designed especially for the purpose.

As for breeding, it's no wonder he's a threat to people's wives. Bushy tails produce one to three litters of two to six young each season, so they can feed plenty of owls and still fill your crawl space with the next generation. Their social structure is polygynous, which means that each male shacks up with a harem of several females. The females, for their part, are capable of running up vertical walls even with young dangling from their mammary glands, and they will often begin copulating within twelve hours of giving birth (two facts that, as it turns out, one should not bring to the attention of human mothers). Finally, pack rats are meaner than they are cute. We aren't talking field mice here. Because of sexual dimorphism in the species, a male *Neotoma cinerea* can weigh in at a whopping six hundred grams, which is about the size of a big burrito—only a ferocious burrito with razor-sharp claws and teeth. In fighting with other pack rats, which he does viciously and from a young age, he'll stand upright on his hind legs and bite and scratch for all he's worth, even leaping into the air to use his powerful hind claws to slash at and lacerate his opponents.

So what advantages are enumerated in the Nature Boy column of my list? Not many. I have an overdeveloped cerebral cortex, which, though helpful for executing such abstract tasks as making lists, is proving virtually useless in the practical conflict at hand. I do find that I have some things in common with Rat Bastard, who is described as "unsocial, solitary, and strongly territorial," but identifying his weaknesses is another matter. I did locate a few general sources devoted to how to get rid of rodents, but all the prescribed methods had attendant perils. "Exclusion" sounded obvious, but it came with the assumption that I knew exactly where they were getting into the house, which I didn't. "Toxicants" wasn't a great option, as pack rats will carry poison bait away and cache it in their dens, sometimes not eating it for weeks or even months; besides, my collateral damage assessment suggested that, considering both the domestic and wild animals around, there were plenty of "non-target species" (including our daughters) to be concerned about. "Biological control" for pack rats is more or less limited to cats, and our cat, Lucy, who has an impressively fat ass and who in any case spends most of her time trying not to become dinner for a coyote, is far too slow to dream of going to the mat with a fierce, burrito-sized street fighter like a pack rat; indeed, Lucy is the kind of feline who would have her paws full in a smackdown with an actual burrito. "Ultrasound repellers" sounded encouragingly high-tech but had been proven ineffective after a very short period. This left only "Trapping," which had plenty of complications. Rat Bastard was too big for a glue board, which seemed cruel anyhow, and a conventional snap trap would certainly catch me or my kid or my obese cat before it ever caught him. And anyway, think of the splatter. I knew my desperation had peaked when I found myself actually considering a plan enthusiastically proposed by my father-in-law, who is an impressively resourceful guy: fabricate a steel mat and wire it to a battery system by which we could electrocute the pack rats.

It was then that the owls showed me the light. Eryn and the girls and I went away for a single night, mostly to get a short break from my ratty nemesis, and when we returned it looked as if a fifty-five-gallon drum of half-and-half had been poured on the peaks of our roof and onto the ground below. "That's bird doo-doo," I explained in answer to Hannah's question, though it seemed inconceivable that anything smaller than a pterodactyl could produce crap this voluminous. "Yay, the birdie went poopie all by his self!" Caroline screeched, hopping up and down. Soon afterward I noticed that for once there were no turds on the porches—not one pellet. Aha! Rat Bastard, I have found your weakness! My presence here had disrupted a predatory cycle and had given *Neotoma* prime digs—not only a good place to hang out but also protection from predation by Ye Olde Nocturnal Raptor. Combining what I learned from reading about wood rats with my feces-induced epiphany about the vulnerabilities of my furry antagonist, I rededicated myself to getting something other than my frontal lobes on the Nature Boy side of the power tally.

How does the genius detective catch the genius criminal? By thinking like the criminal. If I were Rat Bastard, what would I want, and what would I fear? He's got plenty of chow and women, and he doesn't even need to drink, but he has the willies about being out in the open. He needs deep cover to nest, cache food, and thermoregulate—and to avoid being suddenly eviscerated by that silent-winged death from above. And pack rats are fiercely territorial and agonistic. As do other agonistic species, like alligators, they'll live close together but do not like each other much, and they'll fight fiercely for cover when it is scarce. As one study put it, "Possession of a house is so important to wood rat survival that a high level of aggression and solitary house occupancy are basic to the genus." A glance around our property suggested that I'd inadvertently created pack rat nirvana. There were several tarped pallets of rock, old PVC pipe lying around the foundation of the house, and heaps of scrap lumber here and there. Because we heat primarily with wood, there was a pile of stove wood the size of a train car—at least eight cords that I'd hauled, bucked, and split. How many rats might be living inside there? At the top of Rat Bastard's column of advantages over me was the superb cover that my own trash had provided him.

Heartened by these new observations, I decided to run my insights by an expert, if I could find one. After a number of phone calls I tracked down a guy nicknamed "the Ratman" at the state wildlife office. I didn't catch his real name, but everybody I talked to swore he was the pack rat guru in Nevada. When I finally reached him, he turned out to be another of the quirky, knowledgeable desert characters I enjoy so much.

"You up in the juniper? Yeah, *cinerea* for sure. Cute, aren't they? Ever seen them climb? They're amazing!" The Ratman is not only knowledgeable and friendly but also perfectly evangelical about the wonders of wood rats. He talks like a guy with nowhere to be, which is oddly pleasant, and he clearly wants to educate me as well as solve my problem. I go over my observations and options with him, and he concludes that he can help, but first he extorts from me a promise that I'll bring him a frozen pack rat. "Not one that's poisoned!" he insists. I agree reluctantly, though I haven't the slightest idea how I'll keep my promise.

"First, you've got to stop them from getting in," he says. "Then you need to deprive them of protective habitat around your place—that's their real vulnerability. They've got a small home range, so four or five hundred meters is plenty. Then you need to trap like crazy. Listen to the Ratman." Passing over his creepy use of the third person, I proceed to resist the apparent complexity of his plan.

"I can't figure out where they're getting in, Ratman, and I have about six or eight cords of wood I'd have to move. Besides, I'm really not the hunter-trapper type."

"If they're getting in under the roof tiles, stick steel wool or blow foam in there. If they're coming in around the foundation, mortar it up. You have to move all the stove wood—that's ideal habitat. The best trap for *Neotoma* is the two-foot, two-door Havahart." I'm comforted that he's been so humane as to suggest a live trap, when he follows with: "And do *not* go soft and release them! Best to drown them in a trash can." This from a guy who likes pack rats enough to call himself the Ratman.

"I know it's hard to tell over the phone," I reply, "but I'm really not the killing type. I'm one of those tender-hearted environmentalists. You know, a peace-to-all-creatures, live-and-let-live sort of guy."

"Listen, nothing you do will dent the general population—we're just talking about making an NFZ, a *Neotoma* Free Zone, in a five-hundred-meter arc around your place. Besides, you're only icing some of this year's model, the young who are being kicked out of the nests by the big adults. The home nests will still be out there in the scrub. You've got to tear up that woodpile like a coyote and hunt them at night like an owl. Listen to the Ratman. Peanut butter in the trap, then swimming lessons in the trash can. You have to get busy." I thank the Ratman for his help and, at his insistence, renew my pledge to bring him a bushy-tailed Popsicle.

Then, over a solid week of summer, I set out to do everything the Ratman recommended. First I spent several days up on our roof, broiling in the sun as I lay on my belly, spraying foam into every rat-sized gap. The remainder of the backbreaking week was devoted to moving stove wood and debris to another part of the property—fourteen pickup loads in all. As I did so, I found no less than a dozen individual pack rat nests in the woodpile alone—downy soft, palm-sized cups of shredded juniper bark, more delicately woven than a bird's nest. Every night I set a trap, and most mornings I had a hopping mad incarcerated pack rat to deal with. At first I allowed my tender green mercies to trump the Ratman's directive, and I would drive my catch out into the desert each morning for its ritual release. But soon I admitted that the scarcity of quality habitat, the fiercely agonistic nature of *Neotoma*, the extreme climatic conditions, and the summer's bumper crop of dispersing, aggressive young pack rats made this approach a death sentence for the animal, as well as being a very stinky and time-consuming prebreakfast activity for me each day.

And that is how I became a cold-blooded killer of my fellow creatures. Every morning I would wake up, drink a big mug of strong java, trudge off to my improvised trash-can water-tank death chamber, and use the unfortunately named Havahart trap to capture and give terminal swimming lessons to animals that, even if they are shameless stealers of baby pacifiers, are handsome, intelligent creatures that really just want to share our peanut butter.

Perhaps it was my guilt about the fact that my furry pupils invariably failed their swimming lessons that fueled my fascination with them, for as I became a murderer of pack rats I also became their admirer. Once I had evicted the bushy tails from our house and had, after repeated failures, finally managed to keep them out, I read more about *Neotoma*—both in books and in the landscape. I perused scientific studies of wood rats, gleaned what I could, and then hiked out into the desert to make my own observations. I discovered pack rat bones in owl pellets, and I climbed cliffs to examine *Neotoma* nests in granite notches. I identified many pack rat stick houses, which I visited regularly and watched closely, noticing if they had been built up, lined with fresh juniper, or disturbed by predators. Based on exposure, cover, and vegetation, I learned to anticipate where pack rats were likely to live, and eventually I even developed the ability to locate pack rat houses by following their distinctive acrid odor across the sagebrush steppe. I made regular visits to inspect the urination "posts" that pack rats visit repeatedly as a way of sharing olfactory information, and I watched the artistic patterns of their urine streaks emerge on rock faces after rain washed organic materials away, leaving expressionistic striations of dissolved calcium carbonate behind.

As I explained to Hannah and Caroline, the pack rat is no Johnny-come-lately, like the Old World rats whose pedigree dates only to the *Mayflower* and which now infest the sewers beneath every city in America. *Neotoma* is instead a true native, and there are fossil pack rat nesting sites in the Great Basin that have seen more or less continuous use for fifty thousand years. As a result of this long residency—and because pack rats have not changed their basic social behavior since the last ice age—we have learned amazing things from them. Of special value is the pack rat's powerful but indiscriminate penchant for collecting and storing things, often caching them deep within cliff faces and protecting them within stick houses, where the worst weather never reaches. Better still for posterity, it is often the case that generations of *Neotoma* will urinate on the collected materials, causing them to be encased in a virtually impervious, amber-like gem of crystallized pee—a substance the earliest western explorers couldn't identify but thought looked a lot like candy (some who took the confectionary appearance literally reported that the stuff actually tastes sweet but causes a terrific bellyache). Because it is an assemblage not only of food but also trash, a pack rat's midden (the debris pile it gathers in or around its nest) is a wild miscellany of objects that functions as a time capsule of the local environment at the time of collection. What some of us call trash an anthropologist calls an artifact and a paleoecologist calls a macrofossil.

Within the pack rat's trash we have discovered answers to

some of the most important questions we ask of the past. How do we know what level ancient lakes in the West reached, and how have we managed to chart their rising and recession over tens of thousands of years? By documenting the elevations of fossil pack rat middens, the ages of which are determined by studying the easily dated materials they contain. How do we know whether martens or jackrabbits or pikas or rattlers lived in a certain place twenty thousand years ago? Because pack rats collect and store small bones, as well as coyote scat and owl pellets, in which bone fragments of larger animals may be found. How do we know that here in the Great Basin subalpine conifers once grew 1,000 meters below their lowest distribution today? Because the twigs of bristlecone and limber pine are found in ancient pack rat middens that are far lower in elevation than the areas where those trees now exist.

This sort of information isn't important only to paleogeeks. Knowing the relative distribution of various plant species over a period of thirty or forty thousand years allows us to extrapolate changes in climate during that period, which in turn provides a paleoclimatologic baseline against which we can measure current rates of climate change. The pack rat's appetite for gathering trash provides a crucial means to gauge the degree to which the human appetite for consuming fossil fuels is causing a planetary environmental crisis. And we know all this for a very simple reason: pack rats gather trash near their houses and store it safely. The pack rat is a preservationist of the first order, one without whose collections of scat and berries and bone we would be hard pressed to understand the environment of the late Pleistocene and early Holocene periods.

It is no doubt true that one person's trash is another's treasure, but to the pack rat all trash is treasure—and I have discovered that it is in this treasuring of trash, as well as in the trash itself, that treasures are often found. Although we made sure that the pink pacifier I found beneath the house never made it back into Caroline's mouth, we still keep it in a shoebox along with scores of other objects the girls and I have collected from pack rat nests. And while our box of pack rat treasures includes tufts of fur and shards of bone, most of the objects we've discovered in local pack rat houses are rediscovered items—those ponytail holders and bobby pins, flat washers and beer bottle caps that are the unmistakable artifacts of our own unusual twenty-first-century life lived out on this high desert hill. Although the pack rat is a truly wild presence here, he also traffics in domestic goods and in that sense might be considered part of our extended household.

In fact, *Neotoma* and I are still cohabitants of sorts. Although he no longer lives within the walls of our house, he does have his own houses nearby, and we visit each other from time to time. In this truce we both prosper, even if my way of "dealing with him" doesn't involve the apocalyptic extermination Charlie advocated. I realize, of course, that there is blood on my hands. Indeed, I've remembered my debt to the Ratman and have in the back of our freezer, where Eryn isn't likely to notice it, a wrapped and taped butcher-paper package clearly labeled NOT A BURRITO. Despite this frozen corpse, my relationship with my bushy-tailed neighbor is mostly peaceful, and détente has its advantages. I still have my wife and my single-barrel hooch, and he still has his wives and his beer can tabs. If my spare key vanishes occasionally, I trust that my furry neighbor won't use it to let himself in. Perhaps in another fifty thousand years, some earnest researcher may discover that key enshrined in crystalline pee in the heart of an ancient midden and wonder what kind of life was lived behind the long-vanished door it once would have opened.

Chapter 7

Playing with
the Stick

The photograph of Curator Man that hit all the wire services and accompanied most of the online stories is of a tall, thin, well-groomed, friendly looking fellow (the kind of guy you'd actually call a "fellow"), with short hair, prominent ears, wire-rimmed glasses, and what looks like an expensive tie. In his hands he displays an elegantly framed item that in a few moments will become the most prized and celebrated treasure in his museum's collections. Curator Man's proud smile tells us that this is a big day for him. And what is the treasure behind the glass in the mahogany case? The stick.

This stick is at once just any old stick and not at all just any old stick. It is the stick that on November 6, 2008, was inducted into the National Toy Hall of Fame at the Strong National Museum of Play in Rochester, New York. As yet another anniversary of the stick's induction rolls around, I'm reminded of this photo of proud Curator Man, who could not have anticipated the media circus his museum's stick would provoke. When news of the stick's induction was announced in a ceremony and accompanying press release, the story was picked up by hundreds of online news sites and blogs and was even featured prominently in the last sixty seconds of many local TV news programs, right in the slot where the quintuplets usually go—which proves that even quintuplets can have a bad media cycle. Reporters invariably skipped the obvious question, "Is there really a National Museum of Play?" and went straight to the kind of penetrating journalism that helps a benighted public understand the complexities of so important an issue. "What can you do with a stick?" they wondered in print. "Who plays with sticks, and just how do they do it?" Since the stick doesn't come with directions and doesn't cost anything, they worried, how will Americans figure out how to use or value it? And, the tabloid sites asked, what do we *really* know about the panel of nineteen so-called experts whose deliberations resulted in its selection? In short, everyone demanded to know what's so great about a stick.

I'm intrigued by this famous stick for a number of reasons, not the least of which is that I still can't figure out if it is profound or absurd, or profoundly absurd, or absurdly profound. There's a little of the emperor's clothes phenomenon going on here, I think. When I tell people about the celebrated stick, the response is nearly always the same. "You're kidding, right? A *stick*? You mean a *real* stick? Like one you'd pick up off the ground?" There follows a long, uncertain pause. Then, almost invariably, comes the grinning reply: "*Hell, yeah, the stick. Greatest toy ever. Totally brilliant!*" And after proclaiming something "Totally brilliant!" it is difficult for people to turn back. But I do want to turn back, to ask whether the museum's stick was nature masquerading as culture or culture masquerading as nature. I want to return to the moment in which we had to decide for ourselves what to make of the idea that a stick, rather than being viewed as a natural object, needed to be displayed in a museum.

If Curator Man thought any of this was funny, he certainly didn't let on. First, he pointed out that the selection panel of esteemed judges—intellectuals, artists, curators, pooh-bahs of various stripes—had a very difficult decision to make. They also had to adhere strictly to a formally articulated set of explicit criteria when choosing a toy to join the vaunted ranks of already inducted classics like crayons, marbles, the teddy bear, and Mr. Potato Head. To be selected, the toy must: (1) possess icon status, (2) have longevity, (3) encourage discovery, and (4) promote innovation. Curator Man went on to extol the many virtues and uses of the stick: "It can be a Wild West horse, a medieval knight's sword, a boat on a stream, or a slingshot," he pointed out. "No snowman is complete without a couple of stick arms, and every campfire needs a stick for toasting marshmallows." The media's immoderate love of Curator Man and his stick even spawned a widely syndicated "news" story actually called "Notable

Suggestions for How to Play with a Stick," which made it evident that Hannah and Caroline were already as intelligent as at least some journalists.

It is at this point that the strange stick story jumps journalism's slick tracks and begins tearing through the weedy field of American popular culture, no longer under anyone's spin control. In Rochester there was still a stick in a case on a wall, but the story of that stick had gone viral. The first wave of responses to the stick was uniformly positive. What we might call the Good Old Stick! crowd rushed to expand Curator Man's already long list of noble uses for the stick, and they were mighty hard to argue with. I wasn't so impressed that a javelin and a golf club may be considered sticks—finding one so dangerous and the other so dangerously boring as to have no use for either—but a fishing rod and a baseball bat were sticks of an entirely different sort, and it was painful to imagine life without them. What about a conductor's baton or a pair of drumsticks? The fretted neck of my guitar is a kind of stick, and even the wooden combs of my harmonicas are little ten-notched sticks. The more I thought about it, the more impossible life without stick play seemed, and for a while I teetered on the brink of conversion.

But then the intellectuals got involved, and before I could make up my mind about the stick, all hell broke loose. First the developmental psychologists more or less said that kids would all be retarded without sticks, and some careless readers concluded by extrapolation that ADD, ADHD, OCD, LH, SLD, SLI, HDTV, THC, PCP, and

LSD could all be blamed on the condition of tragic sticklessness to which "kids these days" had been so brutally subjected. Evolutionary biologists then asserted that it was the use of sticks that caused humans to develop immense cerebral cortexes, which apparently we needed in order to ensure that the really sharp sticks would poke the saber-toothed tiger and not our brother-in-law—that being the kind of "accident" that might halt activities leading to procreation and would surely have been selected against by evolutionary pressures. The sociobiologists went even further, asserting that the human affinity for sticks was evident in our fort-building behaviors and in our innate desire to have pickets in front of our houses when somebody came over to kill and eat us.

Then, predictably, the closet Luddites—who might best be described as "really old white guys who somehow learned to use social media"—got involved in the debate, and they were so elated to see the triumph of the good old stick that they felt their lives fully vindicated. The excruciatingly detailed "When I was a boy . . ." stories about sticks proliferated so quickly as to crash several servers, even as young IT people scrambled to figure out how a lowly stick could have brought down their networks. These old-guy stick lovers were soon joined by the TV haters, who didn't care about sticks one way or the other but judged them better than what they called the "mind-numbing cancer" of television, never mind that they were sitting in front of glowing computer screens and posting their views on blogs with disturbing names like Turned Off Moms.

At last, the very worst occurred. We eco-geeks got hold of

the story, and that was when the shit that was already hitting the fan began to stick. According to its green defenders, the stick is important not because it is iconic or because it promotes discovery or innovation—indeed, even the detail that sticks might actually be played with by children drops out of the story at this point—but rather because it is "ecofriendly," "the ultimate disposable, biodegradable, versatile, multipurpose plaything." These ecobloggers celebrated the stick as "sustainable, recyclable, and upcyclable." One exclaimed euphorically that "you can even turn it into mulch when you're done playing with it!" which made me imagine tearing a stick from Caroline's little hands and jamming it into my tractor's wood chipper.

I don't want to rain on any parade that puts a humble stick in the lead float—after all, if Silly Putty and the Easy-Bake Oven can make the National Toy Hall of Fame, who am I to whine about the stick having its day in the sun?—but there's something creepy about this whole business. As the viral contagion of the stick story spread, I found myself possessed by a desire to shake Curator Man and his army of zombie bloggers and yell, "Hey! Wake up! Y'all are talking about a fucking stick!" But once the stick's coronation was hijacked, what had been a plaything was transformed into Captain Ahab's doubloon, Hester Prynne's scarlet letter, Citizen Kane's Rosebud: not a window onto childhood play but, rather, a mirror in which obsessed grown-ups saw nothing more than the reflections of their own faces. The stick's induction had been distorted from a celebration of how kids play into an ideological skirmish into which adults brought their own values and obsessions. At this point something in the stick story was lost forever. After all, isn't the beauty of a kid playing with a stick precisely that it is never our stick but always already theirs, that their imaginative powers define its shape, name, and use? It seemed to me that we pathetic grown-ups wanted to usurp the magic of the wand: to name and claim it, to wield it as a shield against time and tide.

That's the first thing that's suspicious about this stick story. Who could be so pretentious as to assume that a bunch of grown-ups—even worse, "expert" grown-ups—could possibly be capable of selecting toys for a National Museum of Play? The real experts, who are obviously the kids, hadn't been asked about any of this—including whether the idea of a National Toy Hall of Fame makes any damned sense in the first place. And what about the fact that all the negative connotations of sticks were being glossed over by these blithe stick enthusiasts? The sordid etymology and usage of the word *stick* offers a powerful reminder that the stick we might imagine as a medieval knight's sword in fact has a double edge. What about "stick-in-the-mud," "stick it to them," or "beat him with a stick"? What about the wonderfully imaginative denigration of a pompous person as having "a stick up their ass" or the fact that soft speaking is enabled only by the carrying of a "big stick"? How about the derogatory slang terms "dip stick," "dumb stick," "dick stick," and "weak stick," or "to give stick," which means to disparage or criticize, or the suggestion that one "stick it" (in their ear or elsewhere)? Or the unfortunate transformation of perfectly decent food like bread and cheese *into* sticks; or, conversely, the use of the stick to skewer and roast things, like squirrels? And what about chopsticks, which Americans would starve if forced to eat with, or the stick shift, which we can't drive, or the 1970s hair band Styx—which isn't quite the same, I know, but still makes my point that for every two sticks lashed together to make a mast or rubbed together to make fire, two others are used to make nunchucks or a crossbow. For every bouncing pogo stick or stirring swizzle stick, every forked dowsing stick or sacred rain stick, some poor stick figure ends up swinging from the hangman's gallows. For every burnished walking stick there is a cancerous fire stick, for every joy stick, a night stick, for every prayer stick, at least one stick of dynamite.

Of course the stick lovers don't tell you any of this. They'd also like you to forget the main thing sticks do, which is to poke your eye out. Even if a lot of things in life are "better than a poke in the eye with a sharp stick," one thing that is not in fact better is actually being poked in the eye with a sharp stick. Indeed, the same people who are now swooning nostalgically over their own stick-blessed childhoods are also yelling at their grandchildren to put down the goddamned stick before they put somebody's eye out. Let's face it, sticks are *dangerous*. And if you look at what kind of imaginative play the old-guy stick lovers valorize, it is invariably martial. One man unironically opined that what he most missed about his lost youth was the nurturing imaginative play by which he "could pretend that a stick was a big bazooka." Bazooka Lover had plenty of company. The most treasured memories of childhood play reported by these respondents featured the stick as rifle, shotgun, machine gun, sword, knife, spear, bow, arrow, harpoon, spear gun, blowgun, and even pipe bomb (good old pipe bomb!). One guy enthusiastically described the good fun he had while attacking his siblings with a stick that he pretended was a "Borg prosthetic arm/gun." Another waxed sentimental over the character-building effects of a spirited round of "Dodge the Stick," a game that, from what I could make out, basically amounts to throwing sticks as hard as you can at another person's head. But in addition to the Good Old Stick! crowd valorizing the violent imaginative and literal uses of the stick, they were also smug. Here is a representative posting: "The toys we in the older generation grew up with, like the stick, fostered the imagination. Nowadays, children sit in front of a computer screen playing video games that teach them violence and disrespect. It's no wonder kids these days are obese and ignorant."

The targets of this abuse didn't waste any time in putting down the Game Boy and chicken nuggets to give Gramps a piece of their mind. To their credit, the folks in this second wave of responses to the stick's ascension were more playful than those in the Good Old Stick! faction. Some mocked the stickophilic sentimentalists with sarcastic remarks like this one: "The sticks we had when I was growing up were way better than the ones they have now." Others used humor to fight back against the characterization of American youth as depraved because they play with computers instead of sticks. My favorite of these technophile back-talkers was the kid who wrote wryly, "I have an old Atari 2600 that I use as a makeshift stick." Yet others used hyperbole to ridicule the violent tendencies of the Good Old Stick! folks. "In a related story," wrote one mockumentarian, "the National Child Toy Safety Commission has issued a recall on the stick, identifying it as the nation's most dangerous toy. The Commission is now in negotiations with leading environmentalists, who make access to sticks easier every year."

One especially witty blogger imagined comments that might have been posted to Amazon.com by consumers who had heard of the stick's new fame and rushed out to buy one. One of these fake postings, from a mom and stick purchaser, describes the trauma suffered by her son after he discovered the troubling indeterminacy of the stick's meaning. She advises that parents "speak to the neighborhood kids in advance to reach a consensus as to what The Stick represents." Another, posted by the wonderful "Grandpa Dan" (who, of course, writes from Florida), reads as follows: "The Stick will never be beat. And it's a great bargain, too! The wife and I bought a single Stick, sawed it into five pieces, and now all our young grandchildren are having a grand time talking on their 'cell phones.'"

But the best was yet to come. The debate about the stick soon spawned a number of playful mock campaigns to have various other items inducted into the National Toy Hall of Fame. Among these nominees were the leaf, bubble wrap, the Popsicle stick, the log, the egg carton, shadows, the pillow, the vibrating dildo, the shoebox, dirt, the snowball, and Pete Rose (after all, Rochester is only 174 miles from Cooperstown). But the mock campaign that gathered the most momentum was the one agitating for inclusion of the rock in the National Toy Hall of Fame. As a first move, the rock advocates appropriated the discourse of racial justice to argue that the elevation of the stick over the rock was a clear case of bias, pointing out that sticks had received preferential treatment for far too long. They also observed that "sticks and stones" had long been associated with one another—in various cultural contexts, including the breaking of people's bones—and it was thus unfair that the stick alone should receive recognition. The rock folks gave hundreds of examples of the wonderful ways in which rocks foster imaginative play. Taking a page from the battle plan of Bazooka Lover and his ilk, for example, they pointed out that a stick's ability to be a gun is in no way superior to a rock's ability to be a grenade. I found this hard to argue with. Finally, the rock people emphasized the precedent of the toy Pet Rock, which in the 1970s swept the nation and made so much money for its creator that the guy became a millionaire overnight and at last achieved his lifelong dream: to own a bar in Los Gatos, California.

The persuasiveness of the rock campaign caused me to wonder not only about sticks and stones but about all the toys that have been inducted into and rejected from the National Toy Hall of Fame. As it turns out, debate has surrounded these selections from the very beginning. When the inaugural class of 1998 included Barbie but not Ken, a group of college students complained of sexual discrimination, arguing that Ken deserves equal billing with his female counterpart—who, they pointed out, is insipid, emaciated, and nip-pleless and, furthermore, has poor taste in purses and terrible gay-dar. Some Marxist critics declared that the induction of the Radio Flyer wagon, the Duncan yo-yo, and the Crayola crayon constituted the baldest form of product placement advertising. Wouldn't the generic wagon or crayon have been good enough, or was the Hall of Fame taking kickbacks from these companies? When Monopoly was the only board game included in that first class, the aficionados of everything from Candy Land to Parcheesi to backgammon went wild—not to mention the evangelical Scrabble-ites, who had plenty of choice words for the Hall of Fame after their snubbery (if that's even a word).

This debate surrounding the choice of inductees became an annual ritual; most interesting is how regularly adult obsessions were reflected in these bizarre skirmishes over toys. While the Ken doll faction was clearly in it for the laughs, the Raggedy Ann fans—who actually call themselves "Raggedy Fans" and who in many ways dis-turbingly resemble a cult—were in genuine fits from the beginning. It wasn't so much that Raggedy Ann, whose oft-recited pedigree dates to 1915, was rejected—it was instead the fact that Barbie, that mindless slut, had been inducted with the very first class. The Raggedy Fans took to the warpath and for four long years endured repeated defeats until, at last, in 2002, came the "magical moment" (their words) when Raggedy Ann became the twenty-sixth toy to join the ranks. During those four years the Ann cultists collected more than eight thousand petitions but still had to endure the humiliation of having been outgunned by the Mr. Potato Head lobby, which, after suffering a similar defeat in the inaugural year, had their man in office straightaway in year two.

My study of inducted and rejected toys also revealed the precedent that indirectly enabled the stick's ultimate success: the surprising choice, in November 2005, of the cardboard box. The box was an influential inductee, because it was the first plaything not produced by a toy manufacturer to have made the National Toy Hall of Fame. Once the humble box had cracked the dam of the hall's logic, other toys not made to be toys couldn't be far behind. The affinity between the cardboard box and the stick was in fact remarked upon by many folks who responded to the stick's induction. One would-be parodist offered the *Onion*-esque headline "Stick Enters Toy Hall of Fame, Cardboard Box Snubbed," only to be informed that, in fact, the box was already in. Many parents liked the choice of the box because it confirmed their observation that no matter how much dough they shelled out for toys, their kids preferred to play with the boxes in which the toys came. As a parent who has spent too much time repairing overengineered toys, I too approved of the box and stick, both of which I added to my personal list of Things That Actually Work, which until that time had included only WD-40, bourbon, and *Moby-Dick*.

I also found it instructive to consider some of the National Toy Hall of Fame's selections in light of its explicit criteria for inclusion. For example, while I'll fight the man who claims that the Slinky doesn't "possess icon status," it is harder to see how the Atari can be said to "have longevity." The Atari was inducted in 2007, by which time it had been obsolete for decades, and to make matters worse the Atari shared the class of 2007 with the kite, which is a three-thousand-year-old toy. It is also difficult to see how some of the inaugurated toys "encourage discovery," unless, as in the case of Play-Doh and Silly Putty, the discovery is simply that it is better if you don't swallow it. And can we legitimately claim that the jack-in-the-box works to "promote innovation," given that playing with this toy amounts to mindlessly cranking it up, scaring the shit out of yourself, and cranking it up again, over and over? It even took the play "experts" until 2009 to admit the ball and until 2013 to open their doors to the rubber duck, thus finally ending their ill-advised stonewalling of two of the most universally beloved toys of all time.

Then there's the problem of the still-rejected toys. I note that after the embattled first year of the National Toy Hall of Fame's existence, when every nut who could click a mouse raised hell that their favorite toy had been left out in the cold, the panel of wise toy experts responded in year two by rejecting both the soccer ball and baseball glove, thus ensuring that they would piss off every person on earth. As with the Raggedy Ann standoff, adult obsessions were at the heart of these debates. For example, after being judged unfit for service in the Hall of Fame for several years running, GI Joe went commando and was carried into the hall in 2004 on a testosterone-driven groundswell of support from advocates whose appeals sounded as if they had been excerpted from speeches by General Patton. Gender politics were equally transparent in the induction the following year of the Easy-Bake Oven, which, though reviled by feminists as a symbol of the subjugation of women within a hegemonic patriarchal system of exploitative domestic servitude, was celebrated by other women as "*really* cute." The museum capped off its long run of poor choices in 2014, when it rejected more than a hundred worthy nominees—including such truly pleasurable toys as the Slip'n Slide—in order to induct the Rubik's cube, which is not a toy but rather a heinous torture device intentionally designed to fatally deprive innocent children of their self-esteem.

I ultimately decided that to settle the troubling matter of the famous stick I would have to consult a real play expert. Hannah seemed to me the right choice. She's thoughtful, asks good questions, and doesn't jump to conclusions about anything other than the need to take care of her little sister and eat ice cream immediately. She has informed opinions about things she has experience with, and clearly she has experience playing. One morning, while driving the girls to school, I told Hannah all about the Strong National Museum of Play, and the National Toy Hall of Fame contained within it, and about the stick. She listened carefully, raising her eyebrows a few times.

"Who are the kids who get to decide which toys are allowed to be in the Hall of Fame?" she asked.

"They aren't kids," I explained. "They're all grown-ups."

"That's weird," she said. Little Caroline nodded in agreement. "Kids have a lot more practice playing. Why don't they ask kids?" I told her I didn't know. Hannah said she could understand why somebody might think of a stick as a toy, since kids could use sticks to . . . and then she breathlessly listed about fifty uses of the stick that had never occurred to Curator Man: a bridge for an ant to walk across, a hole poker for making secret caves, a fencing foil for sister Caroline, a key to a magic ice castle, a cloud scratcher. "Yeah, a cloud scratcher!" Caroline repeated enthusiastically.

Next, Hannah wanted to know how the grown-ups decide what's a toy and what isn't. "If a stick is in there, how about a whole tree, which is better, because most kids love to climb trees. Can that be in there?" I told her I didn't know. Hannah has always loved learning the names of flowers and trees, and so she also wanted to know what kind of stick it was. Was it a stick from a Utah juniper, or a Jeffrey pine, or maybe a Fremont cottonwood?

"Nobody ever said what kind of stick it was," I replied. Now Hannah frowned in earnest. Caroline followed suit, shaking her head side to side as if perfectly disgusted.

"They put it in a museum without even learning its name?" Caroline asked, incredulous.

I was nonplussed by how quickly the girls' simple questions were exploding the pretensions of the National Toy Hall of Fame, and I was quietly embarrassed that their best questions had never occurred to me. But Hannah's next question was especially provocative.

"When kids visit this Hall of Fame, can they *play* with the stick?"

I paused before replying.

"No. They can't. The stick is in a display case on a wall in the museum."

"*Really?*" she asked, her voice alive with genuine surprise. "Why do they call it a Museum of Play if you can't play with the stuff there? Maybe they could make the case with a lid, so you could just get the stick out. Or maybe they could have lots of sticks, so if me and Caroline and a bunch of other kids showed up we could all have a stick to play with. Why don't they do something like that?" Caroline nodded her assent as I once again told Hannah that I just didn't know.

Hannah's critique reminded me of the debate we've been having about modern art since the early twentieth century. Does the display of an object—an African mask, a bicycle wheel, an antique milk jug—deprive that object of its life? When we put a vernacular object in a museum and declare it "art," are we celebrating the meanings of that object, or are we impoverishing our understanding and enjoyment of it? And what becomes of the stick's status as a natural object once we define and limit its use? Is a stick in a case just another elephant in a zoo, another butterfly with a pin through it, yet one more grown-up way of attempting to domesticate the wildness that is inherent to natural play and to the children who benefit from it? Is a stick on display in a museum even a stick at all?

Hannah was still thinking hard, and she sat quietly for a while before reaching her conclusion. "Dad, since the stick isn't made by people, it really is different than a Hula-Hoop and stuff like that. And I think natural things that belong together should stay together, so if the stick is in there, then it isn't fair not to put in the whole tree, plus leaves, and rocks, and everything else around it."

"And bugs too," added Caroline, "but it wouldn't be nice to keep bugs inside like that."

"Right," Hannah agreed. "I think they ought to just leave the stick outside. That way it can be in the wind and rain, which it's used to, and bugs can use it to crawl on, and also kids can play with it."

I'm aware that we've been waxing rhapsodic about the wisdom of children since the romantic poets tromped euphorically around the Lake District (without children, I might add), but this struck me as a sensible verdict, rendered by a thoughtful judge and based on a sound interrogation of the facts. Caroline's energetic nodding in support of her sister's argument suggested that even a little kid could grasp the problem Hannah's logic had exposed. We grown-ups had insisted upon turning the stick into everything from a three wood to a bazooka, but the girls' imaginations had effortlessly, magically transformed it back into a stick.

I suppose we could say that adults crave play, too, and that playing with the famous stick's meanings is the grown-up way of trying to think up something as cool as using a stick as a cloud scratcher. By eliciting the two most powerful forms of nostalgia—the loss of nature and the loss of childhood—the celebrated stick had captured our adult imaginations. But while we were arguing over its meaning, turning its induction into the National Toy Hall of Fame into a cause for celebration or complaint, we also forgot to go outside and play. And I suspect that it is this failure to play—this atrophying of the ability to imaginatively engage nature and then also leave it as we found it—that somehow separates us from our childhoods and perhaps also from our children. Maybe we've been grasping at the stick because we need to recover something that we dropped on the ground a long time ago.

Chapter 8

Freebirds

One afternoon a few days before Thanksgiving, Eryn came home from town with Hannah and Caroline, both of whom had been administered the traditional Thanksgiving myth at school that day. Three-year-old Caroline was as proud as could be of her paper turkey, made from a cutout drawing of her own little hand. And Hannah, the loquacious six-year-old, began blurting out her holiday lecture the moment she came through the door: "Dad, I bet you didn't know that Thanksgiving comes from the Pilgrims and the Indians helping each other a bunch and then having a peace party and eating a really big supper with crazy colored corn and turkeys and those turkeys were *wild*!" With this she donned her construction-paper Pilgrim hat with its big fake buckle and gave me a huge smile.

I took a long sip of my whiskey and tried to formulate a response. The Thanksgiving feast the girls had learned about did in fact occur—at Plymouth Plantation in 1621—but by the following year violent conflict between colonists and Native Americans had erupted, and devastating Indian wars soon swept New England. There weren't many turkeys shared at Mystic River in 1637, for example, when the Pilgrims burned and hacked to death at least four hundred Pequot, mostly women and children, as they slept. The Pilgrim leader William Bradford—who had actually been present at that much-celebrated first Thanksgiving—had this to say about the slaughter: "It was a fearful sight to see [the Indians] thus frying in the fire and the streams of blood quenching the same, and horrible was the stink and scent thereof; but the victory seemed a sweet sacrifice, and [we] gave the praise thereof to God." Just as I was pondering how best to explain this act of violence in a way that might somehow be compatible with the ennobling concept of Thanksgiving the girls had learned at school, Hannah pointed excitedly at the muted TV behind me and shouted, "It's turkey time!" I turned to see that the news had given way to the image of a large white turkey. A turkey at the White House, in fact. A turkey that was about to receive a formal pardon from the president of the United States.

For many people, Thanksgiving is about bringing together family and friends; for some, it is centered around the ancient autumnal harvest festival; for others, it is an opportunity to count and express our most precious blessings; for yet others, it is a holiday devoted to copious amounts of football and alcohol. I believe deeply in all these versions, but for me Thanksgiving is very much about the pardoning of turkeys.

The tradition of the presidential turkey pardon is wonderfully rife with distortion, ambiguity, and error—as all good stories should be—but what is most perplexing about this bizarre ritual is our uncertainty about its origins. Some claim that the turkey pardon began with President Lincoln, who, hoping to promote national unity amid the social fragmentation of the Civil War, did in fact declare our first official day of national thanksgiving in 1863. That same year Lincoln's ten-year-old son, Tad, so the story goes, became so attached to a Christmas turkey that the president relented and agreed to spare "Jack" from the family table. More common is the claim that Harry Truman was the first president to save a turkey, but while Truman was indeed the first commander in chief to receive a holiday gift bird from the National Turkey Federation—a custom begun in 1947 and continued to this day—the evidence suggests that Truman, like most presidents who followed him, hadn't the slightest compunction about eating his gift. It was President Kennedy who first broke with his predecessors by declaring, just four days before he was assassinated, that—despite the sign reading GOOD EATING that the National Turkey Federation had hung around the bird's neck—he would let his fifty-five-pound gobbler live.

Even though President Reagan delivered a few respectable

one-liners about sparing his turkey (he was every bit as charismatic with his bird as he was with that cute chimp in the movie *Bedtime for Bonzo*), the Gipper promptly gobbled up all of his gobblers. And it is here that bird-pardoning lore moves from speculation to historical fact, for in 1989 George Herbert Walker Bush had the honor of becoming the first president to formally issue a pardon to a turkey—an innovative leadership move that no doubt helped to secure his legacy. Since Bush Senior, every president has participated annually in this strange ritual—which held special pleasure for Presidents Bill Clinton and George W. Bush, each of whom embraced the event as an occasion for the kind of political theater that offered welcome distraction from the kind of political theater that occupied them at all other times.

It seemed to me that President Clinton always shot his birds an amorous look while pardoning them, and his uncharacteristic restraint in looking but not touching may have been indirectly attributable to our old friend William Bradford, who, in his seventeenth-century page turner *Of Plymouth Plantation*, carefully documented the execution of one of his fellow Pilgrims for the unpardonable sin of sodomizing a turkey. Bradford's troubling account leaves me with three questions: Can there be anything more disgusting than having sex with poultry? How, exactly, would you go about doing it anyway? Is this really something you ought to kill a guy for? I think it would have been more humane, more punishing, and also more entertaining to simply make fun of him for the rest of his life. It wouldn't take much—you could just gobble a little under your breath as he passed your pew in church. Of course, none of the Pilgrims' distasteful Indian killing or turkey raping stopped President George W. Bush from executing a 2007 pardon for "May" and "Flower," birds whose names offered a clear allusion to Bradford's intrepid congregation.

The tradition of the presidential turkey pardon has continued to evolve in surprising ways. In the early years the exonerated gobblers were sent to Kidwell Farm, a petting zoo in northern Virginia where, as turkey rock stars, they lived a life featuring excessive drug use and constant media attention, but only the brief fame their overbred and steroid-addled condition would allow. Since 2005, however, the ritual has become more surreal: the pardoned bird is now immediately flown to Disneyland or Disney World, where it serves as grand marshal of the Thanksgiving Day parade at the self-proclaimed "Happiest Place on Earth." And if the idea of Americans spending their Thanksgiving holiday at a theme park watching a fat bird lead a Mickey Mouse parade seems depressing, it is encouraging to note that the birds are flown to their new posts first class, so while in transit they enjoy comfortably wide seats and a lot of free gin and tonics. It beats the hell out of that cramped poultry yard with its hormone-dusted cracked corn, and since the birds are so overbred as to find it barely possible to waddle (pardon the pun), much less fly, their trip to the Happiest Place on Earth is in fact the only flight they will ever know.

Soon after he took office, President Obama recognized the surreal quality of the ceremony when he remarked, "There are certain days that remind me of why I ran for this office. And then there are moments like this, where I pardon a turkey and send it to Disneyland." Now that the pardoned bird is a national celebrity, it has become necessary to pardon an alternate bird each year, in case the National Turkey is unable to fulfill its duties—as occurred in 2008, when "Pecan" fell suddenly ill and required his understudy, "Pumpkin," to receive the honors.

In our family it is a hallowed tradition—one as sacred and as ceremoniously performed as cheering on the opening day of baseball season—to witness and celebrate the annual presidential pardoning of the turkeys. Although Hannah and Caroline are necessarily recent participants in this annual custom, I consider myself the Cal Ripken of turkey pardoning, having never missed one since the initiation of the ritual more than twenty years ago. As is the case with other Thanksgiving traditions, I find it helpful to drink while participating in this one, so I annually toast the birds' reprieve with stout tumblers of what I call *Meleagris gallopavo* cocktail, which is Wild Turkey straight up, the "cocktail" mixed in only as an avian pun to sweeten the experience of watching the president talk turkey. After all, nothing is more threatening to one's mental health than to be caught uncomfortably sober when it comes time for the leader of the free world to issue a televised and legally binding pardon to a bird.

Although I have long found the pardoning of the turkeys to be among the more entertaining things to transpire in our nation's capital each year, the levity of this ritual has become compromised by politics. In particular, the vegetarian lobby has complained that the annual pardoning amounts to free advertising for the poultry industry, and it has suggested that the president would set a better example by accepting a cruelty-free Tofurky, whose life before being pressed into a shimmering loaf of gelatinous curd presumably consisted of cavorting innocently through fragrant bean fields while in absolutely no danger of being sodomized. The Humane Society has also objected, making the hard-to-dispute point that turkeys produced by industrial poultry farming have about as unpleasant a life as one can imagine, and while two birds do get to fly first class to Anaheim or Orlando each year, 250 million others aren't so lucky. Each year following the pardoning, PETA is served a generous slice of free media pie when it describes in gory detail the miserable lives of these factory-farmed birds.

My objection to such complaints is certainly not that they are groundless—they must be at least as compelling as the idea that the leader of 300 million people should not waste his time, not to mention his political capital, pardoning a turkey—but rather that they are unpardonably lacking in humor. It is not, after all, a Supreme Court deliberation we are talking about, but rather a turkey pardoning. So here, perhaps, is a useful rule of thumb for animal rights activists: if the president and a turkey are more entertaining than you are, it can hardly be surprising that your client is headed for decapitation. With a little creativity, such activists might dramatize their objections in ways that would be more in the spirit of the event. How about staging a parody of the turkey pardoning in which a PETA activist, costumed as a giant turkey, pardons the sitting president for *his* misdeeds?

The potential for humor here is also suggested by the comic

irony of an actual event involving none other than the media super-star and former governor of Alaska, Sarah Palin. Back in the days before her Fox News stint and failed reality shows and her rewrit-ing of the history of the American Revolution, the governor, having just pardoned a turkey (yes, many state governors also participate in this tomfoolery), waxed rhapsodic on camera about the virtues of compassion and forgiveness, while unbeknownst to her a worker in the background was busy decapitating and bleeding out turkeys. The YouTube video of this interview, which is far funnier than any *Sat-urday Night Live* send-up of it could possibly be, has been watched more than a million times.

If I were to object to the turkey pardoning—which, of course, I haven't the slightest intention of doing—I would do so on the grounds that to render a turkey a fit subject for pardon, we must presume the bird's guilt. To be pardoned, one must first be in violation of some communal law or code. While enjoying Thanksgiving dinner, for example, we don't "beg your pardon" unless we belch, fart, or otherwise violate the community ethic by which the ritual meal is conducted. A pardon is both an expression of mercy and a certificate of absolution; it is both amnesty and exoneration. To pardon, after all, is to forgive. And if we're talking about a turkey, it becomes difficult to discern what criminal or immoral behavior on the bird's part may be said to estab-lish the necessary preconditions for its forgiveness.

Now if Benjamin Franklin had won the argument and the tur-key had become our national symbol, the case might be different. You may recall that wise old Ben claimed that the bald eagle made a poor national symbol because "he is a bird of bad moral character." This, incidentally, from a man who advocated choosing for a mistress an older woman because "there is no hazard of children, which irregularly produced may be attended with much inconvenience"; who invented bifocals so he might focus on prostitutes both up close and from slightly farther away; and who is credited with proffering the timeless verity that "beer is proof that God loves us and wants us to be happy." So much for moral character. Unfortunately, Ben's failed lobbying prevented the fat gobbler from making it onto the presidential seal, though I do still like to imagine a plump tom turkey with an olive branch in one scrabbly claw and a sheaf of gleaming arrows in the other, as if to say: "I'm a jolly, peaceful old bird, but *don't fuck with me*." I would argue that, given its failure to achieve the status of national icon, the turkey—being innocent of everything save its cowardly squandering of the rare opportunity to peck viciously at the president of the United States—cannot in fact be legally pardoned. And if the annual pardon is both presidentially sanctioned and demonstrably illegal, then it is also necessarily unconstitutional and therefore constitutes legitimate grounds for impeachment.

My point here is not that a US president should be impeached for pardoning a turkey—though I won't stand in the way if that's how it ultimately goes down—but rather that we might benefit from asking what human vanity or lust for power inspired the presumption that we *could* pardon a bird. On his final day in office, Bill Clinton pardoned 140 people, including a few whose deeds might lead you to conclude, by comparison, that even the turkey sodomizer wasn't such a bad guy. Although most industrialized democracies on the planet have long since abolished capital punishment, more than two-thirds of US states continue to respond to violent crime with the awkwardly violent response of sending people to the death chamber—not to mention the excruciating frequency with which these killings are not even executed properly. And we still aren't done quibbling about what constitutes torture and whether our nation should sanction its use in extreme circumstances. But, as Thomas Jefferson well knew, it is the political expediency of those in power that defines the extremity of the circumstances. As Jefferson's buddy James Madison wisely observed, men are not angels.

I realize this is pretty heavy stuff to include in an essay about pardoning turkeys—and for that I hope I too may be pardoned—but the plain truth that we *are* so flawed, so very far from being angels, is directly relevant to this story. It is we who burn the village, justify the torture, execute the criminal. How is it that we are so sure of ourselves, so certain about the infallibility of our judgment and authority? I wonder if there is some relationship between our presumption of power and this desire to pardon—even the desire to pardon an innocent, feathered, nonhuman being. I wonder if perhaps we have a vague sense that it is some guilt of our own that must be assuaged: that we, whose power is so often used to judge, might be redeemed by some corollary power to forgive, that exoneration might at the eleventh hour become the bright shadow of a looming condemnation.

Of course the National Turkey—which, for all we know, might

wisely prefer death to Disney World in any case—doesn't require our mercy in the slightest. It is we who need the bird, desperately so, for through its salvation we are permitted to express our deep human desire to grant amnesty to those who would otherwise suffer. From where I sit it is difficult to determine whether the granting of a pardon constitutes an assertion of power or a relinquishment of it. But for allowing us a momentary, if symbolic, reprieve from our role as judge and executioner, we have ample reason to give thanks to these turkeys—so many thanks, in fact, that it probably is a good idea to be on the safe side and pardon one every now and then.

I pour another tumbler of bourbon and look again at Caroline's sweet little handprint turkey. Then I look at Hannah's beaming face, which so clearly registers her innocent excitement that President Obama—with his own two daughters by his side—has made it possible for these otherwise doomed gobblers to go free. I think about that mythic first Thanksgiving that we describe to our children, even as a long shadow of violence threatens constantly to reduce it to historical insignificance. I think of the presidential turkey pardoning being performed in a world so replete with greed and conflict, suffering and injustice. I think of the fact that the ratio of turkeys annually pardoned and given free gin and tonics to those raised under horrendous conditions and unceremoniously decapitated is approximately 1:125,000,000.

"Girls!" I suddenly hear myself exclaim. "This is the best day *ever*! The president has made sure that the turkeys will be set free, and now they get to fly in a plane to Disney World, and they even get to be the stars in the big parade! And today you girls have learned all about how Thanksgiving is a holiday of peace and forgiveness, and soon we'll have a wonderful Thanksgiving dinner of our own. This is truly a day to count our blessings!"

Eryn instantly furrows her brow, as if contemplating whether to take my Wild Turkey away. Then Caroline starts counting aloud, "One, two, free, four!" and Hannah claps her hands and chants, "The birds are free! The birds are free!" I glance at Eryn, who is looking at me as if I've once again started something she will have to finish. It is a difficult moment, I admit. And so I do the only thing I can. I do what I think any father would do under the circumstances. I set my whiskey down slowly. Then I begin jumping up and down, clapping and shouting along with Hannah, and then Caroline follows suit, and, at last, even Eryn joins in: "The birds are free! The birds are free! The birds are free!" Before our celebration reaches its breathless finish, we have segued from our avian freedom chant into "Turkey in the Straw," "Five Fat Turkeys Are We," and, for our big closer, "Free Bird." There is much jamming on air guitar, and when we finish singing we all stand panting, heads bowed, holding our imaginary lighters ceremoniously above our heads.

All too soon my daughters' veneration of the first Thanksgiving will give way to a painful awareness of the Mystic River massacre. In the meantime we will celebrate, not history, which is so often a monument to human failure, but rather myth, which is the necessary dream that a better future might redeem the errors of our past.

Perhaps we each deserve a pardon. Maybe, whether we are doomed prisoner or executioner, we each need to receive that last-minute phone call in what would otherwise be our death chamber. We forgive the birds, and in so doing, we hope desperately that they might forgive us.

PART THREE

Humbling

Two conditions—gravity and a livable temperature range be-
tween freezing and boiling—have given us fluids and flesh. The
trees we climb and the ground we walk on have given us five
fingers and toes. The "place" (from the root plat, *broad, spread-*
ing, flat) gave us far-seeing eyes, the streams and breezes gave
us versatile tongues and whorly ears. The land gave us a stride,
and the lake a dive. The amazement gave us our kind of mind.
We should be thankful for that, and take nature's stricter lessons
with some grace.

—GARY SNYDER, *The Practice of the Wild*

Chapter 9

Finding the
Future Forest

I find it easy to praise the high desert, because it is a landscape so open, wild, and resistant to human inhabitation that it speaks simultaneously to my love of nature, my longing for challenge, and my desire to get in touch with my Inner Curmudgeon. But there are two weeks each July when my idealization of this arid land is tested by the scorching high-elevation sun, and I begin to wonder how anything besides leopard lizards and Great Basin rattlers could make a home in this withering heat. During this period I avoid reading anything I've ever written about the desert, because it invariably strikes me as fluffy pastoral crap. If Wordsworth were here now, he'd lay down his glowing pen and take up a shotgun and a fifth of tequila and head for the shade of a juniper. During these two weeks I have no choice but to relinquish my lyricism and admit the obvious: this place is a baking hell, and I was insane for building a house without air conditioning. This time of year it is easy to understand why the old miners who passed through this area named local landscape features things like Hell's Furnace Hill, Devil Canyon, and Inferno Ridge.

There is, however, summer consolation nearby. From my sweltering perch I can see the distant Sierra Nevada crest, and I don't need John Muir's ghost to tell me how cool and lovely it is up there right now. Fifty miles south of our desert home is one of the most beautiful alpine lakes on earth. Lake Tahoe is often described as a gem, a translucent blue jewel set among the snowcapped peaks that ring its spectacular basin. But this gemlike image of Tahoe as static and isolated disconnects the celebrated lake from the watershed that not only encircles it but also extends downstream from it into the desert below. It might be better to say of Tahoe, as Thoreau said of Walden Pond, that it is not a jewel but rather an eye: something deep, clear, reflective, but also intimately related to a larger living body through a complex arterial system. The Tahoe watershed is spectacular not only for the gem lake at its fountainhead but also for the life it brings to the western Great Basin, these beautiful, blazing landscapes where the snowmelt of the mountains becomes the lifeblood of the desert.

Five rivers drain eastward from the northern Sierra into the Great Basin. From south to north they are the Owens, Walker, Carson, Truckee, and Susan. Each terminates in a lake, marsh, or sink from which it never escapes. This is the origin of the term *Great Basin*:

we live on the extreme western edge of a vast desert from which no water ever reaches the sea. Of these five rivers, our home river is the Truckee, which winds 121 miles from Tahoe to its terminus in Pyramid Lake, the eye of the desert and the final home of that shimmering alpine water. Among the most magnificent desert terminus lakes in the world, Pyramid is a twenty-six-mile-long azure expanse cradled among the bare, glowing hills of the desert and surrounded by formations of tufa—towers of calcium carbonate that stand in surreal poses along the shores of the lake. Pyramid is as ancient as it is beautiful; it is one of the few surviving remnants of Pleistocene-era Lake Lahontan, which at its height thirteen thousand years ago covered more than 8,000 square miles of what is now Nevada. Although Tahoe and Pyramid are in starkly different ecosystems and are separated by 2,400 vertical feet, they are linked by the flowing bridge of the Truckee River. They are sister lakes that share the same origin in Sierra snow and whose fates remain intimately intertwined.

Of the river systems along the eastern flank of the Sierra, none has escaped severe damage, and several are critically endangered. Beginning with the federal Reclamation Act in 1902, enterprising westerners tried to make the desert bloom by replumbing Sierra watersheds in the vain hope that the vast, arid expanses of the Great Basin might be converted through irrigation into a prosperous agricultural empire. The Newlands Reclamation Project resulted in the construction of Derby Dam, which diverted much of the Truckee's flow into the Carson River watershed, where it could be put to use in commercial agriculture instead of "going to waste" out in the desert. This is why Fallon, Nevada, which receives an average of five inches of rain each year, is now known for its trademark Hearts of Gold cantaloupes.

But while the Truckee was being diverted to grow cantaloupes in the desert, the magnificent terminal lakes it fed began to die. Starting in the early twentieth century, water levels at Pyramid and Winnemucca went into freefall, and by 1939 Winnemucca Lake had simply vanished. Once a twenty-eight-mile-long, tule-filled, wildlife-rich lake, today it is an immense stretch of bare alkali flat, a white ghost lake rippled only by wind and sand. After the diversion of Truckee water the native Pyramid Lake Lahontan cutthroat trout—the largest cutthroat in the world, which weighed up to sixty pounds and which at one time was shipped to mining camps at the rate of one million pounds per year—could no longer reach its spawning grounds and began to go extinct. So too the now-endangered Pyramid Lake cui-ui fish, whose critical importance to local Native American culture is reflected in the ancestral name of the Pyramid Lake Paiute people: *Kuyuidokado*, or "cui-ui eaters." As the marshes and lakes of the region dried up and their fisheries collapsed, the great eastern Sierra flyway also began to collapse, with the result that the millions of migrating eagles, ibis, loons, dowitchers, plovers, phalaropes, and other migratory birds that depended on their waters were reduced to a trickle.

The Lahontan cutthroat, Nevada's state fish, provides an inspiring example of the fall and rise of some desert species over the past century. The triple threat of introduced nonnative fish, overfishing, and plummeting water levels posed a severe threat to these fish.

During the 1920s, anglers were landing monster cutthroat here, but by the 1930s this native fish had begun to disappear. Their last river spawn was in 1938, and less than a decade later the Lahontan cutthroat had vanished from Pyramid. The species was federally listed as endangered in 1970. The mistakes we made in managing the liquid gold that is the lifeline of this watershed had resulted in the loss of one of the most remarkable fish species in the West, and now the desert lake was teeming with swimming ghosts.

Thirty years after the cutthroat's disappearance we tried to correct our mistake by attempting an ambitious restoration effort—an example of the sort of creative rewilding upon which the environmental health of the Intermountain West will ultimately depend. During the 1970s, a transplanted population of Lahontan cutthroat was discovered in a remote stream up in the Pilot Mountains on the Nevada-Utah border. Using genetics from late-nineteenth-and early-twentieth-century museum mounts of the extirpated native trout, it was established that the Pilot Mountains population was indeed descended from the original Truckee Basin stock. A hatchery program was established here in northwestern Nevada, and genetically native Lahontan cutthroat trout were raised and, beginning in 2006, reintroduced to Pyramid Lake. In 2014 a long-awaited miracle occurred: the fish spawned in the Truckee River for the first time in seventy-six years. Fishermen are already catching twenty-pounders in the lake. Once vanished, the Lahontan cutthroat trout has become native here again.

"Keep Tahoe Blue" is the rallying cry of folks who care about the integrity of this alpine lake (though "Drink Tahoe Red," which celebrates an excellent local beer, also has a place in our sloganeering lexicon). "Keep Tahoe Blue," which we sometimes render "Mantenga Tahoe Azul," refers not so much to the color of the lake's water as to its clarity. Tahoe's clarity is measured using a Secchi disk, a black-and-white platter, ten inches in diameter, which is lowered down into the water until it finally becomes invisible. Back in 1968, when clarity measurements began, the disk was visible more than a hundred feet below the surface of the water—a remarkable depth, but one that has been decreasing ever since. By 1997 average visibility was down to a mere sixty-four feet, and since then a lot of folks have been working to bring that number back up. It isn't just that we want to be able to see kokanee salmon seventy-five feet down in the blue depths, though of course we do; we also realize that Tahoe's clarity is a prime indicator of the health of our entire watershed.

Despite setbacks, the Tahoe-Pyramid watershed has many advocates who've worked, with some notable successes, to restore these great alpine and desert lakes and the spectacular river corridor connecting them. Activists in the Tahoe Basin are educating the public about the value of minimizing runoff, erosion, and pollution, and ambitious restoration efforts in the Truckee's riparian zone have stabilized stream banks and improved fish spawning areas. One dramatic success story is Anaho Island in Pyramid Lake, which is now protected as a National Wildlife Refuge. Here breeding colonies of many species of gulls, terns, cormorants, herons, and egrets thrive. Anaho is also home to one of the West's largest colonies of American white pelicans, majestic birds that soar above the lake on snow-white wings that span an incredible ten feet. The astonishing sight of a gyre of immense pelicans wheeling in the desert sky is a graceful reminder that the creatures of the Great Basin are utterly dependent upon the Tahoe Sierra waters that nourish them.

Although I'm a confirmed desert rat and would rather camp out in the bright dust of a remote alkali flat than spend a weekend in a chalet overlooking Lake Tahoe, I do know which side my bread is buttered on. The health of the Tahoe Basin and its watershed is our lifeline; if the chalet dwellers don't send us enough water, or don't send it at the right time, or don't send it in decent condition, the ecosystem we inhabit is stressed—and the desert is a place where the margin of survival is razor thin to begin with. Because the closing of an upstream spigot can cause a magnificent desert lake to simply vanish, the stakes could hardly be higher. While I like cantaloupes as much as the next guy, lakes for 'lopes is not a trade-off I am prepared to make. This is why I ultimately decided that in order to help protect the desert I would have to start in the mountains. If forestry practices in the Tahoe Basin could be improved, so would the volume and quality of water we receive down here in the Great Basin. If we manage to "Keep Tahoe Blue," we'll also achieve something less visible but equally important: we'll keep the lifeblood of the desert flowing. If I wanted to see white pelicans in desert skies, I would have to start by working high above me, up in the alpine forests.

I'd been at home in other forests: first in the mixed deciduous woods of my southern Appalachian boyhood and then in the tangled cypress strands and shaded mangrove hammocks of the Everglades detour my life took before I swooned for the high desert. But the stately coniferous forest of the Tahoe Basin looked to me like someone else's woods, its picturesque slopes, open stands, and sculpted boulders too like an advertisement for property you couldn't afford, a ski lodge waiting to be built, a place that only existed for two weeks in August. These are the limitations of vision we carry with us on our scattered voyages through new landscapes. If it bothered me that people so often failed to appreciate the skeletal beauty of the desert, it was equally true that as a desert rat I had failed not only to appreciate the beauty of Tahoe but also to acknowledge my dependence upon it.

I had also been a forest activist in other places, and I had always been especially devoted to watchdogging logging roads—those arteries of pain invading the healthy body of wild country—and helping to ensure road closures and obliteration in the interest of forest health. As an admirer of poetry as well as of forests, my motto had been, in the spirit of Robert Frost, "Two roads diverged in a yellow wood, and I . . . got them both closed." Now it seemed time to get behind the postcard image and try to discover what might be missing from my own way of inhabiting the Truckee River watershed.

As a first step, I contacted a guy named Rich Kientz at the League to Save Lake Tahoe and volunteered to serve as a forest monitor up in the Tahoe Basin. Rich was a good guide and teacher as we took long hikes through forests that were slated to be logged. Like rafting a river just before it's dammed, we walked in the shadow of the tractor and the saw—a long, chilling shadow you could feel falling across something that had reached evening before its time. On some days monitoring felt like little more than measuring the waning life of something inexorably doomed; on others, though, the woods still felt as restorative and quiet and endless as they had seemed when I was Hannah's age.

The objective of the forest monitor is to compare the US Forest Service's plan for logging (the "prescription") to the ecological reality of the forest ("on the ground"). For example, a forest monitor might discover that a riparian zone (or SEZ: "stream environment zone") has not been adequately protected by a logging prescription or might note that the removal of large trees would be inconsistent with the objectives of the forest management plan. A monitor may express concern that tractor logging in certain areas will create excessive soil compaction or erosion, threatening critical wildlife habitat or endangering watershed health. In other cases, a monitor might note that the stated reason for logging an area—heavy fuel loading posing fire danger or die-off from insect kill, for example—isn't justified by observable conditions in the forest. The monitor then communicates concerns to the Forest Service (whose employees are often nicknamed "Freddies" by forest activists). If all goes well, the prescription for logging that tract will be adjusted toward a more sustainable approach to harvesting timber.

One summer afternoon I had just hiked out of a timber sale unit on Tahoe's North Shore with Rich. As we sat on the tailgate sweating, drinking Tahoe red, and looking out over the windy expanse of the sapphire lake, Rich offered a brief explanation of forest history in the basin. During the Comstock era of the mid- to late-nineteenth century, the basin's forests had been severely cut. Ancient ponderosa and sugar pine were the first to go, providing the beams and braces that supported many miles of mineshafts beneath then-booming Virginia City. Almost overnight, a towering ancient forest in the mountains became the skeleton of a labyrinth of subterranean catacombs in the desert. A century later, the clear-cut basin forests have grown up into same-age stands of trees, rather than the mixed-age stands that would have prevailed under an undisturbed forest regime. Within these unnatural same-age forests there is fierce competition for the vital resources of sunlight, water, and soil nutrients—competition that often triggers die-off, especially in thick stands of fir. At the same time, increased human inhabitation of the basin has prompted ambitious fire-suppression efforts, and while a lot of oversized vacation homes have been spared, the forest has become loaded with an unnaturally high concentration of dead and downed trees, which intensifies the risk of catastrophic wildfire—a risk that is exacerbated by drought and by the long-term effects of climate change.

In response to the fire danger posed by this heavy fuel loading, the Forest Service strategy has usually been to log these areas in order to thin dense forests—which are dense precisely because the natural fire cycle has been interrupted—and eliminate the ladder fuels by which a low-intensity ground fire might climb into the canopy and escalate to become a holocaust. Unfortunately, such logging has often proven to be environmentally destructive. The economic reality is that the trees most in need of removal to reduce the risk of stand-replacing fire—dead and downed trees, ladder fuels, jack-strawed ground fuels, and saplings and young trees, especially white fir—are those with the least economic value. In order to make logging pay, it is necessary to cut larger trees, green trees, and pines as well as firs, an approach that often results in a disturbed and less biodiverse forest of mostly younger trees. Add to this the fact that logging commonly causes soil compaction and erosion, destruction of wildlife habitat, and threats to water quality and that it sometimes leaves behind so much residual slash that fire danger is actually increased, and you can understand why concerned citizens worry that the solution is often worse than the problem.

When Rich finished explaining this environmentally destructive cycle of fuel loading, salvage logging, and habitat destruction, we began to wonder aloud what the forest would look like if the Forest Service could afford to manage these public lands according to their own stated objectives of watershed health, wildlife habitat, and fire control.

"To begin with," said Rich, "you wouldn't bring tractors in here. This unit was logged too recently. It's already taken a beating."

"And you wouldn't cut so many big trees," I added.

"Right, and you'd select for dominant species and thin for diversity," he continued. "Basically, you'd be removing ladder fuels and reducing ground fuels to mimic the effects of a low-intensity ground fire."

"I like to close roads," I added, handing Rich another ice-cold Tahoe red. "Could we obliterate a few skid trails while we're at it?"

"Why not?" he laughed. "Let's go ahead and restore those blown-out landing zones too."

Although the impossibility of the plan was painfully obvious to us both, we continued drinking and talking until we had fantasized a massive volunteer effort to hand-thin this part of the forest, sparing it from logging while also managing for key forest values, including wildlife habitat and fire control. It would be a model forest project combining activism and education—a collaboration between citizens and land management agencies that might result in a healthy forest, one that could also provide a baseline against which industrially logged parts of the basin could be compared.

"No problem," said Rich as he gazed out over the lake. "All we need is a workable plan, a team of field coordinators, a shitload of free equipment, an army of volunteers, the blessing of the Freddies, and some juicy media coverage."

That night I had a strange dream. I was standing in a primeval forest in which every tree was marked to be taken—a looming clear-cut with telltale orange blazes on every last trunk—when the markings slowly faded away, leaving a healthy forest of straight, clean, furrowed bark, standing tall and ready to catch the flakes of the first snow.

A tailgate is as good a place as any from which to begin the reformation of the world. Rich wrote an astute proposal, with which he and the League to Save Lake Tahoe succeeded in persuading the Forest Service to remove 240 acres from the planned North Shore timber sale. Instead, we would go in and care for the forest ourselves. From this urge to take care, the Tahoe Forest Stewardship project was born. Collaborating with the league and other groups, we worked out a treatment plan with the Forest Service, begged and borrowed the necessary equipment, recruited a group of team leaders, and had a series of preparatory meetings, usually held out on the forest unit we would be working. All this required a huge effort, but we were buoyed by the fact that so many people were willing to help. My favorite part of the project was working throughout the year with the other field coordinators, a diverse and talented group of foresters, activists, whistle-blowers, fly-fishers, smartasses, ski bums, and rednecks, many of whom combined these various identities to impressive effect.

One year from the tailgate, more than two hundred volunteers participated in the first Tahoe Forest Stewardship Day. Bird watchers, mountain bikers, Boy and Girl Scouts, ROTC teams, teachers, students, and scientists worked side by side to thin dense stands of saplings, eliminate ladder fuels, chip ground fuels, regrade landing zones, obliterate skid trails, and protect wildlife habitat. We had hydrologists, wildlife biologists, and fire ecologists on hand to help volunteers understand forest ecology and to add a crucial educational component to the event. Native Washoe elders also participated, telling their old stories and teaching our kids how to roast pine nuts and how to build a wickiup—an elegant, dome-shaped shelter constructed of arched willow saplings. Even the media coverage was uncharacteristically well informed. As we gathered at the end of the day for hot barbecue and cold beer, there was little left to wish for.

In the intervening thirteen years we have continued our cooperative forest protection work. Indeed, I achieved dubious fame among my fellow field coordinators the year I opted to run volunteer crews at the event rather than go on a honeymoon with my newlywed wife. My rationale, which Eryn agreed with, was simple: What the hell good is a great marriage if you don't have a healthy watershed to enjoy it in? The success of our initial effort resulted in an expansion of the project, which is now conducted annually at various sites around Lake Tahoe. The Forest Service, at first hesitant to work with us, is now enthusiastic about this project as a model of collaborative, community-based forest management. Sensing which way the wind is blowing, the Freddies often send a film crew to the event, not to mention a guy in a Smokey the Bear costume. Having been forced by my wife to occupy half of a horse costume at Caroline's last birthday party—the blazing hot ass half, needless to say—I'm always vigilant about slipping poor Smokey a few chilly brewskies. This act of generosity backfired last year when I discovered, too late, that the bear costume was being worn by a very sweet (and also by that time somewhat tipsy) thirteen-year-old Cub Scout. But even the incensed scoutmaster had to admit that at least my heart was in the right place.

For thirteen years I have continued to return to the patch of forest we worked in that first year of the project. Although, as today, I often bring Hannah and Caroline with me, the presence of those volunteers—by now around two thousand of them—is with me whenever I visit. Even at age seven, Hannah can appreciate what has been accomplished here; and while three-and-a-half-year-old Caroline may not yet get the big picture, she has a sense that this place is special to Dad, and she loves to come along whenever I visit. Thanks to the hard work of a lot of determined folks, this site has now become a dot on the map of what western American writer Wallace Stegner once called "the geography of hope." It is a place that has been given new layers of narrative, and for a change it isn't the same old story of cut-and-run exploitation. The chill of that long shadow is gone from this one place at least, and the forest here is healing itself and learning to hold water again. I'm especially glad that the girls have come along with me today. Their enjoyment of this place reminds me that our desire to care for the world is intuitive and spontaneous.

For Caroline it is a fun ride into the forest in her three-wheeled off-road stroller, though she climbs out pretty often to investigate pinecones and play in the forest duff. At lower elevations I'm struck by the glowing incense of cedars, their thick, aromatic bark reddish, twisted, and dotted with acorn-sized holes. Chartreuse moss adorns the north side of the trees in symmetrical rings. Hannah notices a pair of Steller's jays as they flash indigo through the lower branches of the surrounding trees. The trail steepens, and we pause to rest. I point out a noiseless arc of black and gray gliding into the crown of a big cedar below us: a Clark's nutcracker. Even the girls have a sense that this is a good place to be quiet. It occurs to me that silence, so commonly driven from our daily lives, is another balm that the forest produces, that it stores and holds, as it does water.

In following the trail's grade, we rise above the cedars and into the thick Jeffrey pine forest and then climb higher still, into mixed stands of large white fir and even larger red fir, a tree whose scientific name, *Abies magnifica*, gives a fair idea of its grandeur. On the way to the former site of our volunteer work we pass the telltale signs of previous logging operations: skid trails that disappear like jagged scars into the forest; landing zones perhaps a decade old that remain lunar and nearly unvegetated; piles of slash that weren't worth loading; a scrapped skid cable, splayed out like intestines. But even the areas stripped to bare mineral soil have begun to show signs of life, with small sprigs of stunted lupine struggling to colonize this miniature wasteland in the heart of the forest.

As we summit a ridgeline, Hannah asks the meaning of what for me is a too-familiar yellow sign, nailed high into the bole of a big red fir.

"That marks the border of a timber sale," I reply.

"They're going to cut them down?" she asks. When I nod my reply, Hannah frowns but doesn't comment. Much of what we've walked through today will be auctioned and logged, even as the forest struggles to recover from having been cut over so recently. As we pause to rest, Caroline gathers pine needles into a pile, then places four cones inside it, like eggs in a nest.

When Caroline has finished playing with her nest, she climbs back into the stroller, and we hike ahead, past the yellow sign and into the unit that is not for sale—into the woods that are the home of our by now multigenerational forest project. A magical line is crossed as we step from a world that is up for sale into a world of trees that will be allowed to stand their ground. The forest looks, sounds, even smells different on this side of the invisible line, and you don't have to be an enviro-geek—or even a grown-up—to tell the difference between land that's been abused and land that's been left to do its natural work. Successive winters have piled snow over the old skid trails we worked so hard to repair, pressing organic material into contact with the ground, building soil, rewilding this place. Each spring this forest gets a little better at holding and filtering water rather than shooting it off the mountain in erosion gullies that carry living soils off to cloud the lake and silt the fish-filled river that runs, invisible, in the valley below. Goshawk, California spotted owl, and other native birds have begun to return to their familiar perches in the canopy. I show the girls the berry-spangled scat of a black bear, which now has a recovering home to return to. We all have a place worth returning to—a place that is healing and in healing can somehow make the world feel right again.

It is a slow process, this work of finding home, and slower still for a stubborn desert rat like me. I suppose we need time to see the wheels within wheels of our home ecosystems turn, to understand these landscapes through the slowly deposited layers of sensibility and perception. Bringing Hannah and Caroline to this place—and knowing that I've had the humbling privilege of helping to make it a place worth bringing them to—reminds me that the story of this forest is now braided with the desert strand of our family's life narrative. The rewilding project has helped me attach to this green place and to attach this place to my desert home below. Now when I gaze up to the Sierra crest during a lizard-blistering summer in the Great Basin I visualize not Lake Tahoe chalets but instead this refreshingly cool patch of forest, this fountainhead of my home watershed.

I hope to return to this place during some hot summer in the autumn of my life, when my girls are grown, and walk them through a forest that feels whole again. By then it may even appear as if our volunteers were never here at all, which would be a wonderful legacy of their hard work. By then the skid trails I helped to repair will also be invisible, and the telltale orange markings on the trunks will have slowly faded away, leaving a healthy forest of straight, clean, furrowed bark, standing tall and ready to catch the flakes of the first snow.

Chapter 10

My Children's First Garden

For several years I had been promising Hannah that we would plant a special garden together just as soon as little Caroline was old enough to be able to share the experience with us. Now that Hannah was eight years old and her little sister was four and a half, it seemed that the time was finally right. I had long wanted the girls to have a garden of their own at home. I wanted to share with them a sustainable practice of labor, meditation, and production that has been essential to my life and that I hoped would become important in their lives as well. I wanted them to experience the miracle of a seed germinating, have the satisfaction of seeing things they planted with their own little hands grow to flower and fruit. I wanted not so much to watch my children's garden grow as to watch them watch it grow and to see them grow with it. To quote Ken Kesey, I wanted to help Hannah and Caroline "plant a garden in which strange plants grow and mysteries bloom." And even if some of the strange plants in Kesey's garden were illegal, his admonition to cultivate mysteries speaks directly to the higher law that governs true gardening.

The garden is not only the place where we grow food but also the place where we plant hopes and nurture ideas, where many plans grow from each thought that is sown. The garden is also a metaphor for what is peaceful, harmonious, and productive in our lives, and even our language reveals how deeply our imaginations are rooted in the garden. We celebrate ideas that are *seminal*, because so much can grow from the *seed* of a single thought. When we deeply question our culture's values we are considered *radical*, because we attempt to address problems at their *root*. We work hard to bring our projects to *fruition*, for nothing is sweeter than the *fruits* of our own labor. The garden is the imaginatively fertile ground where we harvest metaphors along with squash and beans.

Without realizing it at the time, in planning my children's first garden I had conflated parenting and gardening in my mind. After all, both are practices of love, attention, and creativity that result in healthy growth. Both require vigilance, nurturing, and care, and both yield sustaining harvests. Gardening and parenting are disciplines of sustainability, acts of faith in the future that must be renewed through daily practice. Of course this is the same sort of thinking employed by people who believe they are ready to have children because they managed to own a dog. Be that as it may, a gardener's universe is all sweetness and light, and the gardener's mind, like his or her garden, must remain an inviolable space that is impervious to the world's heartless logic. I had been a good gardener, and now I intended to use a garden to be a good father.

Even in my glowing optimism, I knew that my children's first garden might present a challenge. In this high-elevation desert we live amid conditions no gardener would relish: short growing season, extreme aridity, severe temperature fluctuations, desiccating winds, ravenous critters of every stripe. This is a place where even our human neighbors sometimes dry up, burn down, or blow away, which hardly bodes well for a pepper. Still, to a true gardener the unplanted garden is ever a canvas before paint, an idea not yet gone wrong, a sweet dream from which he or she has yet to awaken. As with any good idea, the trouble with a garden begins only when we attempt to realize what we have imagined.

As I spent the last nights of winter by the wood stove, sipping bourbon and strategizing to ensure the success of my children's first garden, I realized that the pressure was on. What if the garden I promised these sweet little girls didn't prosper? Given the metaphorical and philosophical significance of the garden, what larger, darker conclusions might they draw about their small place in the hard world if their own garden failed to come to fruition? I had to get this one right, and so I planned carefully. First, I would site the garden on the lee side of our big hill, where the hot wind would be more forgiving, and I'd stake and cage everything that grew upright to provide reinforcement against the scorching afternoon wind known locally as the Washoe Zephyr. I would also go to the trouble of constructing a large garden box out of railroad ties; this way I could backfill the raised bed with the primo double-mix soil I call "black gold" while also discouraging the desert cottontails and, especially, the big jackrabbits that can graze a bed to its roots in the time it takes to fetch an ale. To be safe, I'd wrap the whole garden in an impervious wire fence. In the interest of ensuring my daughters' success as neophyte gardeners, I would also set aside my environmentalist scruples and declare the plot a xeric-free zone where the girls could water to their heart's content. Finally, I would swallow my gardener's pride and grow only hardy, reliable plants, those that are fast growing, difficult to kill, and, if possible, spicy enough to be unpalatable to rodents. As winter waned, I came to think of my children's first garden as "the radish plot," as radishes have long been the mascot vegetable for amateur gardeners: fast, easy, cheap, unfailing, and plenty spicy. In a world of waiting and suffering, the lowly radish signifies short-term gratification and certain success.

When spring came, which it does mighty late at 6,000 feet, I built the garden just as I had designed it. Reminding myself of Rudyard Kipling's admonition that "gardens are not made by sitting in the shade," I worked all day in the glaring desert sun, transforming a bare plot of weedy caliche hardpan into my children's first garden. After the mattock, shovel, rake, spading fork, and field hammer were put up, I grabbed a trowel and hand cultivator and called Hannah and Caroline out to plant their garden. It was a momentous occasion, and I insisted that Eryn photograph this moment for posterity. I still treasure those pictures. In one, Hannah is deep-setting her first tomato plant with all her might; in another, Caroline is broadcasting radish seeds from her little green-gloved hand; in a third the sisters stand together, smiling broadly from behind the frame I built to trellis their beans. Throughout this photo op, though, Eryn's face wore a look of bemusement that suggested pleasure tinged with concern.

"Hey, what's the matter?" I asked as I stepped away from the garden, leaving Hannah and Caroline to water in their new plants. "Isn't this great?"

"I don't know, Bubba, they're pretty into this. Are you sure this is going to work?"

I shot a glance over my shoulder at the girls in their garden, then turned back to Eryn with a look of wounded pride.

"Come on, honey, I've been gardening my whole life. Besides, I've got this nailed. Look at what we're growing," I said, lowering my voice to a whisper. "I've stooped to radishes, for crying out loud. This is foolproof."

Only a fool believes that anything in this broken world is foolproof, and so the proliferation of things called foolproof is proof only that the world has fools and plenty. But the troubles in Caroline and Hannah's garden didn't start immediately. There was a golden two-week honeymoon during which seeds germinated, plants grew, and we gathered around the heavily armored plot to witness our little garden prevailing, even against daunting desert odds. We had planted tomatoes, squash, beans, sweet and hot peppers, collards, basil, and, of course, plenty of radishes. It was an unambitious, low-risk starter plot—a prosperous, shining little garden upon a hill that would make the desert bloom according to promises of old. We showered our plants with well water and attention and screened them with burlap to protect them from the scorching wind. My fence kept out the cottontails and big jackrabbits, just as I had hoped. As our plants grew we also took more pictures, proudly documenting for posterity the triumph of two little girls' first efforts at gardening.

Despite Bobby Burns's admonition that "the best laid schemes o' mice an' men gang aft agley," around our place the mice have aft done extremely well, while it is only my own schemes that have gang very, very damned agley. One aspect of my garden fortress scheme that was not well laid was my failure to foresee that slack spots along the base of my hardware cloth barricade would be virtual highways to the field mouse, which has no difficulty squeezing through a gap less than a half inch in diameter. So the "wee, sleekit, cow'rin, tim'rous beastie" got some seeds, as did the long-tailed, chisel-toothed, hopping kangaroo rats (*Dipodomys microps*) that abound here, foraging nocturnally for just such simple treasures as radish seeds. But this was sustainable damage, and I explained to Caroline that we were just being nice by sharing with our nonhuman neighbors. As an added form of insurance, however, I secretly overseeded the plot, and I tightened the fence carefully in hopes of mending the breaches. Within hours of fixing the fence, though, I discovered a mixed flock of bushtits, chickadees, and sparrows tearing up the seedbeds, and so I rushed to string in a half-dozen aluminum pie tins, which whipped in the Washoe Zephyr and made enough racket to keep out the hungry birds.

The next morning we were happy to find the seedbeds undisturbed, but just as I began to relax into a feeling of satisfaction I noticed that the squash plants had been shorn to the ground. After the time-consuming process of unwrapping various layers of fence, I was at last able to get close enough to the plants to examine them closely. Judging from the size of the lacerated stems and the clean, sharp angle of their cuts, I was certain that bushy-tailed pack rats had been the culprits.

Hope is the coin of the gardener's realm, but it is a devalued currency, worth increasingly less as it is traded against the incessantly rising tender of the gardener's despair. It was several days before I made it to town to get plastic bird netting—which I now needed to keep out not birds but pack rats—and by then I was forced to buy replacement seed and bedding plants for the garden, which had already been substantially ravaged by the birds, mice, kangaroo rats, and pack rats. Indeed, the all-you-can-eat salad bar that was once my children's first garden was now so heavily frequented by rodents that the local great horned owl took up a hunting perch on the peak of our roof. While the final stages of the garden's destruction proceeded apace despite the owl's nightly vigil, I now had the additional chore of cleaning from the sidewalk many overlapping bursts of snow-white owl crap, occasionally accompanied by owl "pellets"—a delicate euphemism for a compact, puked-up wad of undigested fur, bones, teeth, and feathers.

During this time the girls continued to water what was left

of their garden, and they had a great time playing together in the mud—even as I was constantly humiliated by having to explain to their mother why I, the seasoned gardener, was finding it so difficult to grow a few radishes. The ripe fruit of my gardener's pride began to wither on the blasted vine of my children's first garden, and while I was relieved that Hannah and her little sister seemed unfazed by what Eryn had begun to call "the Vegpocalypse," I had no way of knowing how long this grace period might continue. Grace, like good gardening weather, is welcome when it comes, but you're in deep, uncomposted manure if your success depends upon it. At some point, I reckoned, this garden must produce.

Returning from town one day, despondent but with plenty of bird netting and extra-hoppy IPA, I once again unwrapped the various layers of artillery separating the little garden from the cruel world, and we started over. I dug out the root balls of the clear-cut squash and removed the hard stems of the limbless tomatoes while Hannah and Caroline gathered the scattered leaves of the savaged sweet peppers. We retilled and replanted my children's first garden from end to end, and while I was pretty surly about it, the girls remained in great spirits the entire time. Caroline even told me innocently that she wished we could start the garden over "every single day!" When our replanting was done, the girls went in to wash up while I spent another hour reinforcing my defense systems, concluding with the double layer of plastic netting that I draped over the top of the fortress and snapped down with bright yellow bungee cords.

Then I called the girls and sat down in my old aluminum lawn chair, with Hannah at my feet and Caroline on one knee, and stared at my children's second first garden.

I stared, and yet I could see nothing that we had planted. With all the railroad ties, posts, trellises, stakes, tomato cages, hardware cloth fences, burlap windbreaks, shimmering pie tins, panels of bird netting, and neon bungee cords, it was now virtually impossible to see any living thing through the overlapping walls of the garden. I could in fact see no garden at all, but only a hideous monument to my own determination to establish a barrier where my brute neighbors would have none. My children's second first garden looked like a miniature factory, or prison, or maybe the tangled bones of a steel barn after it meets with the tornado's funnel. What the hell kind of garden was that, especially for a kid? "Something there is that doesn't love a wall, that wants it down," wrote Robert Frost in his poem "Mending Wall." I had instead abided by the maxim Frost's neighbor endorses in the poem: "Good fences make good neighbors." If the furry and feathered would just stay on their side of the fence, all would be well. It was a simple concept, and I was exasperated by the lengths I was driven to in order to make sure my kids would have the chance to pull a few radishes.

Discouraged as I was, as a gardener I had been toughened by disappointment as well as by wind and sun. Even the Vegpocalypse, I reasoned, wasn't worse than some other gardening catastrophes I had endured, and as I sat meditating on my failure I was reminded of the heartening words of Thomas Jefferson, one of our most philosophical gardeners. In the garden, wrote Mr. Jefferson, "the failure of one thing is repaired by the success of another." Perhaps, as T. J. suggested, there would be some yet hidden consolation to compensate for these losses. Just at that moment, however, something tragic and unexpected happened—something that fatally radicalized my approach to gardening in the high desert. As I sat in my bent lawn chair, with Hannah leaning against my shoulder, Caroline sitting in my lap, and one half of my ass poking down through the ripped canvas seat, two tiny white-tailed antelope ground squirrels skittered across the rocky patch of dirt that is our "yard," raced beneath us, and ran over my right foot in their gleeful sprint to get to our newly replanted garden. There they disappeared momentarily behind the railroad ties forming the garden box before popping up in the garden itself, wasting no time in starting to crop our squash.

All of this happened in a matter of seconds, but in that moment I felt the swell of failure curl over me in a slow-breaking wave of despair. My gardener's hubris—that profound, unsubstantiated delusion of superiority without which no gardener could long endure his or her trials—had bitten me on the half of my ass that was exposed to the cruel world. In allowing myself to believe that the replanted and rearmored garden was impenetrable, I had foolishly ignored one of the basic principles of fatherhood, a principle so fundamental that it belongs with such core insights as "The only people who like change are babies in diapers" or "When your kid tells you to cover your eyes, do it with one hand and cover your nuts with the other." Humility is the alpha and omega of both parenting and gardening. I had failed to be humble, and in failing to be humble I was now humbled by failure.

In mute frustration I now reckoned that my daughters' ultimate happiness—their futures as good gardeners, great women, excellent human beings—was staked on the uncertain success of the little garden these white-tailed beasts were devouring. And, damn it, they had stepped on my foot. Both the gardener and the father in me now felt called to battle. As I sat with my jaw locked, watching my children's second first garden being destroyed, I could feel that I was about to cross an invisible line—that extraordinary and perhaps violent measures had become necessary. For their part, however, the girls greeted this new problem with screeches of joy. "Daddy! Look at the cute little chipmunks in our garden!" exclaimed Hannah, pointing excitedly toward the ravaged plot. "Hello, friends!" added Caroline, as she held her hands to her face and wriggled her fingers to mimic whiskers.

As the cracked stubs of what were once our plants baked in the heat of a sun whose azimuth had grown troublingly higher in recent weeks, I began a calculated assault on the "chipmunks" that had now become more numerous than flies around our place. The white-tailed antelope squirrel (*Ammospermophilus leucurus*) is a remarkable creature, one whose adaptations to the grueling excesses of the desert environment can only have been shaped by a zillion evolutionary near misses, each one resulting in a crunchy snack for a harrier or coyote. Until you've been in the desert awhile, the antelope squirrel really does look like a chipmunk, though the differences are many and extraordinary. For starters, optimal habitat for the antelope squirrel is sparse juniper, sagebrush steppe, and desert scrub; unlike the chipmunk, it is never seen in the alpine forest. The white-tailed antelope—the species of *Ammospermophilus* most widely distributed throughout the arid West and the one that was chowing down on my kids' second first garden—sports a narrow white stripe from shoulder to rump, has white cheeks, and carries none of those unsightly chipmunk stripes on its face. Antelopes have thin, coarse fur that is light brown with a gray or, as in our local population, reddish tint. The infallible means to distinguish them from chipmunks, though, is by their amazing ability to run with their tail pulled up over their bodies, a feat your average chipmunk could only dream of attempting. The underside of that raised tail flashes as white as the rump of a pronghorn in flight, an unmistakable visual correspondence that is the source of the antelope squirrel's odd name.

The antelope lives up to the name "squirrel" perfectly. *Squirrel* comes from the Vulgar Latin *scuriolus,* which is a variant of the Latin *scurius,* which comes from the Greek *skiouros,* which gives this family its name, Sciuridae, and which is almost certainly the source of the word *scurry.* Antelope squirrels are so small—four ounces or so—that you could mail one across the country for about a buck, but they scurry with such inconceivable swiftness as to make sprinting chipmunks look like they are shuffling from couch to cupboard to get a bag of Cheetos during halftime. Once running, the antelope squirrel—unlike its namesake, the pronghorn—never stops or looks back, instead flying across the earth like a white-flagged shot that vanishes into the ground at hyperspeed.

Unlike chipmunks and even other kinds of ground squirrels, the antelope is active throughout the year, which frees it from the need to hoard food in preparation for hibernation. It is not particularly territorial and in fact will huddle with others of its kind to conserve heat during the winter, so you can't count on them to off one another the way an aggressive, territorial rodent like a pack rat might. They excavate tunnels with multiple entrances, have several burrows in their large home range, construct separate tunnels for food caches and quick escapes, and often appropriate the burrow systems of kangaroo rats, all of which makes them virtually impossible to locate underground. Somewhere in one of those many tunnels the antelope will make a nest six inches in diameter, which it has likely lined with the golden strands set adrift when Eryn brushes the girls' hair outside on sunny mornings. You can't easily starve an antelope squirrel, as they are generalist omnivores that will eat almost anything, from seeds, plants, roots, grasses, and fruits to insects, lizards, and carrion, including the flesh of fellow rodents. Virtually invulnerable to dehydration, they need no free water to survive, instead deriving all their hydration from the plants and bugs they eat. Their kidneys are so highly efficient in saving water by reducing nitrogenous waste that if we were as well designed we could go several years without needing a replacement roll of toilet paper. Around here the little antelopes usually mate in late February and are born around Hannah's birthday in early April—a reproductive cycle that is precisely calibrated to the emergence of leafy annual plants here in the high desert.

What is most amazing about the antelope ground squirrel is its astonishing ability to keep itself cool in the brutal desert heat. Unlike the nocturnal foragers whose lifestyle seems more compatible with this scorching environment, the antelope is diurnal, cruising around above ground even on the hottest days. It has a number of tricks that make this marvelous feat possible. Its water conservation strategies help, of course, as does its habit of keeping its back to the sun and shading its body with its tail and its ability to climb into bushes to catch a breeze. Most important, the antelope doesn't cool itself evaporatively, as humans and most other mammals do, so it isn't water stressed by cooling. For this little squirrel, keeping cool is literally no sweat. Instead, it is so well adapted to the desert environment that it can allow its body temperature to rise to an incredible 110 degrees Fahrenheit—a thermal load that would cause brain damage and likely death in an adult human. When it begins to overheat, it returns to its burrow, splays its legs, drops its sparsely furred belly against the earth, and lets the ground pull the heat right out of its body—after which it pops up again and resumes razing our garden. If they happen to be well hydrated when they heat up, they will also use the neat trick of rubbing saliva on their faces to cool themselves, a behavior that makes me suspect Caroline may in fact be a ground squirrel.

The antelope squirrel's adaptive strategies are so many and so effective as to give it a daunting home field advantage, and as a beer-guzzling mammalian biped with few effective adaptations to desert life I do not feel myself a worthy opponent. After driving to town to buy several live traps smaller than those used to nab pack rats, a backup case of IPA, and a large jar of crunchy peanut butter (which I labeled NOT FOR KIDS), I began my attempt to capture the cute little antelope squirrels. Following some misadventures in which I trapped and released a piñon jay, a kangaroo rat, a bunny-sized desert cottontail, and my own fingers (twice), I did at last discover that the wee squirrels like Uncle Crunkle's Old-Fashioned Peanut Butter at least as well as they like squash stems. During the next two weeks I captured sixteen antelopes—many of which I released on public lands far from my children's garden (some studies claim that this six-inch-long creature will find its way home from several miles away) but some of which received swimming lessons in my improvised pack rat dunk tank.

Having more or less succeeded in my efforts to remove the antelope tribe from the neighborhood of our garden (there was one smug little urchin I never did catch), I raked together what was left of my gardener's self-respect and helped the girls put on their gardening boots and gloves. We completely replanted our plot yet again, which was perfectly fine with Hannah and Caroline, even as I feared that the seasonal window would slam shut on our plants before they could come to fruition. I was now sufficiently desperate that I hatched a plan to photograph the girls next to the plants as they grew, later interpolating these shots of their third first garden with the earlier ones of them planting the actual first garden so as to create the appearance of success where in fact there had been two complete failures. The fact that I had sprung for larger, more developed bedding plants this time would help support the illusion. When I suggested to Eryn that some photo editing might also help out where evidence of the Double Vegpocalypse was inadvertently revealed (for example, I had carelessly planted a pepper where a tomato had been), she smilingly dismissed my idea as only the most extreme of "the many clear signs" that my obsession with my children's first garden had become desperate. Undeterred, I insisted that the plan would work and so took a raft of pictures of my children's third first garden, which really did look quite nice. We then put up our tools, got out the old lawn chair, and sat together, admiring our neat little garden as Venus arced toward the serrated summit crest of our home mountain.

The next morning I awoke before daybreak with a deeply unsettled feeling. I had experienced a disturbingly vivid nightmare in which I stood in my children's garden, leaning at a slight angle but with arms straight out, like a scarecrow, immobilized by a strange paralysis as rodents of every kind crawled up and down my body, even clinging to my beard with their claws as they grinned directly into my bloodshot eyes. In the dream I was in a state of heightened sensory awareness, and I could not only smell the dank fur but feel the tiny whiskers and even the quivering breath of the mice, voles, moles, pocket gophers, kangaroo rats, pack rats, and antelope ground squirrels as they clambered over me. When I awoke I was just beginning to lose sight as one especially enterprising antelope squirrel nibbled on my exposed, unblinking eyeball.

Trying to chase away my bad night with java that I brewed a good bit stronger than usual, I stood at the slider door sipping from my mug and awaiting sunrise over my children's third first garden. At last the ascending Venus dimmed, the sky brightened, and the little plot was bathed in a golden, effulgent light. There it was, suddenly, in all its shining glory, the little garden for my little girls, and I felt that somehow my struggles had been rewarded. Here was the garden I had envisioned, the sweet little plot that would grow with my kids, teaching them to nurture the flower and fruit that bind us to the nonhuman world. Here they would learn the ethic of care that is the highest mark of a moral person; here they would practice techniques of sustainability that would give them healthy food to eat and a harvest basket overflowing with metaphors to live by.

As I was admiring the garden and contemplating my inspiring success with earth-centered parenting, one of the tomato plants suddenly vanished. I quickly scurried back and forth in front of the slider to make sure of what I was seeing, and then I yanked open the door and sprinted to the garden, leaning over the various fences and pressing my face against the nylon bird netting to get a closer view. In the soil directly beneath the center of one tomato cage, which was still rocking slightly, there was a hole where the plant had stood only a moment before.

In that moment I did not cry out, like Job, to the unjust heavens to demand explanation for why I was being punished for a crime I did not commit. I did not observe the natural historical evidence before me in search of a scientific understanding of the depredation nature had here wrought. I did not engage in the inimitable brand of breathtaking, blue-streaking profanity for which I have been reviled by some and celebrated by others. Instead, I felt something deep inside me begin to uncoil, some mainspring in the engine of my tolerance for my fellow creatures irreversibly unwinding, the psychic rivets of my identity as a father and an environmentalist popping off as that spring unwound.

I have only a hazy recollection of what happened next, but Eryn reports that she awoke to see me walking slowly through the house "like a zombie," wearing only lime-green boxer shorts decorated with orange ladybugs, blaze-orange sound-protection muffs over my ears, and carrying my shotgun. I vaguely recall the muffled sound of Caroline shouting, "Daddy has the fire stick!" as I passed the open door of the girls' bedroom, but this too remains foggy. I do remember vividly how different the garden looked when sighted down the barrel to the bead, and I recall the feeling of the trigger moving beneath my finger when it popped its furry little head out of the hole where the tomato plant had recently stood.

It is true that the shot blasted apart the fence on both sides of the garden—creating gaping holes through which other ravenous critters would enter and finish off my children's third first garden in the days ahead. And it is true that the buckshot perforated the leaves of many plants, which hardly mattered since they were soon eaten by the animals that came in through the fence. It is also true that trying to stop rodents is like trying to dig a hole in the ocean: a bucketful of water closes in where every bucketful is lifted out, forever. And it is very true that no knuckle-dragging human is any match for animals that are so brilliantly adapted to this desert environment. It is further true that the proliferation of these rodents was my own fault—not only because the caloric easy money of the garden drew them in, but also because our presence here created a charmed circle that coyotes hesitated to enter. And it is of course true that gun-play in the garden is not especially consistent with the parental and environmental ethic of care I had hoped the garden would teach my little girls. And it is disconcertingly true that once a pacifist nature lover blows something's head off with a shotgun, it generates in him a certain amount of cognitive dissonance, which in turn is deeply threatening to the identity said nature lover may have spent a life-time cultivating. But it is also indisputably true that, when driven far enough, even a father with a firm grip on the ethical steering wheel can rattle off the washboarded road of his own morality and slide into the humbling ditch of hypocrisy.

Wise Cicero, who wrote that "if you have a garden and a library, you have everything you need," clearly didn't know about the California ground squirrel, or he would have had a shotgun too. *Spermophilus beecheyi* is even more remarkable than his little cousin the antelope squirrel, though I did not know that at the time I decapitated him with a fire stick. Almost a foot long, with a tail that can extend another nine inches, often more than two pounds in weight, and a prodigious excavator and vegetarian with a huge appetite, this beautiful monster is a real threat to agricultural enterprises on both the commercial and domestic scale. Females often mate with more than one male, sometimes doing so more than once each season, and may give birth to a dozen or more pups in each litter, a reproductive strategy that keeps them well ahead of hawks and guys with fire sticks. Their digging capabilities are truly impressive. One study found that a single California ground squirrel complex containing only eleven animals consisted of a tunnel system extending more than seven hundred feet, including thirty-three openings, and descending nearly thirty feet below ground.

The ground squirrel's tunnels usually protect it from predators other than rattlesnakes, but even here its defenses are daunting. Adult squirrels are actually immune to rattler venom, so when a buzz worm slithers into a tunnel system it is not unusual for a squirrel to harass it, even kicking sand in the snake's face. And while squirrel pups do not share their parents' immunity to rattler venom, female squirrels collect sloughed rattlesnake skins, masticate them, and lick the snake-scented saliva onto their pups, thus using smell to trick the rattler into thinking the baby ground squirrels are actually fellow snakes and encouraging the predator to seek elsewhere for its supper. The California ground squirrel is fast, agile, intelligent, and resourceful and has vision as sharp as yours. It protects others of its kind with an unmistakable high-pitched alarm call by which it communicates danger across miles of desert—a piercing, surging, metallic cry that now rings in my ears as the soundtrack to my own defeat as a gardener. Although diurnal like its little cousin the antelope, the California ground squirrel goes into estivation (a period of strategic inactivity) when the weather becomes too hot and goes into true hibernation in the winter—a physiological shutdown so amazingly like suspended animation that the animal's heartbeat is reduced to a tenth of its normal rate, and it draws a breath only once every few minutes.

After I learned all this about my neighbor *Spermophilus,* it seemed clear that, as usual, I was overmatched. He didn't need to chew through or climb the wire protection around our garden because he could tunnel under from anywhere he pleased and pop up beneath a tomato plant—which, as the literature on ground squirrel crop damage shows, is among his favorite foods. But everything I read suggested that if I didn't stem this invasion the ground squirrels would overrun the place, undermining the foundation of our house with their tunnels, eating ornamental plants as well as vegetables, spreading fleas that can carry bubonic plague, and perhaps ultimately driving my old pickup to town to buy expensive sour mash with my credit card. They are in fact so destructive to croplands and irrigation systems that it is illegal to release a squirrel that has been livetrapped, and a sense of how far folks will go to try to kill them is suggested by this discouraging remark, which I discovered somewhere in the voluminous antisquirrel literature: "truck-mounted vacuum devices that suck ground squirrels out of their burrows have not demonstrated sufficient efficacy to justify their use." Still, I made up my mind that if my children were ever to have a first garden I would have to try everything this side of burrow vacuuming.

Having already become a gun-wielding killer, at first I decided, like Huck Finn, that "I would take up wickedness again" and so resolved to keep blasting away at my scurrilous neighbors. After all, once you've crossed the line and become a heartless murderer, what are a few dozen perforated corpses, more or less? But Eryn talked me out of the gunplay, not so much by pointing out its incompatibility with the environmental values I aspired to inculcate in my daughters, but instead by reminding me that if I was going to walk around heavily armed I wouldn't be able to drink at the same time—something I prognosticated could become imperative in the battle ahead.

I began with attempts to livetrap the big ground squirrels, as I had their smaller cousins, but they proved too wily to be snared, and as my traps sat empty, my children's third first garden was wiped out completely. At this point I could have acknowledged that after three strikes you're out, but instead I did what my species does best: I chose to believe, foolishly and against all evidence, that nature doesn't bat last, that I could still somehow win one for the humanoids by knocking it into the bleachers in the bottom of the ninth. *Spermophilus* had become my white whale. In a weak moment I went online and ordered a case of Wild Bill's Shure Kill Varmint Hole Fumigating Bombs. I soon prepared a new strategy to defend my children's garden—which, granted, was now an entirely hypothetical construct—by smoking out my subterranean opponent. On Saturday morning I dressed for the occasion, in boots, long pants, long-sleeved shirt, gloves, hat, safety goggles over my eyes, and bandana over my mouth. Eryn observed that I closely resembled the drunken-looking hillbilly Wild Bill, whose scowling visage appeared on the cylinder of each bomb. Carefully following Bill's directions, I first located what I felt certain were all the holes to the squirrels' tunnel system and then began to execute my plan.

For a moment there was a wonderful rush of excitement, as I sprinted from hole to hole amid swirls of fuchsia smoke, dropping lit canisters into the four burrow entrances I had found. The girls stood at a safe distance with Mom. Hannah gave me a two-thumbs-up sign, while Caroline windmilled her arms enthusiastically, like a swimmer warming up for her next event. There followed an ominous hiatus during which nothing at all seemed to happen. As I stood perched over the squirrel hole nearest the house, I finally looked up to see Hannah and Caroline smiling widely and Eryn pointing at something that was apparently behind me. Lifting my goggles from my eyes to my grimy forehead, I turned slowly around. One, two, three, four . . . eleven columns of fuchsia smoke curled gracefully off into the cobalt-blue desert sky. It was a lovely sight, in an *Apocalypse Now* sort of way. Thus was it colorfully brought to my attention that the tunnel system had far more escape hatches than I knew of and that this superb ventilation system had prevented my aerial gas attack from being anything more harmful than a fireworks show for the girls, who in fact liked it so much that they made me a lovely thank-you card out of fuchsia-colored construction paper.

Being averse to using poisons, and having now given up on the trap, gun, and bomb, I had but one weapon remaining in my armory: piss. Relinquishing the treasured idea that a mere human could defeat these squirrels, in my desperation I resorted to an unlikely, indirect form of biological control. The ground squirrel used smell to trick the rattlesnake into believing that *Spermophilus* pups were not what they seemed. What if I could rip a page from the ground squirrels' own stinking playbook and make the scurrilous beast think I was his lethal archpredator, the coyote? Having failed in my roles as Mr. McGregor, Elmer Fudd, and Wild Bill, I now prepared to transform myself into Old Man Coyote. And how is this trickster, *Canis latrans*, known unmistakably to his neighbors in the wild world? By his wicked grin and by the reek of his piss. Having become the first person I know of to mail order a jug of coyote urine, I now possessed both the grin and the pee. And while I tried not to think about just how one would go about collecting a gallon of coyote whiz, I did feel a late surge of hope that my final plan had a chance of working because I was now going with the flow of nature, so to speak, rather than against it. If the crucible of evolution hadn't taught these squirrels to fear gardeners or smoke bombers, it had certainly taught them to dread the loping death that is Old Man Coyote.

The problem with my "desert doggie wee-wee plan," as Eryn unsympathetically taught Caroline to call it, was that in order to test its results, we would have to plant my children's first garden a fourth time, even as I was now virtually certain that after the time consumed by the Triple Vegpocalypse and its attendant skirmishes, frost would kill the garden if *Spermophilus* did not. And so the girls and I spent the next Saturday replanting the plot from scratch, of course using the most humiliatingly large bedding plants that a raided college savings account can buy. While I experienced the replanting as a Sisyphean labor, big sister Hannah effortlessly preserved a Jeffersonian equanimity that demonstrated a healthy resilience of which I was incapable. Little Caroline expressed her happiness that the squirrels had eaten such a healthy dinner. "Daddy, vegetables make them strong too!" she said, holding up her tiny arms in a futile attempt at a bicep flex. Once replanted, the garden had yet again to be rearmored and in fact now looked even more unsightly, especially with the addition of the hardware cloth patches I had wired in to cover the large holes blown out by the buckshot. None of this bothered the girls, who "made rainbows" while watering their new plants, after which we put up our tools and went inside to wait for late afternoon, when I would administer the final deterrent in my dwindling arsenal.

I should admit that as the day wore on I became increasingly nervous about the outcome of my looming experiment and that I drank a fair amount of whiskey in an attempt to knock back my growing uncertainty. Eryn, who is both more sensible and more intelligent than her husband, thought the "desert doggie wee-wee plan" absurd, which seemed inauspicious. I had of course failed in every other attempt, and my poor track record suggested that I was the only creature in my local environment completely ill suited to inhabit it. What could it signify that in my hour of greatest need I had resorted not to the dual consolations of acceptance and prayer but rather to the twin elixirs of bourbon and coyote urine? If I failed in this last and most desperate attempt, I would be forced to admit that I was not only a humiliated gardener, an environmentalist pariah, and an ineffectual father, but also a half-drunk, first-order, second-grade, third-string, fourth-first-garden-planting, gas-, gun-, and pee-toting five-star vigilante.

By late afternoon I was sufficiently lubricated that I should perhaps have reconsidered my plan to resume work in my children's fourth first garden, but I knew that the garden would soon be gone without some form of protection, and I still had a spendy Jug O' Whiz with *Spermophilus*'s name on it. I drained one last whiskey, fetched my secret weapon, and approached the garden with the jug clenched tightly in my right hand. I climbed up onto the garden's railroad-tie frame and balanced myself there, slowly wrapping the fingers of my left hand around the jug's screw-top cap. I paused, taking one last deep breath before cracking the seventh seal.

I still remember how lovely the girls' newly planted garden looked in the glow of the low-angle afternoon sun, how the light breeze rippled the leaves of the tomatoes and squash, how moist and fertile the seedbeds seemed, how neat and well tended the plot appeared. I vividly recall feeling that I was witnessing a perfect garden in a perfect moment, though this transcendental epiphany was no doubt intensified by the blush and tingle of the hooch that had by then loosened all my muscles. I remember how lovely that moment felt, how hesitant I was to twist that cap and lose the wonderful feeling that little garden had raised in me. I remember, with a dreamlike sense of distance, an overflowing feeling that, despite the many trials it had presented, this tender plot was a noble monument to my love for my daughters and for the earth. Maybe, I recall thinking, there is some cosmic plan within which this struggle has been an indispensable part of my own journey both as a father and as a gardener. Then I twisted off the lid.

There can be no word in any human language that even begins to suggest the overpowering, unspeakable stench that exploded from the jug the instant that lid came off. Nothing in human evolutionary biology could have prepared me for this reeking bomb, the first whiff of which instantly flooded my eyes with tears, filled my mouth with a choking metallic tang, and set the whiskey roiling violently in my gut. I felt as if my body had suddenly become a permeable membrane through which the worst stink in the universe was blowing at gale force, carrying off my flesh as it howled through and reducing me to a shattered pile of smoldering bones. This was not just the urine of who knows how many very angry (and presumably catheterized) coyotes, it was a highly concentrated *gallon* of the stuff, and it had been stored for who knows how long in this vacuum-sealed container. I now held, at the end of my quivering, hyperextended arm, a vessel of the kind of stench that could make a gagging human hope to be sprayed by a polecat just to cover it up.

Of course this all happened in a flash, but in the instant that I recoiled from the revolting stink, which blasted out of the jug and attacked my face like a swarm of yellow jackets, I heard that signature metallic chirp of victory ring out from the sagebrush behind me. It was *Spermophilus*, either laughing at me or warning his kin that a thousand coyotes had just simultaneously taken a huge leak. Spinning my contorted face away from the jug and toward that piercing cry, I suddenly felt my boot sole begin to slip on the edge of the railroad tie atop which I was perched. And it is at this moment that time seemed to slow almost to a stop, and I experienced the next few seconds in that frame-by-frame fashion that the human brain reserves for only the most unimaginable of accidents.

I fell for what seemed quite a long time, and I even remember seeing the pee that splashed out of the jug floating in midair, as if in the zero gravity of a space capsule. Eventually the handle of the jug was released from the grip of my fingers, and it too turned slowly in midair, as if it would remain spinning there forever. And then, at last, came the splintering crash of my body as it landed on my children's beautiful fourth first garden, taking down fences and netting and stakes and cages as it did and crushing the plants that by now had assumed a symbolic significance very different from what I had originally intended. As I looked up through my bleary stink tears and through the fragments of the garden in which I now lay, I could just make out a matched pair of sisters in the distance, both of them pinching their noses with one hand and waving at me with the other. And they were smiling. As always, my little girls were smiling.

I scrubbed until I had about peeled my skin off, but Eryn still made me sleep out on the deck that first night. In the weeks that followed I couldn't get near enough to the Superfund site that was my first children's fourth first garden to initiate remediation, though we diluted the terrible pee stench by hosing the garden down from about thirty feet upwind, an ablution that I performed twice each day in order to make it tolerable for the girls to play outside. Five weeks later an early frost hit, and the cold snap knocked the stench down enough that I could approach the wrecked garden to clean it up before the first snow. When I pulled away the broken fences and cages, I found that a few plants had actually survived, unmolested because the not-quite-empty Jug O' Doom still rested openmouthed near their stems. One of these was a tomato plant, and while its tiny yellow flowers were now burned by frost, it had set some fruit, and a single tomato looked pink enough that it might ripen off the vine. I harvested the little tomato, washed it well, and gave it to the girls to put on the sill of their bedroom window. Over the next few days that tomato ripened, and so our family huddled around the kitchen table to celebrate the ritual of the first fruits—well, fruit—of the season, even as a snow sky gathered outside. Caroline took a bite, wrinkled her nose, and said "Thanks for the tomato, Daddy. I don't like it. Can we have a garden again next year? Let's plant pineapples!"

In parenting and in gardening we risk failure every moment of every day, and how could it be otherwise? Through these daily practices of love, humility, and humor we just keep trying, not because our success is certain, but because it certainly is not. We hope, and yet we fail; we fail, and yet we hope. I have promised the girls that we will plant their garden in the spring. And it will again be their first garden, just as every garden is a first garden, just as every day with those we love is a chance to start over, to plant something again.

Chapter 11

The Hills Are Alive

My grandmother's highest compliment for a natural landscape was to say that it was "as pretty as a picture." Even as a kid I remember thinking that this aesthetic was upside-down, that the loveliness of art should be judged according to the inimitable standard of natural beauty rather than the other way around. During the late eighteenth and early nineteenth centuries, well-heeled European travelers scoured the countryside looking for views that would be as pretty as a picture—or, to be more precise, as pretty as a painting. Because they had a certain kind of painting in mind as embodying their standard of natural beauty, these early eco-tourists often carried with them a "Claude glass," a small, convex, tinted mirror that was nicknamed for the seventeenth-century landscape painter Claude Lorrain. When a picturesque landscape was encountered—say, for example, the snowcapped Alps—the tourist would first turn his or her back to the mountains, then whip out the Claude glass, holding it up so as to frame the mountains. The peaks appeared reflected and also color shifted to a tonal range that made them look more painterly. Voilà! Actual Alps not only become pretty as a picture but *become* a picture, as the pleased eco-tourist stands admiring, not the mountains, but rather an image of them that he or she has created. But why must we turn our backs on the land in order to see it in a way that we find aesthetically pleasing? Have we so lost a sense of humility before nature that we've come to love our own representations of the world more dearly than we love the world itself?

It might be fair to say that the Claude glass of the nineteenth century was photography and that the twentieth-century Claude glass was film, since these technologies of representation have profoundly conditioned our landscape aesthetics. They have allowed us to frame the world. As with the Claude glass, there is a sense in which cinema's stylized, controlled, and color-corrected depiction of nature has thoroughly mediated our relationship to the physical world, reshaping our environmental aesthetics and implying that a representation of nature is an improvement upon nature itself. Cinema has the power to show us the environment in remarkably dramatic fashion, but to see the land in film we must temporarily turn our backs on the land itself. To climb into the bright mountains of the screen we must first descend into the dark cave of the theater.

From a very early age I've held the deep and unwavering conviction that musicals—especially movie musicals—represent the most intolerable and misguided aesthetic form in the checkered history of human civilization. In addition to being uniformly hokey and boring, musicals are also cloying and saccharine, which is even more offensive. I make it a policy never to trust a person who would spontaneously break into song for no reason, especially when he's about to begin a knife fight (*West Side Story*), he's adopting an orphan as a publicity stunt (*Annie*), or she's confessing her unwanted pregnancy (*Grease*). It is not simply that the suspension of disbelief required in such cases would daunt Hercules, it is also that it is so obviously inappropriate to croon about things like gang violence, homeless waifs, and bastard children. The world would be a better place if the urge to sing of such things could be soundly repressed—if this upswelling, confessional, tuneful emoting could instead become a stoical moment of shutting the piehole good and tight.

   If I sound testy about this issue of movie musicals, I have good reason. As the father of young daughters, I have been subjected—wholly against my will—to musicals too numerous and nauseating to be enumerated. The most frequently repeated of these abominations is the much-beloved 1965 "timeless classic" *The Sound of Music*, whose perennial popularity confirms every curmudgeonly thing I've ever said or written about my fellow human beings. Indeed, the

National Association of Misanthropes might consider screening this gem at its annual convention, if only to reassure members that they really are on the right track. Despite my personal aversion to the picture, *The Sound of Music* not only bailed out a sinking 20th Century Fox in the mid-1960s but, adjusted for inflation, has gone on to net more than a billion dollars. That's "billion" with a *b*, just like the *b* in "blockbuster," or "banal," or "bullshit."

So much beloved is this appalling movie—which, by the way, won five Academy Awards and was nominated for five more—that the first-ever reunion of its nine principal actors had to be held as part of the final season of *Oprah*. The film was even ranked number 55 on the American Film Institute's centennial "100 Years . . . 100 Movies" list of the most important American films, where it was judged superior to *actual* "timeless classics" including *The Third Man* and *Vertigo, Stagecoach* and *The Searchers, The Gold Rush, City Lights,* and *Modern Times.* Can there be any doubt that Carol Reed, Alfred Hitchcock, John Ford, and Charlie Chaplin—the directors of these amazing pictures—are spinning in their graves? Among the few people ever to tell the truth about *The Sound of Music* was the film critic Pauline Kael, who called it "the sugar-coated lie that people seem to want to eat." "We have been turned into emotional and aesthetic imbeciles," wrote Kael, "when we hear ourselves humming [this film's] sickly, goody-goody songs." In a simultaneous blow to free speech and good taste, Kael was fired from *McCall's Magazine* for the heresy of making this astute opinion public.

I've meditated at length on what disturbs me so much about

this awful film. It isn't simply the gratuitous singing, which is endemic to the form, or the appalling sentimentality of the characters, which I might have predicted, or even that I'm asked to believe that a guy with seven children could be happy instead of insane, even were he not on the run from the Nazis—which, as you'll recall, he is. No, the problem runs much deeper, and it is this: *The Sound of Music* is an expression of my own values. First, there is an emphasis upon the centrality, resilience, and importance of family, which is a principle I hold dear. Then there is, in the romance plot, an assertion of the power of love to pull down interpersonal barriers, including those related to class. This too I believe. And the good guys in this movie seem to feel that the Nazis are bad guys, which I have no difficulty going along with.

But what is the core value at the true heart of this film? It is the protagonist's deep love of nature. You'll recall that the Julie Andrews character, Maria (soon to become Mrs. Maria von Trapp), is from the beginning an irresponsible and negligent nun in training who fails miserably at her religious duties. Why? Because she is so busy spinning around flowery mountaintops in implausibly orgasmic nature reveries. Here we recognize the oldest of the tricks in the book written by Wordsworth and Coleridge, Beethoven and Schubert, Bierstadt and Cole, Emerson and Thoreau: indulge orthodox rejoicing and piety, but while your parents aren't looking just swap out the divinity of God for the divinity of nature. Maria isn't a bad nun. She is a good transcendentalist. She believes deeply in grace and in the divine, but for her the locus of divinity is the Alps rather than the abbey. So moved is she by nature that, well, damn it, she just has to "climb every mountain." And she's none too quiet about it.

If this film reflects so many of my own values, why then do I find it intolerable? You know that feeling that comes over you when you discover that some bloviating asshat is a huge fan of your favorite baseball team or an ardent admirer of your favorite band—when the purity of your ineffable love for something is sullied because it must be shared with an obnoxious knothead? *The Sound of Music* is so incredibly trite that I can't help but resent its superficial dramatization of my own beliefs—particularly my core faith in the spiritual value of nature. Is this how I appear to others, a self-indulgent, dirt-worshipping, gushy, feeble-witted tree hugger who twirls around in fields bursting forth in earth-loving song?

Inspired by their immoderate affection for Maria, Hannah and Caroline propose that we climb our local hill and reenact the opening scene of *The Sound of Music*. As a man who despises musicals and is deeply suspicious of Chautauquans, Civil War reenactors, and department store Santas—all of whom I consider not only counterfeits but also drunkards and pedophiles—I am a poor choice for this mission. But here's the thing: I'm their dad. Among the many blessings of being the father of daughters is the constant opportunity to operate entirely outside my comfort zone. What choice do I have, especially after Eryn, with a wry smile, tells the girls how certain she is that Dad would *love* to be a part of this project? "Daddy even teaches film classes," she says enthusiastically. "I'm *sure* he can help you understand why this movie is so great!" This is my punishment for having married someone with a sense of humor, which now seems less charming than it did during our courtship.

"OK," I finally assent, "but if I help you reenact the 'hills are alive' scene, then I get to choose another scene that someday y'all will help *me* to reenact." When the girls agree, I reveal my choice: the scene in which the dad, a grumpy sea captain, imposes martial discipline upon his children, controlling their every behavior through a series of coded orders tooted out shrilly on a dog whistle. This promises to be a refreshing change from my usual domestic life, in which my agency has been reduced to running the chainsaw and hoisting IPAs.

As we screen the opening sequence of the film in order to observe every excruciating nuance of the "hills are alive" scene, I'm reminded that the movie begins with a montage of lovely establishing shots of the snowy Alps and verdant Salzkammergut foothills—helicopter shots that are plenty respectable for sixties cinema. Just as I begin to enjoy these rich images, however, the aerial camera makes the unhappy discovery of Julie Andrews doing those orgasmic hilltop pirouettes, after which she promptly destroys the moment by bursting into song. It is the kind of cinematic moment that, rescreened a few times, could make spies talk. I find it difficult not to fantasize about some way—*any* way—to make Julie stop. I imagine that the studio helicopter is in fact a helicopter gunship, its sweeping descent toward warbling Maria accompanied by the satisfying rat-a-tat-tat of machine gun strafing. Or perhaps that she might be skewered by the chopper skid, a chirruping Maria-kabob rising joyfully into the clouds. Maria's song, "The Sound of Music," turns out to be a kind of environmentalist anthem, replete with natural images including hills, birds, lakes, trees, breezes, brooks, and stones. The degree to which Oscar Hammerstein's gift as a lyricist has been exaggerated is made evident by the line in which Maria's heart wants to sing "like a lark who is learning to pray." This is a moment so insufferable that we ourselves might pray, along with the hapless lark, that Maria would just shut her von Trapp. But there it is again: my personal belief in the divinity of nature, being expressed in the most saccharine and clichéd manner possible. Of course Hannah and Caroline absolutely love it.

The girls and I make our plans for the reenactment, and Eryn costumes them to look suitably Maria-ish. I fill a day pack with snacks, water, and sunscreen, and we begin our afternoon ascent of Moonrise, the nearby hill that we've so named because it's an especially fine spot from which to watch the rising moon on summer nights. These Great Basin foothills could not be more different from the lush hills of the film's Austrian Alps. Here we push through high desert scrub, including thorny desert peach and scratchy bitterbrush, an unbroken carpet of big sage and rabbitbrush rolling out before us to the distant horizon. It is a desiccated and brown landscape in which we must guard against sunstroke, dehydration, and Great Basin rattlesnakes, which are common on the rocky slopes of Moonrise. Here are no babbling brooks to meditate beside, no azure lakes into which to dip our oars, no trees to stroll romantically beneath, no emerald grass to loll upon.

Nothing here is green, save for the yellowish green of an ephedra bush here and there. The glare of the high-elevation sun is intense as we push up the dusty slope of Moonrise and into the hot blast of the Washoe Zephyr. This is not the land of the Claude glass but rather the land of the emergency signal mirror—not a place for twirling but rather for hunkering down in order to survive.

Wallace Stegner wisely observed that we need to "get over the color green." "You have to quit associating beauty with gardens and lawns," he admonished. Stegner realized that our fantasy landscape remains closer to that of *The Sound of Music* than to the austere geophysical reality of the arid West and that this aesthetic preference has environmental consequences that are all too real. My girls have been raised in this open, windy desert, and they know instinctively that its power lies precisely in its gorgeous starkness, in its effortless resistance to our intentions. This land is sublimely inhospitable, and its grandeur inspires a humility that is the greatest gift it has to offer. Stegner was right. Until we get over the color green we'll remain doomed to view the West through a Claude glass of our own imaginative construction. We'll continue to see the world indirectly, artificially framed, color shifted to conform to an environmental aesthetic that is disconnected from the visceral reality of this astonishing place. Here in the western Great Basin, green is the color of the lawns that don't belong and the money that buys the vanishing water that keeps them that way. The high desert is not the green world of the Austrian Alps, but neither was it meant to be. This is our home landscape, and to us it is far more beautiful than the Alps could ever be.

On the way up Moonrise I ask little Caroline what her favorite part of *The Sound of Music* is. Without hesitating she replies, "I like the part with those bad guys, Daddy. What are they called again?"

"Nazis," Hannah replies.

I cringe. This is the same kid who, during our earlier reenactment of scenes from *The Wizard of Oz*, insisted upon playing the role of one of the terrifying flying monkeys, even in scenes where they had no credible reason to appear. Hoping to shift the conversation, I ask Hannah what her favorite part is.

"I like Liesl the best, especially when she's singing in the rain."

I wince again. The scene Hannah has in mind depicts the courting of Liesl, the eldest von Trapp daughter, by an Aryan messenger boy named Rolfe—a scene in which Liesl croons the insipid teen anthem "Sixteen Going on Seventeen." This awful ditty includes the girl singing sweetly to her Hitler wannabe beau: "I need someone older and wiser, / Telling me what to do." As the father of daughters, this is not the sort of thing I want to hear. I note that this antifeminist narrative isn't much of an improvement over Hannah's favorite kid flick, Disney's *The Little Mermaid*, in which a mermaid girl—basically an aquatic Liesl—disobeys her father, leaves her home place, and relinquishes her own voice, all in order to be with a guy just because he's human.

"Hannah, do me a favor," I implore. "When you're sixteen

going on seventeen, remember that *I* am the one who is older and wiser. Not some boy, *me*! And don't forget that charming Rolfe ends up joining the Nazis."

"Right," interjects little Caroline. "Nazis!"

At last we reach the summit of Moonrise, where we pause in the shade of a granite palisade to hydrate and snack. We are well above 6,000 feet now, and the cloudless cobalt sky shimmers as it can only here in the high desert. The scat of pronghorn and coyote are nearby, and the faint tracks of black-tailed jackrabbits, and some orange lichen that has eked out a living in a fissure in the rock. Once rested, we choose the site for our reenactment, and I clamber up into the cliffs above in order to approximate the film's memorable high-angle opening shot. The girls are down below, practicing their lyrics and poised to pirouette. They look adorable in their corny dresses and makeshift aprons. At last I yell, "*Action!*" and they begin to twirl like crazy, stumbling a little over the rocks, bumping into each other and also into the sage and rabbitbrush. I catch a word here and there as the hot wind sweeps their song away toward Utah. The sere, brown land is treeless and flowerless. In the viewfinder of my camera I frame the little stars of my own life story, spinning in their mountaintop reverie. They are laughing, and dancing, and singing, right here, in this place, among the rattlers and scorpions. It is, I admit to myself, a strange and wonderful kind of musical. In the glare of the high desert sun and the sweep of the scorching wind, the irony of the reenactment suddenly dissipates, and I feel a rush of genuine sentiment. My little girls are dancing in their home hills, and the hills are alive.

Chapter 12

Fire on the
Mountain

Here in the remote western Great Basin Desert we dwell as guests
in the house of fire. Of course wildfire has helped to shape most natural landscapes, but that fact is easy to forget in urban and suburban
settings, while out on this wildlands interface the presence of fire is
tangible. From the windows of our home we look out over open desert that is dotted green with Utah juniper trees but also dotted gray
and black with the charred snags of junipers that have been consumed by flames. We see fire-protected, rocky spots with immense,
seven-foot-tall sagebrush, while other areas have burned over so
recently as to harbor only the sprigs of bunchgrasses, rabbitbrush,
desert peach, gooseberry, bitter cherry, ephedra, and balsamroot. Fire

visits our area almost every summer, and the vibrant mosaic of trees, plants, grasses, and flowers visible on the distant hillsides has in fact been produced by flames. Because its presence on the land is so conspicuous, we tend to think of fire as a neighbor—albeit a neighbor who, like rattlesnake and mountain lion, is deserving of immense respect.

As a parent I've worked deliberately to avoid demonizing fire, just as I've resisted misinformed violence toward maligned endemic species like rattlers and scorpions. Hannah and Caroline understand that this desert place was the residence of coyote, buzzworm, and wildfire long before we chose to make our home here. The girls have come to appreciate these neighbors—to offer respect by giving them a wide berth, but also to learn about them, and never to encounter them with the irrational fear that too often characterizes human relationships with the desert environment and its creatures. I hope this desert will teach my daughters to accept that we are subject to natural forces larger than ourselves and often beyond our control, since it is the humility inspired by that awareness that helps lead us from a blind assumption of dominance toward an enriching imagination of reciprocity with the natural world.

We are fortunate that the desert we inhabit has been sculpted by fire. In a normal fire regime, low-intensity ground fires have substantial ecological benefits. These fires often wipe out invasive plants that compete with fire-evolved natives, and they help to balance the populations of many insects. Their passage opens the way for the growth of grasses and forbs that provide excellent forage for mule deer, pronghorn, and many other animals. The ashes they produce add nutrients to the soil, and there are even species of trees and plants that are unable to reproduce without fire. Unless the land has been excessively degraded by destructive forces such as road building, overgrazing, or previous colonization by invasive exotic plants, the presence of fire tends to catalyze biodiversity and improve ecosystemic health. The fire history revealed by dendrochronology suggests that in a natural fire regime the wildfire cycle here might be as short as twenty or twenty-five years. The northern Great Basin sagebrush steppe is a biome that needs its fire.

Knowing that we are fire's neighbors, we've made extensive preparations for cohabitation. We've designed and built a wildfire-resistant home with a stucco exterior and concrete tile roof, and we've sited our propane tank far from the house and away from trees. We've done extensive fuels-reduction work on our property, engaging in the kind of thinning performed by fire while also decreasing the fuel load available for combustion when the flames do come. We maintain firebreaks and defensible space, and we've landscaped with native plants chosen for their resistance to fire. We've installed freestanding hose bibs on all sides of our home site, and we have a propane generator that can be used to run the well pump and thus provide water to fight a ground fire even if the electricity has been lost (or cut, which often occurs during fires). We've laid out our long driveway with wide turns and a loop up near the house to facilitate access by emergency vehicles. We've even made sure that down at the gravel road our address numbers, which are reflective, are mounted on a noncombustible post. We've done all this because out here we are so far away from help that we can't afford to count on good luck. In our years on this remote hill we've witnessed dozens of fires, and twice we've been evacuated while emergency crews occupied the firebreaks that we maintain with such vigilance. Someday wildfire will return to our home hill, and it is our responsibility to prepare for that day while also respecting fire's ecological value and resisting the urge to view it through the distorted lens of fear.

Ecologists employ the paired concepts of resistance and resilience to understand and describe the effects of environmental disturbance. *Resistance* refers to the capacity of an ecosystem to *retain* its essential structure and functioning despite stressors, which might come in the form of extreme weather, invasive species, human activity, or wildfire; *resilience* describes the capacity of the ecosystem to *regain* its essential structure and functioning once altered by a disturbance, like wildfire. In other words, we should take care not to compromise the health of this desert ecosystem, because its well-being is essential to its ability to withstand and recover from environmental stress. The concepts of resistance and resilience are helpful to us in imagining our own lives as well. If we remain healthy, we're better able to resist illness and disease; in the unfortunate event that by some accident we are overwhelmed by a major environmental stress, our chances of being sufficiently resilient to restore ourselves to health are vastly improved.

When the smoke alarm went off upstairs, Hannah and Caroline had already been asleep for an hour or so, snuggled in their bunk beds in their shared bedroom on the ground floor of the house. Eryn and I were sitting on the stone hearth, enjoying one drink before the warmth of the wood stove, talking over our day and sharing that sweet, brief calm that comes to parents after their children are asleep and before they have themselves succumbed to the day's fatigues. It was Valentine's eve (which happened to be Ash Wednesday), and we had just finished cleaning up from helping the girls make their Valentine's cards, which they would give to their friends at school the following day.

"Here we go again," I said in exasperation, taking one more sip of rye before setting the tumbler down to go deal with the problem.

"I'll check on the girls in case the noise wakes them," Eryn said.

"Thanks," I replied. "I'll get the ladder and see which one it is this time." I had yet to make it through a full year without an alarm going rogue, and while the problem was usually solved with a fresh nine-volt battery, I had also replaced several of the devices that simply wouldn't keep quiet. As I headed down the hall to fetch the stepladder from the garage, I felt certain this was another false alarm—until a second alarm also began to sound from upstairs.

I paused for a single moment before turning on my heel and sprinting down the hall to the stairs, which I took three at a time as I raced up to my scribble den. Although I smelled no smoke, the two alarms continued to blare convincingly in an echoing, alternating rhythm, as if synchronized. As I grabbed the doorjamb and swung myself around the corner and into the room, my eyes went first to my writing table, where my laptop sat open, surrounded by stacks of papers important to the book project I had been working on that afternoon. Beneath the table were piled boxes full of books, notes, papers, and manuscripts associated with the various other projects I had finished in recent years or hoped to write in the years to come. My eyes then shifted a few feet to the left of my writing table. There I saw bright orange and yellow flames several feet high blasting up through a sizable hole in the floor.

The physiology of alarm is not easily translated into words. For a single instant I felt as if the air had been sucked from my collapsed lungs, while my legs had suddenly turned to molten rubber and my mouth was filled with a nauseating metallic taste. And then the adrenaline rush hit with such intensity that it felt as if my body had been struck by lightning from the inside. My breathing suddenly quickened, and I could feel my pulse pounding in my neck and my heart hammering in my ribs. It was then that I smelled the smoke.

"*Eryn, this is for real! Call 911 and get the girls out, NOW!*" I yelled down the stairs. Over the blaring of what were now at least three smoke alarms, I heard her acknowledge me, and I caught a glimpse of her running down the hall toward the girls' bedroom. Turning back into the study, I grabbed the fire extinguisher from the top of a nearby bookshelf, yanked the pin as I ran across the room, and unloaded the extinguisher's contents into the flaming hole in the floor. As I sprayed the foamy fire retardant the flames disappeared, and for a brief, hopeful moment I imagined that the situation was under my control. The instant the extinguisher ran empty, however, the flames shot back up out of the hole, as if I had done nothing at all to discourage the fire. I then scrambled over to the upstairs bathroom, where I removed a second extinguisher from beneath the sink, ran back to the study, and repeated my efforts. Once again the flames vanished only while the retardant was flying, immediately surging back out of the hole as the extinguisher ran dry. It was now clear that the fire was intense and that it was burning within the floor beneath me.

I sprinted down the stairs and then down the hall and into the garage, hitting the garage door button as I dashed out. I grabbed an orange five-gallon bucket from the garage floor, ran to my workbench, and lifted the large fire extinguisher I keep there into the bucket, which I left sitting on the bench. I then jumped into my pickup, started it, and backed out onto the gravel driveway. I jammed it into park, threw open the door, and jumped out.

"*Eryn?*" I called loudly.

"We're out front!" she replied, from around the corner of the house.

"The truck is running here—come get the girls off the hill!"

"Where's the puppy?" she hollered back.

"No time! Get off the hill *now!*" I shouted, dashing back into the garage before I could catch a glimpse of Eryn, Hannah, or Caroline.

Barely breaking stride, I grabbed the plastic grip on the wire handle of the bucket, swung it off the workbench, and ran into the kitchen, leaving the door open behind me. I retrieved a small fire extinguisher from beneath the kitchen sink and tossed it into the bucket. I then sprinted with my bucket to the hearth, where I kept another extinguisher near the kindling rack. As I crossed the living room in a rush to the hearth, I had a strange experience. The fight-or-flight dump of dopamine from my exploding adrenal glands had produced the odd effect of time slowing down, and so even as I worked frenetically, I had bizarre moments in which it seemed that I had paused to engage in leisurely contemplation of a particular image or sensation. Now, as I sprinted across the room, I noticed Eryn's half-full wineglass and her cell phone and my rye tumbler sitting placidly on the stone, as if nothing were amiss. Behind the glass doors of the wood stove lapped our lovely little fire, just as before. The scene looked cozy, and although the thought must have taken only a millisecond to register in my racing mind, I reflected on how strange it was that the fire behind the glass appeared so controlled while just upstairs burned a sister fire that was fierce. This protracted moment of slow-motion perceptual intensity was so dreamlike that it caused me to wonder if I might awaken to discover that this strange fire had been ignited only within the wildness of a dream.

I snatched the extinguisher from the hearth, added it to the bucket, and ran back upstairs with my load. Although I had been gone only a short time, the situation upstairs had grown a good deal worse. The hole in the floor had at least doubled in size, and the flames too had increased, now leaping three or four feet out of the burning floor. Worse still, the room had begun to fill with smoke, and while visibility was decent at eye level, the ceiling was now a wall-to-wall mat of thick smoke. I set the bucket down and lowered myself to one knee next to my writing table, hoping to achieve a low angle that might allow me to blast retardant further up under the floor, toward the unseen source of the flames. I emptied one extinguisher into the flaming hole, and then the second, and finally the third. Each time the flames retreated as the foam splattered into the hole; each time the fire flared up the instant the extinguisher was emptied.

It was clear from the five empty extinguisher canisters and the increasingly intense flames rising toward the ceiling that the fire was raging hot and fast within the floor. I now began to realize, for the first time, that it was entirely possible our home would burn to the ground. The fate of the house would be determined by the outcome of a race between the fire and the people who, unlike me, have the skill and equipment to fight it—people who, because of the remoteness of our home, are a very long way away when you need them most. All I could do was try to slow the spread of the fire, buying precious time until help arrived.

Having exhausted all my extinguishers, I now ran with my empty bucket to the upstairs bathroom, where I slid open the glass shower door and turned the tub faucet on full blast. I jammed the empty bucket beneath it and watched as time once again slowed to a crawl. How long had I been fighting this fire? How long would it take for help to arrive? How many years before this bucket would fill with water—water that fell as if it were a viscous plasma, with a slowness that made me question whether the law of gravity had been repealed? In the eternity it took for that bucket to fill I kept hearing, over and over, the percussion-driven rhythm of the Grateful

Dead surrounding Robert Hunter's provocative lyrics for "Fire on the Mountain":

> *Long distance runner, what you holdin' out for?*
> *Caught in slow motion in a dash for the door.*
> *The flame from your stage has now spread to the floor.*
> *You gave all you had, why you want to give more?*
> *The more that you give, the more it will take*
> *To the thin line beyond which you really can't fake.*
> *There's a fire . . . fire on the mountain.*

I finally lifted the bucket out half-full, left the water running, and ran back into the scribble den. Fearing the collapse of the burning floor, I didn't dare put my weight too close to the blazing, ever-expanding hole. Instead, I stood back and flung the contents of the bucket all over the floor in the general area of the flames. I then ran back and refilled the bucket, again dousing the room, but this time slamming water onto the walls as well as the floor, trying desperately to slow the spread of the fire.

It suddenly occurred to me that although the fire in the wood stove appeared small and controlled, it might somehow be contributing to the fire in the floor above. Filling the bucket a third time, I hauled it downstairs, threw open the wood stove door, and tossed the full bucket of water directly onto the coals and logs that were burning within the stove box. The dousing produced a loud hissing sound, audible even over the piercing blasts of every smoke alarm in the house, as an immense cloud of acrid, sulfurous, ashy smoke billowed from the wood stove and rose up the rock hearth to the ceiling.

I ran back upstairs and continued my bathroom-to-study shuttle run, splashing buckets of water onto the floor, carpets, cabinets, walls, and, eventually, even the stacks of boxes, books, and papers that comprised all of my writing projects. The full wisdom of my adrenaline-driven logic might be summarized this way: "Wet stuff doesn't burn, right?" As the room continued to fill with choking smoke, I finally noticed the flashing lights of emergency vehicles out in the distance, though their movement through the blackness of the desert seemed preternaturally slow. Encouraged by the prospect of help, I resumed my sprint-and-douse dash.

Finally, two firefighters arrived in my study. They were dressed in full battle regalia, complete with helmets, face shields, head-to-toe yellow fire suits, giant fireproof boots and gloves, and air masks with hoses that led to the oxygen tanks they wore on their backs. I was wearing old jeans, a Buddy Guy concert T-shirt, and broken-down trail running shoes. Worse still, I was standing in a flaming, smoke-filled room in a burning house holding a half-full bucket of water. Ignorant of the social protocol surrounding house fires, I wasn't sure if I should toss those last few gallons onto the fire or instead address the men. "Thanks for coming," I offered, sheepishly setting my little bucket down. "Can I do anything to help?"

"Sir, you need to evacuate this structure *immediately*," said one of the large yellow men, who seemed surprised to see me. He then spoke a string of commands into his walkie-talkie. It was clear that my shift was over. In a matter of moments our "home," which had already become a "structure," would be what emergency responders call a "fireground." Reaching the bottom of the stairs, I had to jump aside as three guys hauling fire hoses over their shoulders came rushing in the front door and charged upstairs into the smoke. As I stepped slowly out into the cold, carrying nothing at all, I was surprised at how many emergency vehicles had already arrived: a command car, two fire trucks, a water truck, and a sheriff's deputy car—and I could see more flashing red lights off in the distance.

I stood out in our firebreak, between patches of old snow, shivering in my T-shirt. I first looked west, in the direction I always imagined the fire would come from—the wildfire I had worked so hard to prepare for. Out there in the black depths of the open desert there was no fire save the stars ignited in the moonless sky. I then turned and looked back at our house, where the wild force of fire was traveling through the floors and perhaps also through the walls and ceilings. The power had been cut, but through the unshaded windows I could see the firefighters' headlamps, laser-like, slicing through the thick smoke as they worked in the murky darkness. I heard chainsaws revving and then droning while I caught glimpses of large yellow men cutting holes into the walls and ceilings as they chased fire through the bones of our home.

After what seemed a very long time, the fire captain came over to talk with me. When I asked if they could save the house, he answered only that they would do their best. I waited for a more hopeful prognostication, but none came. The visible flames were extinguished, he said, but the fire was still smoldering within the floors or walls, and they had not yet located it. This sort of fire could blow up quickly, he explained. I asked him about our pets—two dogs and a cat—and he reported that Darcy, our old dog, had been found cowering beneath the water truck, but that the puppy, Beauregard, and Lucy the cat had not been seen either inside or outside the house.

At some point my father arrived, and the two of us stood together in the cold, staring at the house, watching firefighters rush in and out, listening to the sound of chainsaws, receiving no assurances. My dad was the primary designer of our passive solar house, and he worked tirelessly as our general contractor when it was built. It was as efficient, creative, and beautiful a home as any desert rat could ever hope for—the result of a multigenerational collaboration in which every member of our family was deeply and personally invested. Hannah was an infant when we brought her to this place, and it has been Caroline's only home. This was the place where we had built our shared life together—the place our stories came from. And now, as we stood silently out in the cold, thick smoke billowed from beneath all sides of the roof.

While I was battling the fire on my own, Eryn was making sure the girls were safe. Hearing me shout from upstairs, Eryn called 911 and reported the emergency. She then dropped her phone on the hearth and ran to the kids' bedroom, where both girls were sound asleep despite the blaring smoke alarms. She first woke Caroline and instructed her to "give Mommy your best monkey hug," a neat trick by which Caroline can hold on to you with the vice grip of her muscular little legs. With Caroline firmly attached, she then woke Hannah, took her by the hand, and led the girls quickly out of the house, where she sat them on a railroad-tie wall out in the cold February night. Now having a moment to gather herself, Eryn realized that the girls were barefoot and wearing nothing but their pajamas. She told Hannah to put her arm around Caroline and under no circumstances to go back into the house.

"I am coming back, but you two stay together no matter what. And don't come back into the house. That's your job," she told them. Then Eryn dashed back into the girls' bedroom, pulling their robes off the dragonfly-shaped hook on the back of their door and snatching the first shoes she could grab from the closet, which turned out to be the two little pairs of bright green cowgirl boots we'd bought for Hannah and Caroline on our last family expedition across the Great Basin.

Although Eryn had been gone only moments, by the time she ran back outside Caroline was scared and upset, and Hannah was hugging her little sister and comforting her. Caroline is fortunate to have such a caring, loving big sister. After all, the girls had gone from a deep sleep to being awakened to the sound of alarms and hauled out into the dark night without so much as putting their shoes on. They were disoriented and cold. They didn't know where their dad was.

When I appeared with the truck, Eryn brought the girls around the corner of the house in their green cowgirl boots and red bathrobes and piled them into the idling pickup. She then drove down our dark, muddy, half-mile-long driveway, fielding a battery of fearful questions from the girls. What was going on in the house? Why wasn't Daddy coming with us? Was he going to be OK? Eryn's answer to all these questions was to say, over and over and with great confidence, "Dad always knows what to do."

When Eryn reached the bottom of the driveway, she jumped out and propped open our green farm gate with a rebar stake. Then she drove out onto the gravel road, spun the truck around, and backed it up so as to face the road and be just beyond our driveway—a position from which she intended to direct emergency vehicles. During the long wait for help to arrive, she realized that she didn't have her phone, or her glasses, or any warm clothes, or anything at all for the girls to read or play with. And there they sat, with the truck running and the heater blowing, headlights tunneling into the darkness, waiting in the breathless silence of the desert night. The remote location of our house and the hilly topography in which it is nestled prevented her from seeing our place or hearing anything from it, and because she had no way of knowing what might be happening up on the hill—except to know that I was there alone and that there was a fire—it was an agonizing wait.

It was during that lonely, frightening eternity in the truck, waiting for help and knowing nothing, that Eryn gave the girls a gift she has also given me: a magnificent strength born of love. Her courage and poise calmed Hannah and Caroline, helping them navigate this difficult and chaotic experience. As Eryn hugged the girls on the old truck's bench seat, she explained to them that some people would be driving out to help up at the house and that the first one to spot the flashing lights would be allowed to honk the truck horn to greet the helpers. Then she turned on the radio and suggested a family sing-along, which she used to buy time between repeating, in response to Hannah's worried questions, that "Dad always knows what to do."

At last the girls spotted the distant flashing red lights of an emergency vehicle barreling up the gravel road. Eryn declared the competition a tie and told the girls that they could both honk the truck's horn as soon as she started waving a friendly hello to the helpers. Then Eryn climbed out of the truck and stood in the middle of the road, in the middle of the desert, in the middle of the night, and flagged the fire truck with a "friendly wave" that was actually a desperate gesture toward the mouth of our driveway, into which the truck sped without slowing down. Climbing back into the pickup, she then told the girls that it would be important to greet every vehicle in just that way and also to observe the number and types of vehicles so they could report to me later exactly what they had seen. Caroline was especially enthusiastic about the game, and so Eryn and the girls repeated their honking and waving another half-dozen times over the next half hour.

Soon, however, the eerie silence fell once again, and while many emergency vehicles had raced up to the house, none had come back down. The last of the vehicles to arrive looked to Eryn like an ambulance, which redoubled her concern. Because she had no phone, could not leave the girls, and did not want to expose them to whatever emergency operations might be going on at the house, she was once again stranded in the dark without support or information.

At only six years of age and possessed of a naturally buoyant personality, Caroline had no trouble playing along with Eryn's games. Ten-year-old Hannah, however, was a great deal more worried, her concern fueled both by her greater understanding of the seriousness of what was happening and also by her naturally caring and fretful disposition. When Hannah began to cry again, Caroline jumped right in to help out.

"Hannahbug, don't worry. An awesome fireman came to my class, and he was a daddy too! It's all good. You can really trust these guys!" Then Caroline did something that was as remarkable as it was mundane, something that was quintessentially Caroline. First she retrieved my broken sunglasses from the side panel of the truck door—cheap shades I had shown her the previous day when one of the lenses popped out and couldn't be refitted—and put them on. Then she took a bright orange ice scraper from the same door panel. And then she threw her head back, curled her lip, transformed herself into a six-year-old Elvis, and began singing passionately into the ice scraper microphone: "You ain't nothin' but a hound dog / Cryin' all the time!" She rocked out until her big sister, still crying, also began to laugh. And once Hannah had laughed good and hard through her tears, Caroline concluded with a drawly "Thankyah, thankyah vury mush." Hannah had comforted Caroline out in the cold, and now her little sister was returning the favor in her own inimitable way. I still consider Caroline's cover of "Hound Dog," performed in my truck that night, to be one of the greatest acts of resistance and resilience imaginable. Although I did not even witness it, this is my most poignant memory from the night of the fire. It plays over and over in my mind, especially in times of stress. I have kept the broken sunglasses and orange ice scraper microphone to remind me of that moment, of its spontaneous, albeit transitory, triumph over circumstances beyond our control.

After another hour or hour and a half of waiting, a second sheriff's deputy rolled up. Eryn was able to flag the officer down and ask him to radio up to the site for information. He did so and reported that I was safe. In that moment Eryn cried for the first time that night. Soon afterward my mom and dad arrived. When Hannah asked why her grandparents were driving out here in the middle of the night, Eryn replied simply that "G and G always come when we need them." We later learned that a neighbor who picked up news of the incident on her police scanner had recognized our address and called my parents, who rushed out from town as quickly as they could.

"I see you girls will do anything to get a slumber party out of me," said my mother, coolly normalizing the situation for the girls. "Let's the four of us go back to town and have hot chocolate," she suggested.

"Great idea," added my father, with his signature calm. "You girls can sleep at our place while Grandpa goes up to check on things. I'll give your dad a lift to town."

It would be another three hours before the firefighters were satisfied that the fire they had chased through the bones of our house was fully extinguished. Thanks to their expertise and efforts, our home was saved. I used my father's phone to call Eryn, update her briefly, and tell her that we hoped to be back in town by daybreak. No, I hadn't been able to locate Lucy the cat, but I had found the puppy, Beau, far out in the desert and had put both dogs safely in the garage for what little remained of the night. I asked if there was anything she needed from the house.

"My phone and my glasses, if you can find them," Eryn replied. "That's not important," she added, "but please be sure to get the girls' valentines off the kitchen counter. They really want to give them out at school tomorrow."

The next morning, after dropping Hannah and Caroline off at school with their valentines and having discreet conversations with their teachers about what had happened, Eryn and I drove with my folks back out to the house to meet the insurance agent and fire inspector. By the time we arrived, the part of the scribble den floor that had not burned away had already been removed. There were large chainsawed holes in walls and ceilings throughout the upstairs and plenty of visible water damage, but the place didn't look as bad as I had feared it might. We even found Lucy the cat hiding behind the headboard of our bed, where she had weathered the fire's storm. Looking down through the missing floor of the scribble den to the room below felt odd, but all things considered, I found myself thinking that we might come out of this OK.

"This doesn't look so terrible," Eryn said to the insurance agent, hopefully. "What do you think?"

The woman hesitated, choosing her words carefully. "Look, I can see that you guys are coping. I think that's great, really. But at some point this whole thing is going to hit you. I just don't want you to be surprised."

As Eryn continued the conversation with the agent, I gained a better appreciation for what "this whole thing" would mean. Because of extensive smoke damage, every piece of electronics in the house—including the wristwatch I had worn while fighting the fire—would have to be thrown out. Any furniture not made of solid wood or tile would also have to go. Every inch of carpet would have to be replaced throughout the house, and the wood floors, which were water damaged, would have to be sanded and refinished. Every wall and ceiling would need to be scrubbed and repainted. Every piece of clothing and bedding would have to be professionally cleaned. Every single book would need to be hand wiped to remove fine ash and then treated in some kind of ozone chamber to remove the smell of smoke. Water damage had destroyed many of my papers and manuscripts. The items that didn't have to be either discarded or professionally cleaned, which were few, would be hauled away to storage during the many months it would take to complete reconstruction. As for reconstruction itself, most of the stone hearth wall would have to come down, as would the walls in the study and the room beneath it, neither of which would be safe to enter during reconstruction. The entire wood stove system would have to be replaced and substantial rewiring done in several rooms. The only room in the house that had escaped significant water and smoke damage was Hannah and Caroline's bedroom.

Before I could process this information, it was time for a debriefing with the fire inspector. Eryn and my mom continued talking with the agent while my dad and I went upstairs so the inspector could walk us through his findings.

"Your fire started here, under the floor," he said, pointing to a hypothetical spot in the immense hole that now gaped where floor struts had once run. "Then it spread laterally, along the joists. This was a true sill-to-sill burn," he added, showing us the charred ends of timbers adjacent to both the interior and exterior walls of the room. "The ignition source was associated with the wood stove system."

"A chimney fire?" my dad asked.

"Absolutely not. This is one of the safest stack and chase installations I've seen. And look at the condition of that pipe. No overheating there. The fire was caused by the wood stove system and started under the floor. Somewhere in the firebox or joint or pipe, there must have been a leak that released a small amount of heat that rose and gathered under the floor."

"Yeah, but I wasn't burning the stove hot last night. I've had it hotter hundreds of times. Besides, how could a little hot air start a fire?" I asked.

"It's more a matter of time than heat," he answered. "You burn this stove every night for four or five months a year for eight or ten years. Even if we're talking a pinhole, over time the timbers get so dried out that their combustion point is lowered. This fire wasn't caused by overburn in the stove. Just a straw-that-broke-the-camel's-back situation."

"What about the leak, this pinhole? Can you tell where it was or what caused it?" I asked.

"Nope, we'll never know. That's what I'm putting in my report. That we'll never know."

"*Never know?*" I asked in mild frustration.

"Listen," he said, with a hint of sternness in his voice, "I'm a forensic fire specialist, and I've been doing this for a lot of years. If there was a way to know I'd know. It was just bad luck."

"So if nothing could have been done to keep this from happening, it could happen again?" I asked.

"That's right, but this sort of fire is very rare. It's a million-to-one chance," replied the inspector.

"It was a million-to-one chance this time too, right?" I asked.

"That's right," the inspector replied. Then he hesitated for a moment before looking directly at me. "I hear you stayed on the fireground."

"Yeah. Me and a couple of dinky extinguishers and a bucket. Doubt it did any good."

"You see that," he said, pointing to a massive post that had charring within a foot of it. "What does that hold up?"

"Everything," said my father.

"Right, *everything*," repeated the man. "The entire structure of both roofs. That post burns, the whole place comes down. You got more water on this than you might think. Clear signs that you cooled and slowed it. It didn't hurt that you've got so much blown-in insulation in this floor—that helped slow it too. But no question that what you did here saved the house."

A few minutes later I walked outside with the inspector, shook his hand, and thanked him for his time. Before he climbed into his truck I wanted to say one more thing.

"It's bothering me that this was just some kind of bad luck that I can't do anything to control. I mean, if it happened before, it could happen again, or something like it." I paused, searching for words. "I've got kids."

"Yeah," he said, in a tone of genuine sympathy. "I know." Then he climbed into his truck and pulled its door shut. He looked at me through the partially opened window, as if it was he who now had something to say but wasn't sure he wanted to say it.

"Look," he continued. "I said that you saved your place. You did. But you shouldn't have. You know how often a civilian is killed in a house fire in this country? I do, because I've seen it. Every two hours and forty-two minutes. That's 24-7, 365, no time off for holidays." Then he started his truck and drove away.

The experience of a traumatic event can result in a variety of stress-induced symptoms, among which are memory loss, flashbacks, and increased worry about the safety of loved ones. But the most fascinating in a long list of stress effects from trauma is fragmentation, which is produced by the inability to tell the story of a distressing event. This incapacity to narrate the experience may be caused by any number of factors, including a desire to avoid painful recollections, an inability to discern meaning in the event, a concern about judgment from others, or an uncertainty about how to represent oneself in the retelling. But in our inability to tell a story—in our fear that we may get the story wrong, or that we might misinterpret its significance, or that its telling will cause us to reexperience a painful event—we risk allowing the story to tell us.

Of course my retelling of what Eryn and the girls went through while I was fighting the fire is a narrative reconstruction. After all, I wasn't with them. But I must explain that the story of what I experienced while fighting the fire is also a reconstruction, one that has been halting and uncertain and that remains unfinished.

In the wake of the fire I remembered little of what had happened during it, and so I've had to resort to physical evidence and to other people's accounts to reconstruct what actually happened that night. I have indelibly sharp memories of certain things: my first glimpse of the flames leaping out of a hole in the floor, the cozy look of our hearth as I passed it in full sprint, the bizarre sluggishness with which water fell from the tub faucet into the bucket. I remember with odd lucidity the sensation of the smooth plastic grip of the bucket handle in my fist, but I do not remember how it came to be there. Because I must have retrieved the bucket from the garage, that is what I have told you I did. The truth is that I do not know how it came to be in my hand. Perhaps it was given to me by an angel or by a ghost. I know what happened that night only in the way we know black holes—by the meticulous extrapolation of data that remain unverifiable by direct observation. I do not know about the fire in the same sense that I know about things I remember.

During the three years that have passed since the fire, pieces of that night have come back to me, a flash here and a flash there, vanishingly thin, crescent-moon slivers of memory often accompanied by powerful emotion. These memories do not arrive in either priority or temporal order. Rather, they are loose pieces of a jumble, fragments that emerge randomly from the bottomless black box of my brain. And many things remain shrouded in the mystery of blackout. To this day I have no memory of pulling my truck out of the garage or telling Eryn to get the girls into it and off the hill. I learned this part of the story from her later, when she also confessed her fear in that moment. "What if that had been the last time I ever saw you, Bubba?" she asks. It is a question I cannot answer and do not try to. When I later discovered five spent fire extinguisher canisters on the floor of my burned-over scribble den—several of which lay beneath the writing table that held my laptop, which was utterly destroyed by heat, smoke, and ash—I wondered how they came to rest there. I had a memory of using two extinguishers, not five, yet there they were. I recall hurling buckets of water many times but only remember filling the bucket once, and I couldn't say whether I ran my alarm shuttle ten times or a hundred. Nor do I recollect the number or type of emergency vehicles that had arrived at my burning house by the time I walked out of it. That is information I recovered from the girls' close observations. The story I have told you is in fact a composite narrative and a reconstruction. If it remains conjectural and elliptical, it is nevertheless as accurate as I am able to make it.

This partial memory loss has been disquieting, but also disorienting has been the fact that my memories of this important event are not only fragmentary but also disjointed, wrenched from the usual calibration of temporal flow. Some things that occurred within seconds in real time still feel to me as if they took much longer, while other events that took hours feel as if they were almost instantaneous. For example, I had guessed the emergency vehicle response time at well over an hour until I was informed that in real time it was only twenty-six minutes. In my memory my father was with me from the time I walked out of the house, while in real time he did not arrive until much later. This experience, and my difficult attempt to recover it, has introduced me to a concept of time that is disturbingly elastic, subjective, and unreliable. For me, "real time" is considerably less real than it once was.

Even more disturbing is the way the fire has challenged my sense of myself as a father. I love my children more than life, and I hope always to be their protector. I want to remove risk of harm from my daughters' home environment. And I want to believe that when a bad thing does happen, I can arrive at an explanation that doesn't resort to terms like "bad luck" or "one in a million." The fire statistics I later read suggest that, on average, one child in the United States dies in a house fire every single day. Behind that cold statistic is someone's son or daughter, somebody's Hannah or Caroline. Well, sure, we might think, but how likely is it that something like that would happen to *me*? I now understand that this question of probability is the wrong one to ask. I can recall a time when one-in-a-million odds of danger sounded reassuring. That's no longer the case.

If, through no fault of my own, my children's lives can be put at risk by some unidentifiable, inexplicable pinhole, how then am I to keep them safe in this troubled and dangerous world? I understand rattlers and scorpions, blizzards and flash floods, and even wildfires, but I have no battle plan for pinholes—no certainty that I can protect my girls from harm in a universe whose fabric is shot through with invisible, long-odds hazards against which no amount of preparation will ever be sufficient. I feel the prick of those pinholes all around me. But what threat should I throw my little bucket of water on next?

I've called parenting an art of improvisation. Much of the ad-libbing we do involves telling our children that everything is going to be fine when we haven't the slightest idea whether it will be fine or not. This "fake it 'til you make it" aspect of being a parent is imperative, because nothing is more important to a child than reassurance. But the poignancy of our sanguine assertions of security weighs more heavily on me than it once did, because my sense of our perpetual vulnerability is now so visceral. How are we to assure our children that we can keep them safe in a world of perils when there is so much evidence to the contrary? Eryn told the girls that "Dad always knows what to do," and it was exactly the right thing for her to have told them in that moment of crisis. But Dad did not have everything under control. Far from it. I was being humbled by the unbridled wildness of fire.

It may be because our memories of traumatic events are so unreliable that writing is widely acknowledged to be an effective technique in the treatment of stress-induced trauma. Beginning with groundbreaking work in the late 1980s, hundreds of studies have investigated the positive health effects of writing about emotionally difficult experiences. Widely replicated and validated, the results of these studies show clearly that the health benefits of this kind of writing are not only psychological but also physical. Blood tests employed in this research show that those who write about their traumatic experiences develop stronger immune systems, and other tracking data show that these writers feel less pain, use fewer medications, require fewer trips to the doctor, and function better in the daily tasks associated with their roles as workers, spouses, and parents. People who write about traumatic events are a great deal more resilient than are trauma victims who do not create a narrative of their experience.

Although the health benefits of writing about trauma are well established, the underlying mechanisms that make this writing so effective remain uncertain. Some researchers posit that writing allows people a safe distance from which to consider and process their most stressful experiences. Others believe that making an event into a story transforms experience into something that can then be let go of. It is also likely that writing triggers a creative form of imaginative reexperiencing, one that, unlike the traumatic event itself, remains under the writer's control. Whatever the reason, we do know that therapeutic writing is effective in relieving trauma-induced stress and that stress correlates strongly with a wide range of health problems.

The novelist John Berger's incisive observation that the work of a writer is "to struggle to give meaning to experience" has special importance when the experience is a traumatic one. And yet the struggle to make sense—perhaps even to make art—of a difficult experience is foundational to the work of any storyteller. Aren't our lives always elliptical, our memories partial, the ultimate significance of our days uncertain? That is the adventure of experience, its beauty and its mystery. I can testify that fire, which has shaped our home landscape, has now also shaped me. And while I still buck, split, and haul the fuelwood that warms our home, my complicated relationship with fire reminds me that we abide with a wildness that can never be fully comprehended. The story of this fire, like the story of a life, must ultimately remain a narrative reconstruction, however fastidiously it may be told.

As a writer myself, I believe the nearly magical positive health effects of narrating trauma must be related to the way telling a story naturally encourages us to wrest cohesion from the disparate, recalcitrant fragments of our life experience. To write is necessarily to fill in gaps where memory fails or information is missing, to reconcile inconsistent facts and impressions, to fabricate a discernible narrative arc, to weave a tale that expresses significance, or at least to craft a narrative artifact from which meaning might later be made.

Writing must also be performed in a specific voice, from a particular point of view, and thus represents an important choice on the part of the writer—a choice that the writer lacked while living through the event he or she now struggles to understand and represent. For even the teller of a true tale is a narrator, and every narrator must also be a character. Essential to the writer's work, then, are meaningful decisions about who we are and who we will become. I write not to report what has occurred but to transform what has occurred into a story that makes more sense to me than does reality, which I often find ambiguous and uninstructive. What scientists call "trauma writing" I simply call "writing."

So who, finally, is the protagonist of this fire story? He could be a man who was prepared for any eventuality, who evacuated his family safely, who owned five fire extinguishers and knew where to find them and how to use them. That is the resourceful narrator. Or he could be a courageous man, one who refused to flee in the face of danger, whose bravery saved his family's home. That is the heroic narrator. Then again he may be a man who views the outcome of the fire as a miracle, a blessing, an act of salvation perhaps associated with divine intervention. That is the faithful narrator. Alternatively, he could be a man overwhelmed by circumstances beyond his control, who was overcome by an unforeseen hazard, and who is now immobilized by fear. That is the powerless narrator. Or perhaps he is a hostile man who can neither forgive nor forget, who lashes out blindly at the injustice visited by fire upon his family. That is the angry narrator. Conversely, he may be a philosophical man, one who understands the universe to be comprised of a series of events that remain beyond human ken. That is the accepting narrator.

My narrator is only moderately resourceful, and if he is not quite weak, he is far from heroic. He is neither angry nor fully accepting. He places his faith in his family and in this hard desert and in other wild blessings unrecognizable to orthodoxy. But as the teller of my own tale I am empowered to choose who my narrator will be, and after a good deal of consideration of this important question I've finally made my decision. My narrator is . . . a narrator. The man in my story is one who somehow finds a way to tell it. He is a man who must turn an experience over slowly in his hands until he at last discovers the angle from which it shines. My narrator can braid a rope from sentences and cast it down to himself in a dark well of fire; he can climb to safety by grasping at the knots of his own words. I am crafting these sentences in the same scribble den where I encountered the wildness of fire within the sanctuary of home. I am remembering and transforming, braiding and knotting, climbing hand over hand, word by word, from the fire toward the light.

Hannah and Caroline, you are too young to read this unfinished fire story, but someday you will. And when you do, I want you to remember this: my narrator is above all and forever your father. The truth is that he is not a man who always knows what to do. But he will walk with you, beneath these gorgeous, flaming pinholes of light burning in the unknowable darkness of our high desert night.

The V.E.C.T.O.R.L.O.S.S. Project

During the winter of the big blizzard, Hannah was not yet six years old, while Caroline was just two. It was mid-January when the first storm hit, dumping nearly three feet of snow. Another foot fell a day later and almost as much again a few days after that. By the time the weather finally cleared, we were buried. Because we live so remotely, we enjoy no public maintenance of the terrible dirt road whose dead end leads to our home. Worse still is our own half-mile-long driveway, which is slick with perilous caliche mud whenever it isn't packed with snow and ice. Back in those days we had no tractor, and so a big winter storm meant staying put and waiting it out until a few sunny desert winter afternoons could render the driveway passable.

Anticipating the arrival of the first storm, we had parked our old pickup at the foot of the driveway down at the dirt road. If a sympathetic neighbor with heavy equipment cleared the road, allowing us to chain up and make it to town, we would simply hike the half mile up to our house for a day or two until our hilly, curvy driveway melted out enough to offer safe passage. To our surprise, however, a rare cold front settled in, and that day or two turned into a solid three weeks, during which every trip up and down the half-mile driveway had to be made on foot.

We became quite resourceful during those three unusual weeks. I snowshoed groceries up the hill in a backpack that I learned to load as quickly and safely as a store clerk packs a sack. I switched from beer to whiskey to reduce the haul weight of our supplies. When I had to come or go from the house before daybreak or after nightfall, I snowshoed by the beam of my headlamp, following the route of my own deepening tracks. If the snow became too icy, I resorted to strapping crampons onto my boots. When shuttling the kids, Eryn would often carry little Caroline in a backpack, while I pulled Hannah along in the girls' blue two-kid toboggan. Because I sometimes had to haul both girls up and down the hill myself, I devised a harness system by which their toboggan was connected by ropes to straps that I wore crossed over my chest and shoulders. Using this arrangement, I learned to walk in an entirely new way, leaning into the hill, driving hard with the toes of my boots and the tips of my ski poles as I pulled the girls the half mile up to the house each afternoon. In the mornings I reversed my route, using my harness and ropes to ease their sled down in front of me so as to keep it from schussing away. I soon became as adept as a plow horse, maintaining my rhythm and balance as I slid Hannah and Caroline down to the truck each morning and towed them up to the house every afternoon. For their part, the girls devised a system of their own: Caroline sat between Hannah's knees, with big sister's arms wrapped around her for a "seat belt."

We felt quite isolated during that time, when our home existed as a desert island floating high in a shoreless sea of snow. Huddled by the wood stove, with the electricity sometimes on and sometimes lost, Eryn and I wondered aloud when the sun would return. It was hard work hauling stove wood through the deep, wind-driven drifts, and each night my aching lower back reminded me that every loaf of bread and pint of rye, each library book and school project that came or went from the house, required an arduous trek. But what I remember most vividly from that time is how much fun we had with Hannah and Caroline, who were convinced that coming and going from home by toboggan was as good as life could get. The girls soon referred to me not as Dad but rather as Snow Donkey, and as the days turned into weeks they began to despair that warmer weather would deprive them of an experience that had become the highlight of their winter.

One afternoon, while I was grunting my way uphill with my giggling progeny in tow, Hannah offered a comment that captured the novelty of the entire three-week adventure. "I asked around at school today," she told me. "Do you know how many other kids get to start every day by sledding down a mountain? *None!*"

"You're right, Bug. This is pretty cool, isn't it?" I admitted. "Maybe we should do something special to make sure we never forget how fun this was. It's hard to imagine right now, but someday all this snow is going to be gone."

"How about if I show CC how to make a snow angel?" Hannah suggested.

"Bug, show me the angel!" Caroline replied, enthusiastically. With that Hannah took her little sister's hands, helped her up from the toboggan, and then plopped her down in a spot that, if not for several feet of snow, would have been in the middle of our driveway. There she splayed Caroline's snow-booted feet and mittened hands until the kid looked like a four-armed, bright purple starfish. Then she helped Caroline to flap her arms and legs up and down in the snow, after which Caroline took over and did plenty of energetic flapping of her own. There was laughter all around, and when Hannah and I each grabbed a mitten and lifted Caroline back to her feet, we discovered that she had created a striking little work of snow art. Where her arms had flown, the snow did in fact resemble wings in motion, while the pattern left by her flailing legs impressed the snow with twin marks that looked like a pair of ringing Christmas bells.

Within a week the snow was gone and with it any visible sign of Caroline's angel. But if her snow art was short-lived, my recollection of it has not been. In the many years since that blizzard I have walked over the angel spot many hundreds of times, and I never pass it without reflecting on that beautiful winter's day and the small ritual of appreciation we devised to celebrate it. Caroline's snow art was ephemeral, but my memory of it is indelible. Every trace of her angel is gone, but the angel is not.

A storied landscape is one in which memorable associations have been forged between specific places and the meaningful experiences we've had in those places. Looking out across our home desert, I see layers upon layers of these associations—strata of rich experiences now so textured, so interwoven with the land, as to have created the fabric of a shared life. Here is where Hannah saw her first pronghorn. There is where fire crested the ridge. Here is where I discovered the paw prints of that wayward Sierra bear. There is where the redtail dropped a live rattlesnake from the cloudless sky. Here is the juniper where the great horned owls nested last year. There is the spot where Caroline became, for one cherished, unforgettable moment, an angel.

Take a moment to imagine the landscape you now inhabit or, alternatively, a treasured landscape from your past. What memories have you attached to that place? How has that place helped to shape the person you are today? How have your experiences there informed your way of seeing yourself, your family, the place itself? Now try this thought experiment. Imagine a landscape—every landscape—in which emotionally, intellectually, aesthetically, or spiritually significant vernacular experiences are geographically located, recorded, and commemorated. What might a place like that look like? How would our imagination of the landscape change if the small but vitally important events that happen to regular people every day were neither privatized nor erased but instead communally celebrated—memorialized in our conception of our local geography? "I was engaged to be married here, standing waist-deep with her in this snaky slough in the Fakahatchee swamp." "My sister had a life-changing realization there, under that broken-topped cottonwood tree across the arroyo." *You* had an intimation of mortality or immortality *there*, you fell in love, or perhaps you breathed your final breath right *here*—on *this* spot. Now go further: imagine a map of the world containing an individualized, place-based record of every important vernacular experience that has ever occurred. We, our people, our sons and daughters, were born here, somewhere, in a place. Someplace is where we experienced ineffable joy or grief; *some place*, a poignant, hidden place unmarked on every map. In the cartography of memory—the cartography of the spirit—our local landscapes are rich with such invisible associations.

Imagine from your childhood a place that is rich with layers of memory, experience, and imagination. This is not simply a place *where* things happened, it is a place *because* things happened—the events of perception, memory, and experience cause this place to glow forth from an otherwise undifferentiated quotidian geography. Even if they build a light-spewing Walmart on your place, would the place beneath it be any less hallowed? If we pave paradise and put up a parking lot, wouldn't you still care about the exact place where you were born, or fell in love, or where you will die, even if it were entombed in asphalt? Shouldn't we somehow mark the spots where we gave or received compassion—where we witnessed the triumph of the better angels of our own or a fellow traveler's nature? Some of us believe we should.

Allow me to briefly explain the inspiration, goals, and benefits of a new environmental and emotional global mapping project called v.e.c.t.o.r.l.o.s.s.—an acronym that stands for Vernacular Experiential Cartographic Traces on Regions, Landscapes, or Specific Sites. The project seeks to map—in both space and time, and both in narrative forms and through accurate Global Positioning System (GPS) coordinates—the precise locations of transformative vernacular experiences. Our project aims to significantly change how landscapes are mapped, described, and remembered, and it has the potential to influence not only the ways places are conceived, named, and marked but also how they are treated. At present, we are using seed grants to conduct a pilot version of the project.

Phase one of v.e.c.t.o.r.l.o.s.s. involves gathering significant place-based vernacular narratives, however brief or informal, accompanied by a set of GPS coordinates identifying the exact spot upon which the described event took place. In the project's second phase we construct precise maps of various scales depicting landscapes as they have been animated by potentially innumerable vernacular experiences. The third phase involves GPS-matrixed cartographic draping (to use the technical term), through which we generate experientially specific layers of mapped data that can be overlaid, like multiple transparencies, to allow for more sophisticated terrain visualizations. For example, here is a map of all the spots in the township of Washington Park (in Washington County, Washington) where people reported falling suddenly, hopelessly in love. Now we can "drape" over this love map any other data set— say, a map of all the places in the township where someone picked up a beautiful rock, or saw a ghost, or witnessed the sun break through the clouds in absolute majesty. The fourth phase requires that we project these draped data sets along an infinitely extended temporal axis. So here is a map of all the places in your town where someone now long gone experienced a transformative moment of inspiration or, conversely, a painful moment of religious doubt. As our data sets proliferate over time, we can successively drape onto this other maps depicting different sites and events in the same area over time. For example, we can overlay on the inspirational moment or religious doubt map an infinite number of other maps—say, maps of Native American geoglyph or of hidden veins of iron ore, of copper bootlegger kettles, or of the powdered bones of buried dogs.

We do not presently have adequate technology to achieve the fifth and final phase of the project, but we're confident that we soon will. This fifth phase is built upon the platform of all the accrued and draped vernacular event cartographies I've described—it is a kind of single meta-hyper-draped map—but also extends to include the record of all important events in the nonhuman natural world. Of course we can already map a fossil bed or earthquake fault, but we do not know the precise spot where, about ten thousand years ago, the last American cheetah crushed the skull of a pronghorn antelope in her jaws and filled her gut before lying down to die beneath the glowing light of the Pleiades. We know that this event did occur; we simply don't know precisely where and when. In its fullest articulation, this final phase of v.e.c.t.o.r.l.o.s.s. is so ambitious as to be difficult for some people to imagine. But who wouldn't want to know the location of the exact branch upon which the last passenger pigeon to survive in the wild built its nest?

If phase five sounds unrealistic, consider this: we've already mapped the imbricated labyrinth of the human genome. And we mapped the human genome because that's what we *wanted* to map. We made a choice about what to observe, record, and remember— just as every map is a mirror that reflects, in its scale, frame, and minutiae, the cartographer's values and sensibility, fears and dreams. Or consider that we have an excellent record—through written accounts, photographs, and video—of the precise spot on the particular tree where the ivory-billed woodpecker, long believed extinct, was once again sighted, thus bringing a momentary infusion of hope to the world. *That* place in the forest, at *that* moment on *that* day, can be located in space and time—it can and has been recorded—so as never to be forgotten. To map such a place in time is vitally important for spiritual as well as scientific reasons, for what would it say about us as a people if we simply forgot which tree it was or which day? What if we felled that tree and made ammunition crates from it because nobody bothered to remember?

Now simply extrapolate from this example. All that is required for the success of v.e.c.t.o.r.l.o.s.s. phase five is that we make a collective commitment to continue this sort of attentiveness for the next, say, ten thousand years, after which, if we have cared enough to notice, we should know the exact location of each sparrow's fall—of every flash of black and red and ivory that restores hope to the world—at least within the sphere of human observation. To extend our project's scope beyond the radically circumscribed sphere of human observation will be our children's work.

The v.e.c.t.o.r.l.o.s.s. pilot program involves the collection of what we call "vernacular witnessings," which are GPS-located narratives of meaningful personal experiences in place.

For example, here is vernacular witnessing number 780, received by text on October 14, 2014—and, of course, accompanied by accurate GPS coordinates: "I had just come off the flight after visiting my mother in LA. As I was going through the security gate a man in front of me began to stagger, and a woman—his wife, I'm sure—tried to hold him up, but he fell forward onto the floor, then rolled, clutching his chest and moaning. The poor woman was so scared, and she started screaming for help. I'll never forget the look of terror on her face. The security guards ran over and cleared people back, and the EMTs arrived quickly, lifted the man onto a stretcher, rushed through a security door to an ambulance that almost in a single motion pulled up, loaded the gurney in, and sped away. There was this odd silence for a few seconds. Then one of the guards bent down and picked up a pen that had fallen out of the man's breast pocket and slid it into his own breast pocket. After that they just started running everybody through again, and in less than a minute there was absolutely no trace of the man. I sat on a bench and tried to calm myself down. Anybody who got in that line even a minute later had no idea what had happened there, and by the end of the day thousands of people had stepped on the exact spot where his cheek had hit the floor. Maybe millions have stepped there by now. And I don't even know if he lived or died. Shouldn't there be a trace of him—some trace?"

And here is vernacular witnessing number 1270, received by e-mail with GPS coordinates on April 9, 2016. "My wife was pregnant with our first kid, and we were right around the due date when her water broke in the middle of the night. So I jump up and I'm tired and mixed up, like when you wake up from a weird dream and then realize you're still dreaming it. So I run around grabbing our stuff up, and then we head out the front door. It's real frosty outside. I turn on the porch light, and we start walking down the walk to the truck. In the eaves of our house, right over the walk, there's this swallow's nest—just mud and sticks and horsehair. Barn swallows. They've been there five years running and raised up a batch of young every year and two batches last year. Even though they crap on the walk I never wanted to chase them out—especially with those babies in there. So I'm walking to the truck to drive into town for my kid to get born, and as I'm walking a feather falls out of this nest, somehow, and it drifts down. Well, without changing my stride I just catch it in my hand and keep going. That next morning our daughter was born, and healthy. I know it sounds like a steaming pile of horseshit, but that's what happened. And that's *where* it happened—right there, between the front door and the truck, under that nest."

V.E.C.T.O.R.L.O.S.S. has already generated a number of provocative research questions that will guide the future of the project. Here are several of them:

QUESTION 1

What is the nature of vernacular experiential hot spots and clusters?
Our initial research suggests that an exhaustive analysis of any single geographical spot over time is extremely revealing. For example, as we gather more data and begin draping data set upon data set, map upon map, we find that certain places have been especially active loci of significant vernacular events. Even preliminary layered cartography reveals, for example, that in the past half century a variety of important events have occurred at one spot on a high bank above the north bend in the Washington Run River (near Washingtonville, Washington): thirty-seven people saw the full moon rise, twenty-two people had good ideas, twelve performed acts of kindness, eight people had sex (two of them for the first time), four wrote all or part of a song or poem, three children saw their first shooting stars, two couples were engaged to be married (though years later one of those couples decided, on the same spot, to divorce), and one pregnant woman went into labor. Yet comparable draped data sets for a similar bank on the next bend of the Washington Run reveal a sort of experiential wasteland. Here two day hikers contracted giar-

diasis, and one old fisherman caught a catfish that already had a hook in its mouth. Nothing more—at least so far.

Obviously, extending our analysis into the future might produce very different results. We hope that enriched data and increasingly sophisticated analysis will help us explain the nature of these mysterious vernacular hot spots within local landscapes. Once we have a complete map of these unusual places, we feel it would be appropriate to construct holographic memorials that convey the remarkable richness of these places over time. Obviously it will be necessary to develop and integrate mobile apps for use by the many who will make pilgrimages to these special places.

QUESTION 2

Is there also a vernacular landscape of missed opportunities?

On April 6, 1327, during "the first hour of the day," in one particular spot in the Church of St. Claire in Avignon, France, Francesco Petrarch cast his eyes upon Laura, a young woman whom he would never know but a mere glimpse of whose beauty would inspire in him a lifetime of radiant poems. On the one hand, this is obviously a transformative vernacular experience in a local landscape; on the other, it is also a poignant missed opportunity. While we have had good initial success gathering vernacular witnessings of events that did happen, we also seek a way to map those events that *didn't* happen—or, put otherwise, to chart events that might have occurred but did not.

Imagine a windy, dust-colored crossroads beneath a single power line, under an immense sky, in the middle of a vast ocean of sagebrush.

Here a young man waits in the dry wind for the bus that will take him to town for the weekend. On that bus is the woman with whom, unbeknownst to him, he is about to fall deeply in love. Perhaps one of their children will cure cancer or negotiate peace in the Middle East—who can know? In any case, these two people are destined for a lifetime of shared affection, perhaps fifty fine Christmases together. As it turns out, however, this crossroads is not the locus of the significant vernacular experience. That spot is a mile and a half up the road, where the bus sits motionless at the roadside while its driver sweats in the desert heat as he changes the left rear tire, which has just blown out. The man, becoming impatient, at last walks back to his little house. Twenty-two minutes later the bus speeds by. Will the man eventually die after a long and empty life? Perhaps not, but who can know? The crossroads at which the man stands must now be placed on a different kind of vernacular map—a map of missed opportunities. That is, the spot where the man is not standing when the bus passes is a vitally important place in a global matrix of places where life-changing events almost happened. We hope to develop more sensitive mechanisms to record such incidents, since we cannot depend upon vernacular witnesses to record events that did not occur. Do you have such missed appointments in your own life? In time, v.e.c.t.o.r.l.o.s.s. might help you to find out.

QUESTION 3

Is there an unexperienced inch of ground on earth?

While the answer will depend upon the temporal and experiential parameters we establish for our inquiry, this question remains extremely important to our project's staff. We ask one another this: When v.e.c.t.o.r.l.o.s.s. is complete, will it be a map of everything? Most of our researchers now agree that, assuming sufficient temporal depth in the model, results will show that every point on earth, however remote or minute, has at some time been the site of some significant human experience. But there are still a few holdouts, mostly among the senior researchers, who cling to the perhaps romantic belief that somewhere on earth (maybe only in a few spots, they acknowledge) there exists some bit of ground—a few centimeters, perhaps, of tundra, ice, or rock—that yet remains unmarked by human experience. The search for these unexperienced vernacular landscapes has become a specialty for certain researchers, whose quest is not for sites of vernacular experience but rather for the mythic purity of a place that remains free from them. On one thing, however, we all agree: if such places do exist and can be located, they will need to be placed on an entirely new kind of map.

QUESTION 4

Can the project's findings be used to protect places?

If you are Native American and can prove that a developer's planned golf course is about to be constructed atop your people's ancestral burial ground, you have at least a chance of saving your sacred site. But some of the v.e.c.t.o.r.l.o.s.s. scientists have taken this kind of resistance to a radical extreme. These researchers—closet activists, really—are motivated by the belief that the project, in proving the richness of vernacular experience in places, can provide ammunition to the enemies of development. I might as well confess that I am one of these people.

Consider this. Even in our current judicial system certain relationships between people and nature are constitutionally protected as expressions of religious freedom. I once read of a case in which some folks prevented construction of a Walmart in their local forest by persuading a judge that they used that forest as a place to pray. The day after reading the article I joined the Universal Pantheist Society (I've been a dues-paying member ever since) and began documenting my devotional use of my favorite place—a hanging canyon hidden at 8,000 feet in the forked embrace of the split summit of my home mountain. I now have hundreds of pages of dated journal entries describing the spiritually illuminating experiences I've had in this high, wet canyon here in the heart of sage country, and I've taken more than seven hundred photographs, now spanning almost fourteen years, of myself "praying" in front of juniper and mountain mahogany, pack rat nests and granite boulders, the perennial spring at the head of the canyon, the carcass of a mule deer freshly killed by a mountain lion.

When they try to build the ski lodge or drill the fracking well there, I'll be ready. I have demonstrable evidence that I am a long-term member of a recognized religious sect (we pantheists even have a newsletter) and that my religious freedom would be threatened if I am deprived of this specific site. And because I worship all the natural elements of this montane desert ecosystem in their complex relationship to one another, my conscience will not allow me to sacrifice even a single serrated leaf of a snow-bent cottonwood, or a button from the vibrating tail of a Great Basin rattler, or a tuft of reddish fur from the ear of a coyote pup crossing this high meadow full of snowberry on its way to seek shelter among the aspen. I won't burn your church, you don't pave my mountain. I have incontrovertible evidence, and I'll take my case to the Supreme Court if I have to.

Now extrapolate from this to your own important place. If V.E.C.T.O.R.L.O.S.S. can scientifically prove that your place is comparably rich with associations that are crucial to your faith—whatever that faith might be—then it might help you make the case that they should not build the Walmart on the spot where your grandfather set the cornerstone of his farmhouse, or where your son caught his first glistening brook trout, or where your little brother saw a tanager flash scarlet in the emerald canopy of a shagbark hickory . . . or maybe that spot on the summit of Moonrise where your daughter, on her sixth birthday, discovered the curving, bone-white arch of a perfect mule deer antler.

In mathematics, a *vector* is "a quantity that has direction as well as magnitude," and it is represented symbolically by "a line drawn from its original to its final position." Each of our lives is also a vector whose representative story line—the narrative of its trajectory through time and space—can be plotted only along the points of our significant vernacular experiences in place. The tragedy of our age is how discontinuous and fractured that line has become, how in desperation we are forced to splice its missing fragments together with misinformation from distorted, alien maps that omit or obscure the lost story of our own being in the world.

I have a dream that someday the v.e.c.t.o.r.l.o.s.s. witnessing archives will occupy hundreds of acres of buildings full of vaults in which all of our most important vernacular experiences are expressed and located, never to be lost. Numberless letters, e-mails, postcards, text messages, tweets—even scribbled cocktail napkins or photographs of drawings etched with sticks into damp sand—each with a small story and an accompanying set of numbers that describes a specific location in space. Countless moments of illumination and disappointment and transformation, placed carefully onto a fully textured map of the living world. Even in its earliest phases, the project has demonstrated that every map, however fastidiously drawn, obscures a rich, invisible landscape of important vernacular associations with the land. And these local experiences do not simply accrue in places over time, piling up like stones in a rising cairn that marks a trail along the ridgeline leading to the future. Instead, the vernacular landscape is a palimpsest, a page of geo-experiential manuscript upon which holograph records are written, overwritten, erased, elided, interpolated, inserted, canceled, and then written again, sometimes in languages not yet spoken, sometimes in a forgotten language.

I believe that the infinitely draped cartography of significantly experienced places, if it is ever completed, will simply be the map of all that is holy. Every spot it depicts will be sacred ground—will be the site of some otherwise invisible deer antler or snow angel. And who among us would not kneel, if in kneeling we could touch a furrow of bark from that tree where the shining ivory bill momentarily reappeared, ghostlike, from the world where all that is lost is said to remain forever? Only then will we finally know what to tell our children when they ask. We'll tell them that all of the earth is a reliquary—that every chip of bark and stone and bone turned out to be a chip of the true cross. If they don't believe us they can check the map, where the first thing they will discover is the place and moment of their own birth, so precious to us, already recorded there.

Reading Group Guide

I. In the book's Pre-amble, the author contrasts his own epic hikes in the high desert with his daughters' long-held ambition to climb a modest local ridge they call Moonrise. Ultimately, he concludes that the experience of hiking with his daughters is "more fascinating and valuable than any heroic male wilderness adventure could possibly be." (p. xxix). What is the impact of the contrast between these two forms of experiencing wilderness—solitary male adventure vs. a father hiking with his daughters?

2. The book's opening chapters, "Endlessly Rocking" and "The Nature within Us," reveal that the author has real fears about whether he is prepared to be a good father. Why is he so hesitant about becoming a parent? How does he ultimately confront concerns that he will be inadequate as a father?

3. Much of this book is concerned with the author's developing identity as "the father of daughters." How might the book have been different if Branch had instead been the father of sons? How might the book's story have changed had it been told by a mother of daughters or a mother of sons?

4. Branch writes that "Laughter is the sound we make in the moment we acknowledge, perhaps even begin to accept, our own mistakes or inadequacies" (p. xxxi). He even claims that "laugher generates the flexibility and acceptance that are necessary for one to develop patience and express love" (p. xxxii). How does humor

function throughout the book? Would you agree that humor has the power to make us more accepting and resilient? What are the limits to the power of humor to help us in our lives?

5. In his endorsement of *Raising Wild*, Pulitzer Prize–winning poet Gary Snyder writes that the book "points forward, not back," and he describes it as "hopeful." What do you think Snyder meant in describing the book as pointing forward?

6. Although the book is often both funny and hopeful, a number of chapters offer serious contemplations of potential loss. For example, "Tracking Stories" examines what might be lost if pronghorn antelope were to be extirpated from the author's local landscape, while "Fire on the Mountain" examines the near loss of Branch's family home to fire. Why are these contemplations of loss important to the larger story told by the book? How can they be reconciled with the book's lighter, more hopeful tone?

7. The key to this book is its setting in the remote, high-elevation Great Basin Desert, which the author describes as being "among the most extreme landscapes in North America" (p. xx). "This place is not remarkable in spite of its blizzards and droughts, its fires and floods, its rattlers and scorpions," he writes. "It is astonishing because of them" (p. xxiii). If the high desert landscape is so inhospitable, why does he value it so highly? Why does he want to inhabit this extreme environment—and raise his children there—if it is such a difficult place to make a home?

8. At many points in the book, the author contrasts the way adults and children see the world. "There is something about adult perception, however finely honed it might be, that struggles to attain

the sense of possibility that is instinctive to children," he writes (p. 104). Do you agree that children retain a "sense of possibility" that has become less accessible to adults? What are examples of things children can imagine that grown-ups have a harder time envisioning? What might adults learn from a childhood sense of possibility?

9. Although *Raising Wild* is a book about the author's life with his family in the high desert wilderness, it often reaches out to make contact with popular culture. For example, "Playing with the Stick" offers a humorous look at the induction of the stick into the National Toy Hall of Fame, while "The Hills Are Alive" takes a comical approach to examining the musical film *The Sound of Music*. How do the chapters that work with pop culture relate to the chapters that more directly discuss Branch's experiences with his children in their home desert? For example, what does "Playing with the Stick" suggest about the differences between adult and childhood perceptions of nature, a theme important throughout the book? How does "The Hills Are Alive" challenge our assumption that green landscapes are superior to arid landscapes, which is another key issue in the book?

10. For many of us, a garden is an important domestic site where nature and culture meet and overlap—a place where we try to understand nature but also shape it to our own purposes. What representation of the garden emerges in the chapter "My Children's First Garden"? What are the author's ambitions for his children's garden? How are those ambitions thwarted? How does Branch respond to his repeated difficulties in this troubled garden? Do you consider the garden described in this chapter to be a failure?

11. The author addresses his book's title this way: "We tend to think that something that is 'raised' cannot also be 'wild' and that

something that is 'wild' must not have been 'raised.' (Think salmon here.) But rather than figure the wild as other than and apart from the family, this book explores the ways in which living as a family in a wild landscape reveals the wildness at the heart of both childhood and parenthood" (p. xxvii). How does Branch conceive of the relationship between domesticity and wildness? Would you agree with his sense that the wild and domestic can coexist, or do you instead consider them mutually exclusive?

12. Henry David Thoreau, whom Branch quotes and refers to a number of times, once wrote that "In wildness is the preservation of the world." However, this quotation is often incorrectly rendered as "In wilderness is the preservation of the world." What is the difference between wildness and wilderness? Can one exist without the other? In what ways does *Raising Wild* explore the relationship between wildness and wilderness, and what does the book ultimately say about the distinction between the two?

13. Near the end of the chapter called "Fire on the Mountain," the author discusses the scientific consensus that "People who write about traumatic events are a great deal more resilient than are trauma victims who do not create a narrative of their experience" (p. 250). Why do you think writing about emotionally difficult experiences has been shown to be so therapeutic? What is it about retelling the story of a traumatic event that makes that event more endurable, perhaps even more comprehensible, to the writer?

14. How would you reply if asked to categorize *Raising Wild* by genre? Is it creative nonfiction? Memoir? Humor writing? An essay collection? Nature or science writing? Regional literature? Is it a parenting book? How might you read the book differently

if you were to first identify it as being an example of one or another of these genres?

15. Very late in the book the author addresses his readers directly, inviting them to try a specific thought experiment: "Take a moment to imagine the landscape you now inhabit or, alternatively, a treasured landscape from your past. What memories have you attached to that place? How has that place helped to shape the person you are today? How have your experiences there informed your way of seeing yourself, your family, the place itself?" (p. 259). Now actually try this! How have your experiences or memories of this special place influenced your identity and your view of the world? How might you be a different person had you never encountered this unique place?

Acknowledgments

Writers are very much in need of friends, and I have been fortunate to have so many in my life and in my corner. Here I offer my sincere thanks, along with equally sincere apologies to anyone I may have neglected to include.

Among fellow writers of environmental creative nonfiction, my thanks go to Rick Bass, Paul Bogard, John Calderazzo, SueEllen Campbell, Laird Christensen, Casey Clabough, Jennifer Cognard-Black, Chris Cokinos, John Elder, Andy Furman, Dimitri Keriotis, Ian Marshall, Kate Miles, Kathy Moore, John Murray, Nick Neely, Sean O'Grady, Tim Palmer, Bob Pyle, David Quammen, Eve Quesnel, Janisse Ray, Suzanne Roberts, Chris Robertson, Leslie Ryan, Terre Ryan, Gary Snyder, John Tallmadge, David Taylor, and Rick Van Noy. Very special thanks to David Gessner, John Lane, and John Price, whose support has been decisive.

Thanks also for the encouragement I've received from other friends in the environmental literature community, including Tom Bailey, Patrick Barron, Jim Bishop, Kate Chandler, Ben Click, Nancy Cook, Jerry Dollar, Ann Fisher-Wirth, Tom Hillard, Heather Houser, Richard Hunt, Dave Johnson, Rochelle Johnson, Mark Long, Tom Lynch, Kyhl Lyndgaard, Annie Merrill, Clint Mohs, David Morris, Dan Philippon, Steve Railton, Heidi Scott, Robert Sickels, Dave Stentiford, Jim Warren, and Alan Weltzien.

I've been fortunate to benefit from productive collaborations with many talented and industrious editors. Following are a few of these folks, along with the magazine or press at which they worked at the time I received their help: Chip Blake, Jennifer Sahn, Hannah Fries, and Kristen Hewitt (*Orion*); David Gessner, Ben George, and Anna Lena Phillips (*Ecotone*); Stephanie Paige Ogburn, Jodi Peterson, Paul Larmer, Tay Wiles, Michelle Nijhuis, Diane Sylvain, Cally Carswell, Emily Guerin, and Kate Schimel (*High Country News*); Kate Miles (*Hawk & Handsaw*); Chris Cokinos (*Isotope*); Nick Neely (*Watershed*); Rowland Russell (*Whole Terrain*); Nancy Levinson (*Places Journal*); Jamie Iredell (*New South*); Mike Colpo (Patagonia's *The Cleanest Line*); Tara Zades (*Reader's Digest*); Justin Raymond (*Shavings*); Jeanie French (*Red Rock Review*); Bruce Anderson (*Sunset*); Caleb Cage and Joe McCoy (*The Nevada Review*); Fil Corbitt (*Van Sounds*); Jason Leppig (*Island Press Field Notes*); Brad Rassler (*Sustainable Play*); Barry Tharaud (*Nineteenth-Century Prose*); Greg Garrard (Oxford University Press); George Thompson (GFT Publishing); Jonathan Cobb (Island Press); and Boyd Zenner (University of Virginia Press).

I want to express my sincere gratitude to the terrific team at Roost Books, whose work on *Raising Wild* has been exemplary from the start. Thanks to assistant editor Julia Gaviria, copy editor Diana Rico, and proofreader Emily White for seeing the manuscript down the final stretch, and to art director Daniel Urban-Brown and designer Jess Morphew for making it a thing of beauty. My thanks to sales and marketing manager KJ Grow, publicity director Steven Pomije, and publicity and marketing coordinator Stephany Daniel, whose excellent work has helped this book to find its readers. Most important, I offer my deepest and most heartfelt thanks to my editor Jennifer Urban-Brown. My collaboration with Jenn has been among the most productive and enjoyable of my career, and I can only hope that folks who believe that a writer's relationship with their editor must be adversarial might someday be as fortunate as I have been in having such a supportive, patient, and insightful partner in their work.

It is fitting that *Raising Wild* should have found a home at Shambhala, given the strange and wonderful way in which my own path and that of the press came to cross. Shambhala Publications emerged from Shambhala Booksellers, which began in 1968 in the back of the storied Moe's Books, on Telegraph Avenue in Berkeley. Back in early August 2002, my wife, Eryn, and I were on our way from the high desert over to the San Francisco Bay to root for the Giants as they took on the Pirates. As usual, we left time to visit the Berkeley Hills and peruse the shelves at Moe's. It was there, as I admired the plates in a beautiful edition of Audubon's *The Birds of America*, that Eryn emerged from the bathroom waving the small wand of a pregnancy test above her head. Through the wand's tiny window we caught a glimpse of our future: two parallel magenta lines that gave the first indication we would become parents. The kid presaged by that magic wand at Moe's Books turned out to be Hannah, who is now twelve years old. She and her little sister, nine-year-old Caroline, are the figures at the heart of *Raising Wild*, serendipitously published by Shambhala, which also traces its origin story to Moe's.

Closer to home, I'd like to offer thanks to fellow Great Basin writers Bill Fox, Shaun Griffin, Ann Ronald, Rebecca Solnit, Steve Trimble, Claire Watkins, and Terry Tempest Williams, with a nod to the desert writers who led my way: Mary Austin, Ed Abbey, Ellen Meloy, and Chuck Bowden. Thanks to my colleagues in the MFA program at the University of Nevada, Reno: Steve Gehrke, Ann Keniston, Gailmarie Pahmeier, Susan Palwick, and, especially, Chris Coake. And thanks to my students in the courses on American humor writing, place-based creative nonfiction, and western American literary nonfiction that I taught during 2014, 2015, and 2016.

I have also been encouraged by the stalwart readers of my "Rants from the Hill" essay series at *High Country News* online, where more than a hundred thousand folks have been kind enough to spend five minutes with my unusual way of seeing the world.

Among Reno friends, I've received valuable support from Pete Barbieri, Mike Colpo, Fil Corbitt, Dondo Darue, David Fenimore, Daniel Fergus, Mark Gandolfo, Betty Glass, Torben Hansen, Aaron and Diana Hiibel, Kent Irwin, Rich Kientz, Tony Marek, Ashley Marshall, Katie O'Connor, Eric Rasmussen, and Meri Shadley. Special thanks to my closest friends, Colin and Monica Robertson and Cheryll and Steve Glotfelty. The most significant support I have received outside my family came from Cheryll, whose encouragement has been essential to my growth as a writer.

I am blessed with a family that is exceptionally tolerant of my eccentricities and ambitions, my fierce sense of place and idiosyncratic sense of humor. On the other side of the Sierra, thanks to our Central Valley people: O. B. and Deb Hoagland, Sister Kate and Uncle Adam Myers, Troy and Scott Allen, and all the cousin critters. Here on the Great Basin side of the big hill, more thanks than I will ever manage to express go to my folks, Stu and Sharon Branch, who have directly or indirectly enabled everything I've accomplished in life. My wife, Eryn, is all I ever dreamed of in a partner—loving, patient, smart, creative, funny, generous, and encouraging; this book could never have been written without her constant support.

I often tell our daughters that "it takes a family to make a book." The dedication of a book is the most sincere gesture of gratitude available to a writer, and I have dedicated *Raising Wild* to Hannah and Caroline, whose wild desert upbringing inspired it. I hope my record of our shared experiences up on this high desert hilltop will seem to them even sweeter as the years go by.

Credits

Many of the chapters in this book had their first life as essays published in magazines, though the versions that appear here are very much expanded and revised (and in several cases retitled). Information on first publication (and, as necessary, original titles) appears below. I am deeply grateful to these magazines and their editors for their support of my work.

"Endlessly Rocking." *Ecotone: Reimagining Place* 2, no. 1 (Fall/Winter 2006): 20–37.

"The Nature within Us." Originally published as "Couvade Days." *Whole Terrain: Reflective Environmental Practice* 15 (2008): 44–47.

"Tracking Stories." Originally published as "Ghosts Chasing Ghosts: Pronghorn and the Long Shadow of Evolution." *Ecotone: Reimagining Place* 4, nos. 1 and 2 (January 2009): 1–19.

"Ladder to the Pleiades." In *Let There Be Night: Testimony on Behalf of the Dark*, edited by Paul Bogard, 74–84. Reno: University of Nevada Press, 2008.

"The Adventures of Peavine and Charlie." Originally published as "The Adventures of Peavine and Charlie: A Journey through the Imaginative Landscape of Childhood." *Orion* 30, no. 1 (January/February 2011): 58–63.

"The Wild within Our Walls." Originally published as "Nothing

Says Trash Like Packrats: Nature Boy Meets Bushy Tail." In *Trash Animals: The Cultural Perceptions, Biology, and Ecology of Animals in Conflict with Humans,* edited by Phillip David Johnson and Kelsi Nagy, 139–49. Minneapolis: University of Minnesota Press, 2013.

"Playing with the Stick." Originally published as "Sticking with the Stick." *Hawk & Handsaw: The Journal of Creative Sustainability* 5 (2012): 68–73.

"Freebirds." Originally published as "Freebirds: A Thanksgiving Lesson in Forgiveness." *Orion* 30, no. 6 (November/December 2011): 44–49.

"Finding the Future Forest." Some passages in this chapter are derived from the following two sources: "Lifeblood of the Desert," *Tahoe Quarterly* (Fall 2007): 55–57; "Finding the Forest," *Orion Afield* 3, no. 4 (Autumn 1999): 10–14.

"My Children's First Garden." Originally published as "My Child's First Garden." *Hawk & Handsaw: The Journal of Creative Sustainability* 1 (2008): 56–65.

"The Hills Are Alive." *Places Journal,* January 2012. https://places-journal.org/article/the-hills-are-alive.

"The V.E.C.T.O.R.L.O.S.S. Project." *Isotope: A Journal of Literary Nature and Science Writing* 5, no. 2 (Fall/Winter 2007): 2–9.

About the Author

Michael P. Branch is professor of literature and enviornment at the University of Nevada, Reno, where he teaches creative nonfiction, American literature, environmental studies, and film studies. He has published five books and more than two hundred essays, articles, and reviews, and his creative nonfiction includes pieces that have received Honorable Mention for the Pushcart Prize and been recognized as Notable Essays in *The Best American Essays* (three times), *The Best American Science and Nature Writing*, and *The Best American Nonrequired Reading*. His work has appeared in many magazines, including *Orion*, *Ecotone*, *Utne Reader*, *Slate*, *Places Journal*, *Whole Terrain*, and *Red Rock Review*. His widely read monthly essay series, "Rants from the Hill," has received more than one hundred thousand page views at *High Country News* online (hcn.org); a book-length collection of those essays is forthcoming from Roost Books.

Mike lives with his wife, Eryn, and daughters, Hannah Virginia and Caroline Emerson, in a passive solar home of their own design at 6,000 feet in the remote high desert of northwestern Nevada, in the ecotone where the Great Basin Desert and Sierra Nevada mountains meet. There he writes, plays blues harmonica, drinks sour mash, curses at baseball on the radio, cuts stove wood, and walks at least 1,200 miles each year in the surrounding hills, canyons, ridges, arroyos, and playas.